Making News

Making News

One Hundred Years of Journalism and Mass Communication at Carolina

TOM BOWERS

UNC
SCHOOL OF JOURNALISM
AND MASS COMMUNICATION

Printed in the United States of America on FSC-certified paper
with 30% post consumer recycled content.

ISBN 978-0-8078-3331-5 and 0-8078-3331-2

Library of Congress Control Number 2008911548

Design and production by Chris Crochetière, BW&A Books, Inc.

Facing page: Horace Carter's newspaper, the *Tabor City Tribune,* won
the 1956 Pulitzer Prize for standing up to the Ku Klux Klan. He later
donated the prize to the School of Journalism and Mass Communication. *(Photograph by Brownie Harris, School of Journalism and Mass
Communication, UNC–Chapel Hill. Reprinted with permission.)*

Publication of this book was made possible by
W. Horace Carter '43 and Russell M. Carter '71.
Horace Carter is a Pulitzer Prize–winning
community journalist and civic leader. His son,
Rusty, is a leading businessman and former
UNC trustee. Both are graduates of our school,
philanthropists, and true Tar Heels.

Contents

Preface and Acknowledgments

Jean Folkerts, dean of the School of Journalism and Mass Communication, asked me in 2007 to work with her as the school prepared to commemorate the 100th anniversary of the first journalism course at UNC–Chapel Hill. She suggested that I might write a history of the school. At the time, the school's written history consisted of two paragraphs that had been printed in school catalogs for many years. I had no idea that I would find so much material and that this story would grow to nearly 300 pages in length. I also did not anticipate that I would find the project so rewarding, and I am grateful to Jean for giving me the opportunity to be a historian so late in my career. Jean is an accomplished historian in her own right, and I appreciate her encouragement.

I began my research by reading the *Tar Heel*, the UNC student newspaper, from its first issue on Feb. 23, 1893, to beyond the formation of the Department of Journalism in 1924. I read every page of every issue, looking for stories about UNC journalists and journalism courses. Sitting at a microfilm reader in a dark room in the North Carolina Collection at Wilson Library made me feel as if I were in a time machine, living through that period as if I had been a student or faculty member. I found stories about journalism at Carolina, but I also became immersed in (and distracted by) stories about the nascent athletic program, accounts of debate tournaments (which were as important as athletic contests back then), military training on campus during World War I, and the tragedy of the Spanish influenza epidemic. What I learned about journalism at Carolina during those formative years provided a basis for the remainder of my research. University and school catalogs gave me an official timeline and showed annual snapshots of the life of the department and the school.

When I started the project, I did not know that the personal papers of three of the important figures in the history of the school—Oscar Coffin,

Neil Luxon, and Holt McPherson—were in the manuscripts department of Wilson Library at UNC–Chapel Hill. Their extensive correspondence among themselves and with scores of friends, colleagues, and students filled in details and gave me background and personal stories for this history. Those personal papers were supplemented by the papers of other people and archival records of university officials.

This book was immeasurably enriched by oral-history interviews of former students and faculty members who gave me more information than I could use in the book: Jack Adams, Harry Amana, Trudy Atkins, Rich Beckman, Bill Beerman, Ty Boyd, Joe Brown, Lester Carson, Horace Carter, Bill Cheshire, Alex Coffin, Richard Cole, Lois Cranford, Wayne Danielson, Lawrence Ferlinghetti, William Friday, Roland Giduz, Dorothy Helms, Walter Jackson, Allen Johnson, Wayne King, Walter Klein, Jock Lauterer, Jim Mullen, Rolfe Neill, Roy Park, Karen Parker, Ernie Pitt, Carol Reuss, Ken Sanford, Stuart Sechriest, Mac Secrest, Donald Shaw, Bill Snider, Jim Wallace, Clarence Whitefield, Roy Wilder, Jo Woestendiek, Ed Yoder, and Jan Yopp. In addition, Speed Hallman interviewed Virginia Doughton, and Jan Yopp interviewed me. The recorded interviews and written accounts of them are available in the Park Library of the School of Journalism and Mass Communication. The school has created a virtual history museum at www.jomc.unc.edu/history, and it includes many photographs, documents, and data about the school.

After I wrote an initial draft of the manuscript, several generous colleagues read it and made useful suggestions: Jean Folkerts, Richard Cole, Frank Fee, Donald Shaw, Speed Hallman, Jan Yopp, and Jo Bass. I am grateful for their many comments and suggestions, but I accept responsibility for any errors in content or conclusions. I am grateful, too, for Jan Yopp's insistence that she write a section about me in Chapter 13.

My research was made much easier and more enjoyable by the helpful cooperation of many individuals. In the School of Journalism and Mass Communication, Speed Hallman, associate dean for development and alumni affairs, accompanied me on many trips to conduct interviews and was a sounding board for ideas; Benji Cauthren, then assistant director for development, answered many queries about graduates of the school; Barbara Semonche, then director of the school's Park Library, gave me access to her collection of memorabilia; Kyle York, assistant to the dean for communication, and Morgan Ellis helped with photographs; Fred Thomsen, director of information technology and services, and his staff provided much-needed technical support; Dottie Howell, associate dean for business and finance, obtained photographs; and Ken Hales, accounting manager, located important financial information.

My many enjoyable hours in the manuscripts department of the North Carolina Collection in the UNC–Chapel Hill Library were made pleasant and productive by the cheerful assistance of Matt Turi, Robin Davies, and their staff. Keith Longiotti, Stephen Fletcher, and Jason Tomberlin of the North Carolina Collection were extraordinarily helpful in my quest for photographs of persons and buildings. In the UNC General Alumni Association office, Julie Trotter, Tracy Chrismon, and Martha Mills cheerfully pulled alumni files and gave me space to read them.

C. David Perry, assistant director and editor-in-chief of the University of North Carolina Press, was extraordinarily generous with advice about getting the book distributed by UNC Press.

At BW&A Books, Barbara Williams and Chris Crochetière were exceedingly helpful at every stage of the process of producing the book. Brent Winter, my copy editor, cared as much for the manuscript as I did and improved it immeasurably. An author cannot ask for more. Like mine, theirs was a labor of love.

Most of all, I shall be forever grateful to my wife, Mary Ellen Bowers, for being my inspiration, supporter, adviser, and editor throughout the entire project.

Tom Bowers
Chapel Hill, North Carolina
October 2008

Foreword

Of all the writers who taught and practiced their craft in Chapel Hill's journalism classrooms over the last 100 years, no one was more suited than Tom Bowers to chronicle the story of journalism education at UNC. Tom spent 35 years of his professional life in the classrooms and administrative offices of Howell and Carroll halls. He knew many of the faculty members who taught here over the last 50 years, and he was the first stop for students in need. Scores of alumni recall his calm, capable assistance when the spelling-and-grammar exam or the swim test threatened to block their paths to professional success. While he is famous for taking care of the minutest details and keeping the school on an even keel over the course of nearly four decades, those of us on the inside know he played a quiet but crucial role in shaping the personality and direction of our school once he entered administration in the late 1970s.

To tell this story of journalism education at UNC–Chapel Hill, Tom logged hundreds of hours in the university's archives, crisscrossed the state to interview alumni, and talked with current and former faculty and administrators. He also drew on his rich insider's knowledge of the institution and the people who helped us become one of the best, if not the best, schools of journalism and mass communication in the nation.

The result is a fascinating story of genius, progressive ideas, hard work, and—in one notable instance—failure. What sets us apart is that our leaders, from the still-revered Edward Kidder Graham to the indomitable Richard Cole, understood that the world and the profession were changing. These visionaries led the charge and challenged students, faculty, and university administrators to follow. But somehow, amid the smoke and clamor left in the wake of these hard-charging change agents, our school kept in warm, personal touch (to borrow a phrase from Edward Kidder Graham) with its students. A glorious cast of personalities, including names such as Coffin, Spearman, Sechriest, Byerly, Shumaker, and Stone, coached, prodded, provoked, and occasionally praised the young people in their care to prepare them for the world beyond this sheltered place. Everything they did was for the students. And the students, whose only charge was to go forth and serve the state, delivered.

It has been a joy for me to enter the warm and big-hearted Tar Heel journalism community, meet alumni, and learn about the history of our school. *Every* graduate tells me how important our school has been and how wonderful our faculty are. *Making News: One Hundred Years of Journalism and Mass Communication at Carolina* gives me an even stronger appreciation of the J-school ties that bind as it tells the story of our century-long mission of service to the people. I'm certain that your experience within these pages will do the same for you.

Jean Folkerts, Dean
Chapel Hill, North Carolina
August 15, 2008

"The beginning of journalism is just coming in the South. For rapid advancement and attainment of power and fame, no calling offers such opportunities as does journalism in this state. Prior to five years ago, there was no interest in the journalism of the college. Since then each year has seen a number of young men interested in college journalism, and the number is steadily growing. These men have seen the opportunity that college journalism work offers for preparing to make good in life and for developing individual culture."—*Edward Kidder Graham*[1]

1. Origins in the English Department

Anticipation was high when Professor Edward Kidder Graham greeted the students in the first journalism class at the University of North Carolina on Sept. 9, 1909.[2] UNC students had been active in journalism for more than 15 years, and they were anxious to have a journalism course. Graham had whetted their appetite with his comments at the 1907 banquet of student journalists. Their interest in journalism was serious, and several former UNC journalists were working at many leading newspapers in the state and nation without having had journalism education or training. Graham, 33, had been editor of the UNC student newspaper and was a strong supporter of the newspaper and other journalism activities as a popular faculty member and dean of the College of Liberal Arts. Four years later, he would be named president of the university and would enlist journalism classes in his campaign to extend the boundaries of the campus to the boundaries of the state through public service. Nine years later, he would be dead, a tragic victim of the Spanish influenza epidemic that swept the world and the campus.

Journalism instruction on campus would flourish, however, as new courses were added and a separate academic department was created in 1924. The department would grow from one faculty member to eight,

1. "The Journalists' Banquet," *Tar Heel*, Feb. 14, 1907, 1.

2. According to the university catalog, lectures began on that date in the fall 1909 term.

survive a failed attempt at national accreditation, and achieve status as a school in 1950. It would establish a reputation for training many journalists at North Carolina newspapers as well as specialists for a wide range of media. With inspired leadership, the school augmented that reputation to become one of the best in the country. Now, 100 years later, it has more than 800 students and nearly 50 faculty members and is known around the world for excellence as a leader in journalism–mass communication education.

This is the story of how that happened. It is a story of strong leaders who shaped the program through their vision and personality. It is a story of one dean who was portrayed in a novel and another dean and a faculty member who were featured in nationally syndicated newspaper comic strips. It is a story, too, of how external forces, including North Carolina newspaper executives, pressured the university to change the journalism program and made an implied threat to ask a rival university to start a program if UNC did not change. It is the story of a dean whose dedication to excellence in an academic program dramatically changed a school that had paid more attention to practical journalism work than to academics. It is the story of deans who built on that excellence and maintained it through turbulent campus times. It is the story of another dean who greatly expanded the scope of the school and raised millions of dollars to support its drive for excellence. The story is built from archival research, secondary sources, and oral histories that capture the factual and anecdotal development of the school and its national reputation.

The *Tar Heel* and the University Press Association

The tangible origins of journalism at UNC can be traced to the student newspaper, the *Tar Heel,* which was founded in 1893.[3] At about the same time, enough students were serving as correspondents for their home-

3. The University of North Carolina was founded in 1793, making it the first state university in the United States and the only one to graduate students in the 18th century. A literary journal, the *North Carolina University Magazine*, was first published in 1844, and similar magazines with that and other titles appeared sporadically throughout the university's history, according to Levi Brown in "Journalism in the University of North Carolina" (bachelor's thesis, University of North Carolina, 1910). The first issue of the magazine was criticized for including news items deemed suitable for a weekly newspaper but not for a magazine, according to Louis R. Wilson in *Chronicles of the Sesquicentennial* (Chapel Hill: University of North Carolina Press, 1947), 286. Battle said in his history of the university that a newspaper called the *Chapel Hillian* was published around 1889 but disappeared before the *Tar Heel* came

town newspapers to organize the University Press Association. Those two activities eventually led to a desire for journalism courses, and Graham and other university leaders obliged.

The University Athletic Association published the first issue of the *Tar Heel* on Feb. 23, 1893, in part to build student support for the athletic activities that the association organized. A statement in the first issue said the university needed a weekly newspaper and the association saw itself as the way to meet the need. Illustrating how athletics and journalism mixed at the time, the first editor, Charles Baskerville, was also a star halfback and manager of the football team. Although it was published by the Athletic Association, the four-page paper that appeared every Thursday devoted itself to the larger interests of the university and promoted itself as the "best, quickest and surest" way for advertisers to reach students.[4] In 1894, a group of students opposed to the influence of fraternities in the Athletic Association started a rival newspaper, the *White and Blue*, but it was absorbed by the *Tar Heel* in 1895.[5]

The newspaper's editorial offices were in a storeroom next to the old Methodist church on Franklin Street.[6] It was printed in a separate location: the facilities of the University Press. Five faculty members had incorporated the University Press in February 1893: John Manning, Francis P. Venable, J. W. Gore, R. H. Whitehead, and Collier Cobb, who managed the operation on the ground floor of the New West building. Wilson said the company was ambitiously called the University Press even though it was not part of the university. In addition to commercial printing, the press printed journals and official university publications as well as the *University Magazine* and the *Tar Heel*. The university purchased the company's assets for $2,000 on Dec. 31, 1899, and moved its operations. The growing Department of Pharmacy needed the space occupied by the print shop in New West, and university officials were also concerned about the fire danger of having the press operations in the building. In 1901 the university built a one-story brick building for the University Press near the site of the current Phillips Annex building next to Carroll Hall, so the current School of Journalism and Mass Communication is close to the site of early journalistic activities on campus. The print shop included an old Babcock cylinder press and a small job press that were powered by an

on the scene. Kemp P. Battle, *History of the University of North Carolina, Vol. II: From 1868 to 1912* (Raleigh: Edwards and Broughton Printing Co., 1912), 454.

4. "The Tar Heel," *Tar Heel*, Feb. 23, 1893, 1.

5. "Athletic Association Meeting," *Tar Heel*, March 7, 1895, 1.

6. Wilson, *Chronicles of the Sesquicentennial*, 297.

unreliable steam engine connected to the nearby power plant. The antiquated cylinder press was so loud that people on nearby Cameron Avenue could tell when the *Tar Heel* was being printed.[7]

Wilson said the university accommodated the private enterprise because it was a convenient and inexpensive service that also provided training and employment for students who were interested in becoming journalists. The printing shop was a stimulating atmosphere, and students competed for the coveted positions there.[8] They included Oscar Coffin, who would be the first dean of the School of Journalism; while he was a student, he earned 15 cents an hour as a typesetter. He recalled that the shop had two cases of 11-point type for the *Tar Heel*, German and French type for scholarly journals, and Greek type for course examinations. He especially remembered two cases of 10-point italic type he used to set the names of bones in a syllabus for Professor Charles Magnum.[9]

Sports coverage dominated the *Tar Heel* through its first several decades. The front page was devoted primarily to sports stories, and editorials were often about athletics. Intercollegiate football got the most attention, followed by baseball, tennis, and track and field. An 1898 editorial asked why the game of basketball had never been introduced to the university.[10] Ten years later, 20 students who had played high school basketball formed a basketball association and collected $18 to support their effort.[11]

Even before the *Tar Heel* was established, some UNC students were campus correspondents for their hometown newspapers in North Carolina. A campus directory of organizations in the first issue included the University Press Association, headed by its president, Howard E. Rondthaler. The association's purpose was to spread news about the university, and administrators encouraged the students because they publicized the university throughout the state. In the absence of a news bureau, which was not created until 1918, the university relied on the student press association. They met regularly on Fridays and received news from William Cunningham Smith, an assistant in the university library, who conferred with President Edwin A. Alderman to assemble news for the students.[12] The *Hellenian*, the university yearbook from 1890–1900, and its successor, the *Yackety*

7. Archibald Henderson, *The Campus of the First State University* (Chapel Hill: University of North Carolina Press, 1949), 306–07.

8. Louis R. Wilson, *The University of North Carolina, 1900–1930* (Chapel Hill: University of North Carolina Press, 1957), 19.

9. Henderson, *Campus of the First State University*, 307.

10. "Basketball," *Tar Heel*, Jan. 11, 1898, 2.

11. "Basket Ball Men Organize," *Tar Heel*, Oct. 15, 1908, 1.

12. "Reporters at the University," *Tar Heel*, Oct. 10, 1896, 1.

Yack, sometimes included the University Press Association in pages about student organizations. Such pages showed 12 members in 1893, 30 in 1896, 22 in 1897, 14 in 1898, 13 in 1899, 8 in 1900, 9 in 1901, 21 in 1903, 8 in 1906, 18 in 1907, 57 in 1910, and 53 in 1911, when the listings stopped. Members sent their newspapers more than 50 stories a week in 1911, and some sent several reports a week to daily newspapers, but most were correspondents for weeklies.[13]

Students may have acted as correspondents as early as 1875, however. In 1926, Judge Francis D. Winston, who had graduated from UNC in 1879 and had been a state legislator, lieutenant governor, U.S. attorney, and university trustee, told members of the North Carolina Press Association (NCPA) that he had been a correspondent for the *Raleigh News* during his junior year at UNC in 1875.[14] Another student correspondent was Quincy Sharpe Mills, who was a correspondent for the *Charlotte Observer* and the Richmond, Va., *Times-Dispatch* before he graduated in 1907. One of his favorite teachers was Edward Graham, who seemed to have sparked Mills' interest in journalism. When Graham was about to be installed as university president, he wrote to Mills: "If I could have about a dozen of you fellows that I used to teach—or I'll make it two dozen—I would be willing to let all the college presidents and 'stuffed prophets' go somewhere else, and we would have a real good time just among ourselves."[15] Mills worked for the *New York Evening Sun* as a reporter and editorial writer from 1907 until 1917, when he resigned to enlist in the U.S. Army for service in World War I. He was killed by a German artillery shell in France on July 26, 1918.[16]

In 1898, the association urged students and faculty members to put news items in a box on the door of the bursar's office, a plea that did not generate additional news copy.[17] The group's 1906 banquet was attended by UNC president Francis P. Venable and Cobb, who spoke about the importance of the country newspaperman. Venable told the students the work of newspapermen was vital to the university and that the university had always tried to make their jobs easier. He advised them to go home after graduation and run a country newspaper. J. E. Latta, professor of electri-

13. "Press Association Is Big Thing," *Tar Heel*, March 11, 1911, 1.

14. North Carolina Press Association, proceedings of the 1926 annual convention, 28–29.

15. James Luby, *One Who Gave His Life: War Letters of Quincy Sharpe Mills* (New York: G.P. Putnam's Sons, 1923), 75.

16. A bequest from his mother in 1956 established the Quincy Sharpe Mills Scholarships that are still awarded in the School of Journalism and Mass Communication.

17. "The University Press Association," *Tar Heel*, March 22, 1898, 2.

cal engineering, was toastmaster for the evening, and he was identified in the story as someone "closely identified with the work."[18] Louis R. Wilson said Latta and subsequently Wilson himself served as a "press committee" that supervised the students and functioned as a news bureau for the university.[19]

Sixteen men representing 20 newspapers attended the 1907 banquet. The guest of honor was Graham, then a faculty member in the Department of English, dean of the College of Liberal Arts, and former *Tar Heel* editor, who talked about the growing importance of college journalism: "The man who sees every side of life in this country, and the man who has the most power in the nation today is the newspaper man." That was especially true in North Carolina, he said, and for rapid advancement and attainment of power and fame, no calling offered as much opportunity as journalism. Until five years earlier, he said, there had been little interest in journalism at the university, but the number of interested students had been steadily growing. Students saw the opportunity that journalism offered for a good life. He admonished them against doing too much routine work: "Express *yourself* [emphasis in text] in college journalism—it is the expression of your individuality that counts."[20]

In the same issue that reported on the banquet, the *Tar Heel* reviewed a trade journal article that painted college journalism in a positive light, saying it trained students to think and express their thoughts and prepared them to enter journalism after graduation. Students who made the most of that opportunity had a good working foundation on which to build, the reviewed article said.[21] That review and the story about the Press Association banquet seemed to be attempts to alert the faculty and administration to the need for journalism instruction. Cobb spoke to the Press Association later that year and said he had never lost interest in journalism since his college days. He talked about advantages of journalism for individual self-development and the importance of the Press Association for telling people in North Carolina about the university.[22]

The interest in journalism on campus was serious, and many former students from the Press Association and the *Tar Heel* had become jour-

18. "Newspaper Men Banquet," *Tar Heel*, Feb. 22, 1906, 1.

19. Wilson to Gordon Gray, Aug. 10, 1953, Norval Neil Luxon Papers #4585, Southern Historical Collection, University of North Carolina at Chapel Hill Library.

20. "The Journalists' Banquet," *Tar Heel*, Feb. 14, 1907, 1.

21. "On College Journalism," *Tar Heel*, Feb. 14, 1907, 1. The reviewed article was by Warwick J. Price and appeared in a magazine called the *Journalist*.

22. "Press Association," *Tar Heel*, Sept. 19, 1907, 1.

nalists after they graduated: Ralph Graves (class of 1897), Sunday editor of the *New York Times*; R. E. Follin (1897), city editor of the *Charlotte Observer*; W. T. Bost (1897), Raleigh correspondent for the *Greensboro Daily News*; Charles Phillips Russell (1903), city editor of the *New York Call* and a future journalism faculty member; Victor L. Stephenson (1905), the *New York Evening Post* and the *Charlotte Observer*; S. H. Farabee (1905), editor of the *Hickory Daily Record*; Quincy Sharpe Mills (1906), editorial writer for the New York *Evening Sun*; and Oscar Coffin (1909), editor of the *Raleigh Times* and future chairman of the Department of Journalism and dean of the School of Journalism.[23]

First Journalism Course

The serious interest in journalism, the hints in the pages of the *Tar Heel*, the number of students working on the newspaper staff, and the students in the Press Association combined to create a desire for journalism instruction at the university. One can easily imagine the students at the 1907 Press Association banquet approaching Edward Graham and other university officials after the banquet to ask that a journalism course be offered. Their request almost certainly got a sympathetic ear because of the university's need for publicity in the state's newspapers. Consequently, English 16, Journalism, first appeared in the university catalog[24] for the 1909–10 academic year, although the news was not reported in the *Tar Heel*. The fact that a journalism course was taught in the English department was not unusual. The earliest college journalism courses were about writing, which was taught in English departments, and journalism programs at other universities across the country had similar origins. College-level journalism instruction in the United States began in 1869 at Washington College (later renamed Washington and Lee) in Virginia. The program, championed by college president Robert E. Lee, included scholarships and internships but lasted only one year, probably because of Lee's death in 1870 and opposition from leading newspapers. Other early programs and curricula were located at the University of Pennsylvania (1893) and the University of Illinois (1904), and the first school of journalism was founded at the University of Missouri in 1908.[25]

23. "Getting the News to Campus is a Good Sized Job," *Tar Heel*, Feb. 22, 1921, 1.

24. *The University of North Carolina Catalog, 1909–10* (Chapel Hill: University of North Carolina, 1909), 52.

25. Joseph A. Mirando, "The First College Journalism Students: Answering Robert E. Lee's Offer of a Higher Education" (paper presented to the History division of the

Professor Edward Kidder Graham taught the first journalism course at the University of North Carolina in 1909. He was professor of English and dean of the College of Liberal Arts at the time and was university president in 1913–18. *(North Carolina Collection, University of North Carolina at Chapel Hill Library. Reprinted with permission.)*

Graham taught the two-credit course in addition to English 3, Advanced Composition, the prerequisite course. The catalog described English 16 as "the history of journalism; the technique of style; the structure of the news story; and the study of modern journals," including discussions and practical exercises. The location of Graham's classroom is not known, although it was probably Smith Hall. It had been built for $10,000 in 1853 and was named for General Benjamin Smith, governor of North Carolina in 1810 and a generous benefactor to the university. Originally called Library and Alumni Hall, the building had multiple functions: university library, ballroom, and site for commencement exercises and meetings of alumni and trustees. It had classrooms on the main level and an agricultural chemistry laboratory in the basement. By 1907, Smith Hall was inadequate as a library because it was too small and because many of the books were so high on bookshelves that they were inaccessible to students and faculty members.[26] After a new library, Hill Hall, was completed in 1908 and the books and shelves had been cleared out, Smith Hall was used for English and journalism courses as late as 1916 and was converted to the Playmakers Theater in 1925.[27]

Graham was a logical person to teach the journalism course. As a student, he had been president of the Athletic Association, associate editor of the *Tar Heel* in 1896, and editor-in-chief of the *Tar Heel* in November–December 1897 before graduating in 1898. As a faculty member, he had

Association for Education in Journalism and Mass Communication, Washington, D.C., Aug. 9–12, 1995.)

26. Arthur S. Link, *A History of the Buildings at the University of North Carolina* (honors thesis, University of North Carolina, 1941), 47, and Henderson, *Campus of the First State University*, 44, 144, 148. In April 1865, at the end of the Civil War, a contingent of Union cavalrymen "occupied" Chapel Hill and the university and stabled horses in several buildings, including Smith Hall's basement.

27. Henderson, *Campus of the First State University*, 145.

Smith Hall, ca. 1907. Journalism courses were taught in Smith Hall in 1916 and prob-ably earlier. *(North Carolina Collection, University of North Carolina at Chapel Hill Library. Reprinted with permission.)*

supported students in the University Press Association and extolled the importance of journalism to them. He was also the thesis adviser for Levi Brown's 1910 account of the early days of journalism at UNC.[28] As dean of the College of Liberal Arts, Graham was in a position to respond to stu-dent requests to create a journalism course, especially because he was so well-liked by students. A story in 1908 about his impending marriage said he was "one of the strongest men in the faculty and universally respected by the students, who recognize him as a friend, a gentleman, who will give a square deal under all circumstances, and a teacher of rare ability."[29]

Graham also had ties to a family of journalists in Chapel Hill. Accord-ing to the 1900 U.S. Census, he was a boarder in the home of Mrs. Julia Graves at the present site of the Carolina Inn. One of her sons, Ralph, had graduated in 1897 and worked on the *Tar Heel* at the same time as Graham; Ralph later became Sunday editor of the *New York Times*. A younger son,

28. Brown, "Journalism in the University of North Carolina."
29. "Prof. Graham to Wed," *Tar Heel*, June 11, 1908, 7.

Louis, lived in the home while Graham boarded there. Louis graduated in 1902 and also worked at the *New York Times,* was manager of Parker and Bridge publicity company, and worked for New York city government before returning to Chapel Hill to teach journalism.

Graham's role in the development of journalism education in North Carolina was later recognized at the NCPA meeting in 1919 in a 12-stanza poem by William Hill, which ended thusly:

> Weed well his grave, here sleeps a man so true,
> 'Tis well to honor him,
> So bright a gem (alas! we find so few,)
> His fame shall never dim.
> And as we think, of all that he hath done,
> To build and hearten youth,
> We now can see, the victory he won,
> For God, and Man, and Truth.[30]

Little is known about the students who took the early courses, but an editorial note in 1911 said the editors had given responsibility for one issue to students in the journalism course: L. A. Brown, F. Hough, J. B. Halliburton, and T. P. Nash Jr. According to the note, the editors jokingly disclaimed responsibility for libel suits that might result from the experiment.[31] Brown received his bachelor's degree in English in 1910, writing an undergraduate thesis about the history of journalism at UNC prior to that time—with Graham as his adviser—and may have taken the journalism course as a graduate student. After receiving a master's degree from the university in 1911, Brown was a Washington, D.C., correspondent for the Raleigh *News and Observer,* White House correspondent for the *Philadelphia Record,* and director of publicity for the U.S. Committee on Public Information in 1917–18. He later wrote for several publications, was president of Lord, Thomas, and Logan advertising agency in New York City, and was public relations director of Pan American Airways when he died in 1947. When the university raised money in 1931 to build Graham Memorial Building to honor Edward Kidder Graham, Brown donated the considerable sum of $80,000.[32]

Despite their low numbers on campus at the time, women were on the

---

30. North Carolina Press Association, proceedings of the 1919 annual convention, 25–26.

31. Editorial note, *Tar Heel,* Feb. 22, 1911, 2. A similar note about a class of 14 students appeared on Dec. 11, 1913.

32. Wilson, *The University of North Carolina, 1900–1930,* 289, 420.

Tar Heel staff, and at least one may have been in an early journalism class. Mary MacCrae, the first woman admitted to UNC and the daughter of Law School dean James C. MacCrae, was associate editor in 1898, Hazel Holland was managing editor in 1901, Louise Wilson was associate editor in 1911 (and may have been the first woman to enroll in a journalism course), Watson Kasey[33] was associate editor in 1912, and Anna Liddell was associate editor in 1915.

According to the catalog, Graham taught the journalism course again in 1912–13. In the intervening years of 1910–12, and again in 1913–15, the course was taught by Professor James Finch Royster, a Shakespeare expert in the English department.[34] He had a bachelor's degree from Wake Forest and a Ph.D. from the University of Chicago and had joined the English faculty in 1907. As a relative newcomer, he may have been assigned to teach the journalism course when Graham was named president of the university in 1913. Nothing is known of Royster's journalism background, but he was related to Vermont Connecticut Royster, who graduated from UNC in 1935 and became editor of the *Wall Street Journal* before returning to the university to teach in the School of Journalism in 1971–86.

A student prize was also created in 1909 to stimulate excellence in journalism. E. R. Preston, a Charlotte attorney, created the Preston Cup

James Finch Royster taught journalism in the Department of English, 1910–15. He later became dean of the College of Liberal Arts and dean of the Graduate School. *(North Carolina Collection, University of North Carolina at Chapel Hill Library. Reprinted with permission.)*

33. Kasey was identified as Miss Watson Kasey in the newspaper.

34. A university catalog is not the same as a schedule of courses in a given term. Course descriptions in the catalog are limited in length for reasons of space and cannot convey the true nature of course content or approach. The catalog lists courses in the curriculum and individuals who normally teach them. In a specific term, however, a particular course might not be offered, or another person might teach it. Edward Graham was named university president in 1913, so Royster may have taught the course in 1912–13.

in memory of his brother, Ben Smith Preston, and the prize continued to be awarded until 1931. According to Brown's history of journalism at UNC, Ben Preston was a former UNC student who died sometime before 1910 while working as a reporter on the *Atlanta Georgian*.[35] Records of the UNC General Alumni Association indicate that Ben Preston attended one summer session in 1905.

Stories in the *Tar Heel* offered some indication of class sizes and suggested that the journalism course was taught with practical elements in those early years. Royster saw the value of field trips and cultivating relationships with state newspapers. In 1911, he took five students to visit the *News and Observer* and *Daily Times* in Raleigh. They left Chapel Hill by car at 10:30 a.m. to go to Durham to board a train to Raleigh, and they returned to campus at 4:30 the next morning. After talking to editors, touring the facilities, and accompanying reporters on their jobs, they enjoyed a dinner hosted by *News and Observer* editor Josephus Daniels at the Yarborough Hotel.[36]

Student journalists felt they were spending enough time on publications to deserve academic credit. In 1912, the editorial boards of the *Tar Heel* and the *University Magazine* petitioned the faculty to give two hours of academic credit to the editors to make the positions more important and to compensate editors for their efforts. The outcome of their request was not reported.[37]

35. Brown, "Journalism in the University of North Carolina."
36. "The Embryos of Fourth Estate," *Tar Heel*, Dec. 19, 1911, 1.
37. "Petition to the Faculty," *Tar Heel*, Feb. 20, 1912, 1.

"I am enjoying the peaceful life, loaf-
ing much but working a little on plans
for teaching journalism—about which
I feel at sea to a degree that I confess
to no one."—*Louis Graves*[1]

2. Growth, Tragedy, and Recovery

Major changes occurred in the next 10 years, including the addition of
new journalism teachers and courses and the creation of a journalism certificate program. The university was so serious about its emerging journalism program that it sent a faculty member to another university to learn
more about teaching journalism and hired a former newspaperman to
teach journalism. World War I and the Spanish influenza epidemic affected the campus and the journalism program, but the rebounding interest in journalism led the university to create a separate academic department in 1924.

Richard Thornton and Expansion

Professor Richard Hurt Thornton was apparently hired in 1915 to teach
journalism courses in the English Department, because he immediately
started teaching those courses and rarely taught others. He replaced James
Finch Royster, who taught journalism for two years before resigning in
1915 to go to the University of Texas. (Royster returned to UNC in 1921 as
a Kenan Professor of English and taught until his death in 1930.)

Thornton was instrumental in creating new journalism courses and

1. Louis Graves to Ralph Graves, July 31, 1921, Louis and Mildred Graves Papers
#4010, Southern Historical Collection, University of North Carolina at Chapel Hill
Library.

drawing attention to the importance of journalism education. Years later, his widow wrote to Chancellor N. Ferebee Taylor to clarify her husband's role in teaching journalism courses. She said he spent the summer of 1916 at the University of Wisconsin to study its journalism program because Wisconsin and the University of Missouri had the two best journalism programs in the country. According to her recollection, Thornton taught the journalism courses in a classroom on the second floor of the old library building (Smith Hall). Mrs. Thornton said her husband taught 50 to 60 students in courses in reporting, news editing, and feature writing, and the *Greensboro Daily News* gave the students an entire page every Sunday for their articles. She said two well-known Japanese journalists were in his classes, as was Billy Polk, who later became chief editorial writer for the *Greensboro Daily News.*[2]

In 1915, the number of journalism courses in the Department of English was increased to four options in English composition courses, but the term "journalism" was not used in the course titles, and the title of English 16 was changed to "Debating." The *Tar Heel* was also acknowledged as part of the journalism curriculum:

English 27–28. ENGLISH COMPOSITION. THE WRITING AND ED-
ITING OF NEWS. "The first term is spent in writing news and in studying the make-up of newspapers. Weekly news assignments are given in addition to written work in class. Many of the more important American newspapers are studied in detail. The second term will continue news writing and also take up the editing of copy. Junior and senior elective; also open to sophomores on the staff of the 'Tar Heel.' Both terms, three hours." Taught by Richard Hurt Thornton.

English 29–30. ENGLISH COMPOSITION. EDITORIAL AND FEATURE
WRITING. "Editorial policies and problems associated with the weekly and daily newspaper will be given attention. A study of the short-story methods as applicable to feature writing will be made in the second term. Junior and senior elective. Both terms, three hours." Thornton.

Signaling a significant step toward the creation of a journalism department and major, the catalog also announced that students interested in

2. Nina Thornton to Taylor, July 19, 1976, Nelson Ferebee Taylor Records #40023, University Archives, University of North Carolina at Chapel Hill Library.

journalism work could earn a certificate in journalism by taking certain electives from various departments in the College of Liberal Arts and completing the four journalism courses.[3] Such certification presumably aided graduates who sought newspaper jobs.[4]

Louis R. Wilson said Thornton was the first person at UNC to perform some of the functions of a news bureau. Wilson added, however, that Thornton's efforts were not well-received by the state's newspapers, and Wilson claimed to have written most of the news releases about major university events himself.[5] Thornton's journalism program had expanded enough by 1915 that Edwin A. Greenlaw, chairman of the Department of English, asked Graham for dedicated space for the journalism course, including storage for newspapers and periodicals used in the course, and a laboratory classroom where students could write.[6]

Newspaper Institute

With support (and likely a mandate) from Graham, Thornton extended the reach of the journalism program in 1916 by working with the NCPA and the North Carolina Association of Afternoon Newspapers to organize a Newspaper Institute for the state's newspapers to discuss their problems and plans for improvement. The newspaper people arrived on campus on Thursday, Dec. 7, for sessions in the Dialectic Literary Society Hall in New East building on Friday and Saturday, and the institute ended at 1 p.m. Saturday. It was held annually at UNC until 1989, when parking problems on campus prompted the NCPA's officers to move it to another location. The concept was revived at the school in 2001 with the Newspaper Academy, a daylong program of training and education for newspaper reporters, editors, and advertising staffs.

The staff of the *Tar Heel* was needed to publish the *Press Institute Daily*, a newspaper for institute attendees, so a journalism class produced that week's issue of the student newspaper. The institute newspaper included

3. *The University of North Carolina Catalog 1914–15* (Chapel Hill: University of North Carolina, 1914), 58.

4. The university revived the certificate concept in the 1990s, when the School of Journalism and Mass Communication offered three-course certificates in business journalism and sports communication.

5. Wilson to Gordon Gray, Aug. 10, 1953, Norval Neil Luxon Papers #4585, Southern Historical Collection, University of North Carolina at Chapel Hill Library.

6. Greenlaw to Graham, May 3, 1915, archives of the Department of English #40081, Southern Historical Collection, University of North Carolina at Chapel Hill Library.

wire-service copy and was the first daily newspaper published on campus, albeit for only three days: Dec. 7, 8, and 9. The United Press Association provided wire service copy, and a Linotype Model 19 typesetter was provided by the Mergenthaler Linotype Company of New York, with the consent of the Noell Brothers of the *Roxboro Courier*, who had purchased the machine. Leroy F. Alford, production superintendent of the Raleigh *News and Observer*, was a volunteer Linotype operator, and the paper was printed by the University Press on campus. The student staff, which operated out of the *Tar Heel* office in the YMCA building, consisted of W. T. Polk, editor-in-chief; C. G. Tennent, managing editor; and C. B. Webb, business manager.

In addition to news about the institute, the newspaper included national and international news—especially about the fighting in World War I—and reprints of articles about newspapers that had appeared in other publications. Four Chapel Hill merchants—Foister's, A. A. Kluttz, Patterson Drugs, and Carolina Drug—advertised in each issue. Mergenthaler used half-page ads to promote the Model 19 that was used to produce the newspaper and to say it could be purchased for $2,700.

NCPA president E. E. Britton of the *News and Observer* wrote about the importance of the institute. He said men and women of North Carolina newspapers were assembled on campus not for entertainment, but "to better equip themselves for service, that the papers which are the products of their brains, their energies, their resources, may better serve their clients."[7]

William H. Taft, former president of the United States, opened the institute with a speech to more than 600 people in Gerrard Hall on Thursday night, but his topic was U.S. foreign policy, not newspapers. Graham welcomed the group on Friday morning and said the university and newspapers needed to work together to "solve the great problems of the people in both prosperous and stunted communities." He said the university belonged to "no one class of people, but to men in every walk of life." He added that such a statement could not have been made 30 years earlier, when the university was supported largely by private means, with many of its buildings funded by private subscription. In the last 10 years, he said, the university had become a public institution "free to all men." A third stage had been reached, he added, and the university was begging men to come to the university to learn. The newspapermen had been invited to the university, he said, "not to be taught by us, but that we may be a medium through which knowledge may be spread and given to the great bulk of the people which both newspapers and the university try to reach."

7. Britton, "Service Above All," *Press Institute News*, Dec. 7, 1916, 2.

The university and newspapers should cooperate to relieve and solve community problems, he said. "Just as the university is the product of the ideas and feelings of the community in which it is, so it is with the newspaper," he concluded.[8]

Thornton explained to the group how he taught his journalism courses. "College-trained journalists are no longer the exception but have become the rule," he was quoted as saying in a story that mistakenly identified him as head of the Department of Journalism.[9] Professor E. C. Branson of the *University News Letter* spoke about "The Newspapers and North Carolina," and Oscar Coffin of the *Raleigh Times* spoke about "The Handling of State News." Other speakers included Walter Williams, dean of the School of Journalism at the University of Missouri, and Talcott Williams, director of the School of Journalism at Columbia University.

Reports of the number of newspaper people at the institute varied. The institute newspaper said more than 100 attended, but its list of registered attendees included only 39 names.[10] The *Tar Heel* also said more than 100 attended, and an editorial said the success of the institute illustrated the need for an expanded journalism curriculum at the university. The student newspaper's writer described the atmosphere in colorful terms: "Long cigars with noted newspaper men have been wreathing the YMCA building in smoke the last three days. For the State Newspaper Institute has been with us."[11]

Thornton was also involved in efforts to create an association of collegiate journalists in North Carolina. At a 1917 meeting in Chapel Hill when the North Carolina College Press Association was formed, he proposed that students should receive academic credit for work on college publications and cited the Department of Journalism at the University of Kansas as a model.[12]

War and Influenza

Two global events affected journalism instruction at the university in 1917–18: World War I and the Spanish influenza epidemic. The United States entered the war in April 1917, and journalism courses were curtailed

8. "President E. K. Graham Welcomes Journalists." *Press Institute News*, Dec. 8, 1919, 1.

9. "Newspaper and the Community Discussed; Session Opens," *Press Institute News*, Dec. 8, 1916, 1.

10. "Complete Registration List Given Here," *Press Institute News*, Dec. 9, 1916, 3.

11. "Newspaper Men of State Meet Here," *Tar Heel*, Dec. 9, 1916, 1.

12. "State College Press Association Organized," *Tar Heel*, April 17, 1917, 1.

in 1917–18 because of military activities on campus. Before he left campus to serve in the U.S. Navy, Thornton persuaded the *Greensboro Daily News* to provide space for student editorials.[13] Many UNC students took military courses, joined the Student Army Training Corps, conducted drills and maneuvers, and dug practice trenches at the edge of Battle Park near Raleigh Road. Some dormitories were called barracks, and the Army opened a post exchange on campus. The *Tar Heel* did its part to conserve paper by reducing its type size and the number of pages from six to four. The student newspaper lamented the fact that most students said they did not have time to read newspapers: "We are not keeping up with what is going on in the world at a time when history is being made faster than ever before, and we are supposed to be some of the best informed youth in North Carolina."[14] The end of the war on Nov. 11, 1918, brought an end to most military activities on campus.

The worldwide Spanish influenza epidemic also had an impact on the university. More than 500 of the approximately 1,000 students enrolled at the time became ill with the flu, and three died.[15] The *Tar Heel* printed the names of the victims in black-bordered boxes at the bottom of page one, one victim per issue. A three-week quarantine of patients was lifted in October 1918 when the epidemic was waning, but 35 victims were still in the infirmary. Two university doctors had become ill, and second-year medical students had to help care for the sick. An editorial note implored professors to open classroom windows to let in healthful fresh air.[16]

The greatest tragedy of the influenza epidemic at the university was the death of 42-year-old president Edward Kidder Graham on Oct. 26, 1918, five days after he contracted influenza and only three days after the *Tar Heel* had reported that the influenza epidemic on campus was waning. A note on page 1 of that issue mentioned another notable victim: "Mr. T. C. Wolfe, managing editor of the *Tar Heel*, left the Hill last week to be with his brother, reported very ill with pneumonia at his home in Asheville."[17] That note almost certainly referred to author Thomas Wolfe's visit to his brother Ben, whose death was portrayed as the death of Ben Gant in Wolfe's novel *Look Homeward, Angel*.

13. "Students' Editorial Work Wins Publicity," *Tar Heel*, Feb. 2, 1918, 1; "Comment by Students in Editorial Writing at the University of North Carolina," *Greensboro Daily News*, Jan. 20, 1918, 4; Feb. 3, 1918, 4.

14. "Newspapers," *Tar Heel*, March 2, 1918, 2.

15. Louis R. Wilson, *The University of North Carolina, 1900–1930*, Chapel Hill: The University of North Carolina Press, 1957, 275.

16. "Influenza Situation Is Rapidly Improving," *Tar Heel*, Oct. 23, 1918, 1.

17. Ibid.

Rebirth in 1919

After curtailing journalism courses during the war and the influenza epidemic of 1917–18, the English Department offered three journalism courses in 1919, and the student newspaper hinted that even more courses were likely: "Journalism is one of the post-war courses being offered in the university which is proving to be quite a success from many angles." The story described the courses: news writing, in which the students wrote for state newspapers on timely topics dealing with the various aspects of the university (English 27); news editing, which covered the study and preparation of manuscripts for publication (English 28); and feature stories (English 29).

Thornton had considered returning to Chapel Hill after the war, but Greenlaw told him there would not be enough work for him because class enrollments in journalism were small and Greenlaw could accommodate those students in his own course. He also advised Thornton to get practical experience in journalism, saying it was absolutely necessary for him if he wanted to get ahead in the field.[18] Thornton did not return to the university, and he later became president of Henry Holt publishing company, where he worked with such authors as Carl Sandburg, Thomas Wolfe, Robert Frost, and Vachel Lindsay.[19]

Clarence Addison Hibbard began teaching journalism courses in 1919. A news story identified him as "head of this department in the English department" and said he was qualified because of his extensive experience as a newspaper correspondent in Japan.[20] In offering the position to Hibbard, Greenlaw said he wanted him to teach "an elementary course in journalism, consisting of about thirty-five men, which should run through three terms."[21] Hibbard was also considering a job offer in Canada but chose to come to Chapel Hill. He said he would consult during the summer with Willard G. Bleyer, head of the University of Wisconsin's journalism program, before he came to Chapel Hill.[22] Greenlaw told Hibbard a month later that he would teach the three journalism courses (English 27, 28, and

18. Greenlaw to Thornton, Dec. 16, 1918, English department archives.
19. "Thornton Writing Program," Lynchburg College Web site, http://www.lynch burg.edu/thornton.xml, accessed May 29, 2008.
20. Hibbard left UNC in 1930 and went to Northwestern University, whose Web site said he had taught at several government schools in Japan and was a newspaper correspondent from 1909 to 1914. See http://www.library.northwestern.edu/archives/findingaids/addison_hibbard.pdf, accessed June 1, 2008.
21. Greenlaw to Hibbard, May 6, 1919, English department archives.
22. Hibbard to Greenlaw, May 8, 1919, English department archives.

29) to 25 men five days a week. He also said Hibbard and his wife could rent a new bungalow in Chapel Hill for $20 or $25 a month. The house had water, electricity, and a good location. It lacked a furnace, but Greenlaw said that would not be a problem because it had a fireplace and an adequate supply of pine and oak firewood.[23]

Lenoir Chambers, who had graduated from UNC in 1914 and received a master's degree from Columbia University, was listed as a professor of journalism in the College of Liberal Arts. He did not teach any courses but was director of the university's News Bureau and editor of the *Carolina Alumni Review* in 1919–21. The first summer school course in journalism, in 1919, was designed for high school teachers. The textbook was *Dillon's Journalism for High Schools*, and students in the course got experience by writing for the *Summer School News*. Summer courses in journalism were not offered for many years afterward.

The student newspaper was optimistic about the future of journalism instruction at the university, saying the journalism "department" would get permanent quarters, including a reading room, in the basement of Alumni Building as soon as the Electrical Department moved into the new science building (Phillips Hall). The news story read like an editorial, expressing hope for a "school" that would compare favorably to others in the country. It cited the large number of articles by current students that had appeared in newspapers in North Carolina and other states. The story said the new "department" and the new School of Commerce showed that educators in the state had responded to demands of the times and had given young people in the state what they wanted at UNC instead of making them go elsewhere. The story

Clarence Addison Hibbard taught journalism courses in the Department of English, 1919–21. He patterned his courses after those in the Department of Journalism at the University of Wisconsin–Madison. *(North Carolina Collection, University of North Carolina at Chapel Hill Library. Reprinted with permission.)*

23. Greenlaw to Hibbard, June 5, 1919, English department archives.

boasted that journalism students at UNC took only five percent of their courses in journalism, compared to 15 percent in the "big schools of journalism in the large Eastern universities." Despite what the story said, the university had not yet created a department of journalism.[24]

The journalism program had an international flavor in 1920. Two Japanese students at UNC, a Mr. Kita and a Mr. Taketomi, both graduates of Waseda University in Tokyo, were enrolled and had expressed interest in journalism and economics. Taketomi planned to study journalism at Columbia University the following year, and a former Japanese student named Nagano was editor-in-chief of the Hochi *Daily News*.[25]

Journalism activities on campus were described in a *Tar Heel* story in an orientation issue for new students in 1920. It identified three publications—the *Tar Heel*, the *Tar Baby*, and the *Carolina Magazine*—in addition to three journalism courses in the English department. The story said graduates of 1920 had found jobs with newspapers, including N. G. Gooding, city editor of the *Morning New Bernian* in New Bern; C. T. Leonard, reporter at the *Greensboro Record*; H. G. West, editor of the *Chairtown News* in Thomasville; and E. W. G. Huffman, on the staff of the *Greensboro Daily News*.[26]

Meanwhile, Hibbard continued teaching through the spring term of 1921, guiding the rejuvenation of the North Carolina Student Press Association and garnering the praise of a major state newspaper. In February, 16 students representing 11 colleges and 13 publications met on the UNC campus and were welcomed by President Harry Woodburn Chase and Professor Frank Porter Graham. Hibbard told the student journalists how to make their newspapers vital: choose an editor-in-chief with executive ability, stress good layout and design, develop a nose for news, make the newspaper vital to its readers, have a definite policy or platform, use human-interest stories, and print as many names as possible.[27]

Hibbard's approach to teaching journalism drew the attention of at least one newspaper in the state. An editorial in the Gastonia *Daily Gazette* praised him for putting the theory of the classroom into practical use and said students were not satisfied with the "mere monotony" of classroom work. Instead, they prepared "live" news stories from the university

24. "School of Journalism Important Feature in Our Greater University," *Tar Heel*, Dec. 6, 1919, 1.

25. "25 Foreign Students Are Enrolled," *Tar Heel*, Feb. 7, 1920, 1.

26. "Work in Journalism Has New Impetus," *Tar Heel*, July 20, 1920, 4.

27. "Editors of North Carolina College Publications Meet; Organize Press Association," *Tar Heel*, Feb. 8, 1921, 1.

and sent them to newspapers of their home county. The editorial said students were getting real experience and citizens were learning about the university. It also said many newspapers were using such stories instead of regular news bulletins, implying that the students' work took the place of the former University Press Association or even the News Bureau.[28] The editorial referred to a department of journalism even though a department had not been created. Hibbard was still teaching other English courses and was also vice president of the North Carolina State Council of English Teachers.[29]

Professor of Journalism in the English Department

Journalism at UNC reached a significant milestone in 1921 with the hiring of Louis Graves as head of the News Bureau and the first person to hold the title of Professor of Journalism in the Department of English. Graves, the first journalism teacher at UNC to have significant newspaper experience, replaced Hibbard, who continued teaching American literature in the English department, and Chambers, who left the university. The student newspaper heralded the significance of Graves' appointment, saying it meant that one man was to devote all of his time to journalistic work. Graves, the story said, was "an old Carolina man who finished here in 1902. He was born and raised in Chapel Hill. He was a great football player and perhaps the best tennis player in the university."[30]

Graves, newly married to the younger sister of Edward Kidder Graham's late wife,[31] moved back to Chapel Hill in the summer of 1921 and prepared for his new duties. One of his first actions was to join the NCPA, and he spoke at an NCPA meeting on July 28, where he was introduced as being "connected with the School [*sic*] of Journalism at the university." He himself called it a school in his speech about "Journalistic Talent for the Future in North Carolina," and he solicited the assistance of every newspaper in the state in developing the budding program.

"The craft of newspaper writing has suffered from a vagabond atmosphere which used to surround it," Graves said, "and writers used to be

28. "State Press Praises Teaching of Hibbard," *Tar Heel*, March 8, 1921, 4; "Real Teaching," *Gastonia Gazette*, Feb. 17, 1921, 2.

29. "Hibbard Is Honored by English Teachers," *Tar Heel*, March 11, 1921, 4.

30. "Graves Is New Head of Journalism Here," *Tar Heel*, June 7, 1921, 2.

31. Graham's wife, Susan Moses Graham, had died in 1916, five years after their son, Edward Kidder Graham Jr., was born and two years before her husband died. Louis Graves and his wife, Mildred Moses Graves, raised the son, who went on to have a career in higher education.

looked upon as freaks, a sort of strolling minstrel, drunkards, etc.; and even yet you find people who look upon the journalist as hanging around the fingertips of reputable society." More preparation should be given to training in journalism, he advised, "so that those who are to do newspaper work will be absolutely clear about the duties when they come to a newspaper office, and the school of journalism is the solution." A journalism teacher should teach what news is and how to present it, he said, and how to read copy and write headlines, and his courses would include news writing, headline writing, copyediting, proofreading, and feature writing. Students would study history and economics in addition to journalism and would learn that there is "no writing too good for newspapers." The overriding emphasis would be on "practice, practice, practice."[32] The attention to history, economics, and practical instruction continued throughout the history of the journalism program.

Louis Graves was the first professor of journalism in the Department of English, in 1921–24. He was also head of the News Bureau at UNC until he resigned to publish the *Chapel Hill Weekly*. (*North Carolina Collection, University of North Carolina at Chapel Hill Library. Reprinted with permission.*)

Later in the convention, the NCPA commended efforts to start a school of journalism at Washington and Lee University as a memorial to Robert E. Lee. The NCPA also applauded the establishment of "schools" of journalism at UNC and the State College of Agriculture and Engineering (now called North Carolina State University) in Raleigh and pledged cooperation with both.[33] Neither university had established a school of journalism at that time, however. UNC would create its Department of Journalism in 1924 and its School of Journalism in 1950. N.C. State University never had a school of journalism, although it offered journalism courses

32. North Carolina Press Association, proceedings of the 1921 annual convention, 18–19.
33. North Carolina Press Association, proceedings of the 1921 annual convention, 41.

in its business school in the 1920s. In 1931, the Consolidated University of North Carolina was formed from UNC–Chapel Hill, N.C. State University, and N.C. Women's College, and the School of Engineering at Chapel Hill and the business school at N.C. State were closed.[34] That led at least a few people to mistakenly believe that UNC–Chapel Hill had swapped its engineering school for a journalism school.

Louis Graves told his journalist brother Ralph of the *New York Times* about the NCPA meeting and bragged that he had delivered an "eloquent speech" on the great future of the teaching of journalism in North Carolina. To his brother, however, he confessed apprehension about his new role and revealed his plans for teaching the course. He said that if he were at a loss for what to say in class, he would simply command students to write something. He also asked for his brother's suggestions, especially for the names of journalists who might be traveling through North Carolina and who could be persuaded to talk to the journalism students.[35]

At the start of the fall term, the student newspaper had high expectations for Graves, saying he had been given the task of raising the newly established department to a footing equivalent to other departments at the university. Despite what the story said, the university had not created a department of journalism, and the error may have been an example of students' not understanding what an academic department was. It is also possible that university officials were using the term loosely or may have told students that a department was being planned.[36]

One of Graves' early changes was to modify the journalism curriculum in the English department, and he created three courses:

English 27. NEWS WRITING. "An elementary course in the writing of various types of news stories. Members of the class are encouraged to write stories on subjects of interest to the State papers, and some of these productions are published. A prerequisite for English 28."

English 28. NEWS WRITING AND NEWS EDITING. "A continuation of English 27. The drill in news writing continues, and the conditions of work imposed grow more nearly like those in a newspaper office. Beginning of instruction in the editing of news (copy-reading). A prerequisite for English 29."

34. Louis R. Wilson, *The University of North Carolina Under Consolidation, 1931-1963: History and Appraisal* (Chapel Hill: The University of North Carolina Consolidated Office), vi, 36.

35. Louis Graves to Ralph Graves, July 31, 1921, Louis and Mildred Graves Papers.

36. "Faculty Increased by Sixteen Persons," *Tar Heel*, Oct. 4, 1921, 1.

English 29. NEWS WRITING, NEWS EDITING, FEATURE WRITING.
"A continuation of English 28, including instruction in the writing
of feature stories."[37]

As hard as he tried, Graves was unable to live up to expectations for
the journalism program because he was also running the News Bureau
and making plans to start his own newspaper in Chapel Hill. In his second term on the faculty (spring 1922), Graves melded his teaching and
News Bureau duties by assigning his students to send news releases to
state newspapers, which prompted negative reactions from some people,
including Chambers. It is not clear whether the objection was to having students do Graves' work for him or to a fear that students were un-
qualified, but Greenlaw did not think the objections were too serious to
be overcome. Graves would be responsible for the students' work, and
Greenlaw said he should use special forms for news releases, similar to
the forms used at the universities of Missouri, Kansas, and Wisconsin.
The main difficulty would be with the athletic teams, Greenlaw said, and
Graves would have to monitor those stories himself. Greenlaw assured
Graves he could find some "hand-picked men" whose work could be sent
directly to the newspapers. He also said Graves would render a great service to the university if he could improve the relationship of the university to the state press.[38]

The student newspaper said Graves had written stories himself the previous term, but he no longer had the time to do it. In his defense, Graves
may have seen this as an opportunity for students to get practical experience and to get their stories published. He said the field for journalism
work at the university was almost unlimited and predicted rapid growth
for it, adding that he had plans for a department in the next two or three
years. The story also reported that Graves held a reception for student
journalists at his home.[39]

Graves made it easier on *Tar Heel* staffers and student correspondents
for state newspapers when he allowed them to get credit for their work
through a new course, English 30, "Advanced News Writing."[40] Near the
end of the spring 1922 term, the *Tar Heel* reported that 16 students in the

37. *The University of North Carolina Catalog 1921–22* (Chapel Hill: University of
North Carolina, 1921), 266.
38. Greenlaw to Graves, Dec. 16, 1920, English department archives.
39. "Student Newspaper Men Send Out Carolina News," *Tar Heel*, Jan. 20, 1922, 1.
40. "Tar Heel Board Gets Handout from Faculty," *Tar Heel*, Feb. 3, 1922, 1.

feature writing class had been getting three or four articles published each week.[41]

Less than a year later, a *Tar Heel* editorial lamented the scarcity of publicity outside the state about the university, and it said this situation presented an opportunity for students because the scope of the News Bureau had been too limited. The circumstances, the editorial said, offered a chance for the "Department of Journalism" to do work that would benefit the university and give students important experience.[42]

Meanwhile, Graves' plans to start his own newspaper reached fruition with the first issue of the *Chapel Hill Weekly* on March 1, 1923. He told the student newspaper that he hoped his journalism students could contribute articles to his newspaper.[43] He announced a few days later that he was purchasing his own printing press and would install it in the basement of the Strowd Building in Chapel Hill so he could print his paper in Chapel Hill instead of Durham. He hired A. E. Shackell, a student with printing experience, to help him.[44]

The journalism program suffered from neglect while Graves was occupied with the *Chapel Hill Weekly*. In October, a *Tar Heel* editorial complained about the lack of journalism courses and said there was support on campus for a daily newspaper. It said the university was large enough for a daily newspaper and that all journalism students should work toward that goal. It closed with the observation that the university had offered no journalism courses that year.[45] A few weeks later, another editorial said Graves had attempted to make up for the fact that no journalism courses were being taught by starting an informal journalism club for *Tar Heel* staff members to discuss newspaper work and try to improve the paper.[46]

C. B. Colton, *Tar Heel* editor that year, apparently wrote the editorials. In February, he wrote that the journalism offerings in the English department had met with limited success. According to him, 50–60 students at UNC were interested in journalism careers, but they had limited opportunities and were looking to other schools outside North Carolina, which hurt the state. "It is no wonder," he wrote, "that North Carolina is woefully weak on self publicity when her largest educational institution gives no

41. "Journalism Class Does Good Work This Year," *Tar Heel*, April 30, 1922, 3.
42. "Tell the World About Us," *Tar Heel*, Jan. 12, 1923, 2.
43. "Chapel Hill Weekly Makes Its Appearance," *Tar Heel*, March 6, 1923, 1.
44. "Chapel Hill Weekly to Be Printed Here," *Tar Heel*, March 9, 1923, 4.
45. Editorial note, *Tar Heel*, Oct. 16, 1923, 2.
46. Editorial note, *Tar Heel*, Nov. 6, 1923, 2.

instruction in a profession that is the molder of thought in this country." He added that the university was probably aware of the shortcoming and wanted to create a school of journalism when the proper men and funds could be found. The person chosen to run the program should have theoretical and practical preparation, the editorial said.[47]

47. "Why North Carolina Has No Press Agent," *Tar Heel*, Feb. 15, 1924, 2. The title of this article was remarkably similar to that of a book written in 1924 by Irvin S. Cobb, a humorist and columnist for the *Saturday Evening Post* and *Cosmopolitan* magazines: *North Carolina, All She Needs Is a Press Agent* (New York: George H. Doran, 1924).

3. Department of Journalism

It was unworkable to have a professor of journalism in the English department teach journalism courses and run the News Bureau, so in 1924, the university answered student demands and created a separate Department of Journalism in the College of Liberal Arts. The first department chairman lasted only two years, but his successor built a program that became an important part of North Carolina journalism and laid the foundation for even greater impact and prestige.

Gerald Johnson

With a front-page story on May 27, 1924, the *Tar Heel* announced the creation of the Department of Journalism, saying that although university officials had kept a "sphinx-like silence," students had heard rumors about plans to open a Department of Journalism for the 1924–25 academic year. The report said Gerald W. Johnson, an editorial writer for the *Greensboro Daily News*, had agreed to be chairman of the department and that a construction company had developed plans to build a nine-room house for him and his family.[2] Johnson was a North Carolina native and a 1911 graduate of Wake Forest University who had started the *Davidsonian* newspaper

1. Quoted in Wint Capel, *Shucks and Nubbins* (Chapel Hill, N.C.: CapeCorp Press, 2000), 15.
2. "G. W. Johnson to Head School of Journalism," *Tar Heel*, May 27, 1924, 1.

Gerald W. Johnson, first
chairman of the Depart-
ment of Journalism,
1924–26. *(North Carolina
Collection, University of
North Carolina at Chapel
Hill Library. Reprinted with
permission.)*

in Thomasville, N.C., in 1910 and worked for the *Dispatch* in Lexington,
N.C. When classes started on Sept. 19, 1924, the two journalism courses
had more students than expected—13 in the basic course and four in the
advanced course, with five women among the 17 students.[3] The department was temporarily located on the second floor of New West, above the
student newspaper offices and below a room where the UNC wrestling
team practiced.[4] The department moved to Alumni Building two years
later.

The Department of Journalism first appeared in the university catalog in 1924 as part of the College of Liberal Arts, and graduates could receive a Bachelor of Arts in Journalism. Johnson was the only professor in
the department, and he taught two courses each term from the six-course
curriculum:

3. Thad Stem Jr., *The Tar Heel Press* (Raleigh: North Carolina Press Association,
1973), 177.
4. "Gerald W. Johnson Is New Department Head: Infant Department of Journalism
Finds Itself a Very Popular Baby," *Tar Heel,* Sept. 20, 1924, 1. See also Capel, *Shucks
and Nubbins,* 55. New West was constructed as a dormitory in 1860. Arthur S. Link, *A
History of the Buildings at the University of North Carolina* (honors thesis, University
of North Carolina, 1941), 53.

1. NEWS WRITING. "A course in elementary news writing, including practical work in the class room and outside assignments. Prerequisite for Journalism 2. Five hours a week, fall quarter."

2. NEWS WRITING AND EDITING. Prerequisite, Journalism 1 or the equivalent. "A continuation of the work of Journalism 1, with the addition of some instruction in copy-reading and head-writing. Prerequisite for Journalism 3. Five hours a week, winter quarter."

3. NEWS WRITING AND EDITING. Prerequisites, Journalism 1 and 2 or the equivalent. "A continuation of the work of Journalism 2, but with more emphasis on copy-reading and head-writing, and with the addition of some instruction in make-up. Five hours a week, spring quarter."

10. DESK WORK. "This is a course for advanced students in the problems of deskmen and executives. It includes also practice in special article writing. Three hours a week, fall quarter."

11. PUBLIC OPINION AND THE NEWS. "A study, based largely on contemporary newspapers, of prevailing methods of handling various types of news, with some attention to the theories of Walter Lippmann and others. Three hours a week, winter quarter."

12. POLICY AND RELATIONS. "Comparative examination of news—as distinguished from editorial—policies of various newspapers. Study of the relation of the newspaper man to the general public. Editorial writing. Three hours a week, spring quarter."

Journalism majors had to complete the same freshman and sophomore requirements as other B.A. students at the university: three courses in English; three in each of two foreign languages; two each in history, mathematics, and science; and two electives. The overall degree requirements emphasized a strong background in the arts and sciences, and only six courses out of 40 (15 percent) could be in journalism. In addition to completing the six journalism courses in their junior and senior years, journalism students had to complete courses in advanced English composition, economics, national government, state government, American history, and North Carolina history; an advertising course and a resources and industries course taught in the Commerce Department; a course about the use of books; and a sociology course. The emphasis on a broad liberal arts

New West, ca. 1929. From 1924 to 1926, the Department of Journalism was on the second floor, above the student newspaper offices and below a practice room for the wrestling team. In the 1890s, the University Press, which printed the student newspaper, was on the north side of the first floor. *(North Carolina Collection, University of North Carolina at Chapel Hill Library. Reprinted with permission.)*

education with a minimal number of journalism courses has been characteristic of the school ever since.[5]

As the journalism teachers before him had done, Johnson stressed practical fundamentals in his courses. Shortly after launching the department, he spoke to a group of students on campus about "Journalism as a Profession," saying journalism could not really be called a profession because a journalist was not independent. He said the field of journalism was growing in North Carolina, but the work was "grinding, hard and constant."[6] A few weeks later, O. J. Peterson of the *Chatham Record* in Pittsboro came to Chapel Hill on personal business and visited Johnson's journalism class. The visit was deemed worthy of a story in the student newspaper, in which

5. *The University of North Carolina Catalog 1924–25* (Chapel Hill: University of North Carolina, 1924), 149, 182.

6. Lucy Lay, "Gerald Johnson for Journalism," *Tar Heel*, Nov. 6, 1924, 1.

Peterson was described as a veteran newspaperman of the "good old days" of the profession.[7] In 1925, the university's extension division announced a contest for high school journalists, which was created to improve the quality of high school journalism. The story did not mention the Department of Journalism.[8]

Johnson was not destined to remain at the university. The *Tar Heel* reported on Feb. 11, 1926, that he had submitted his resignation and would join the staff of the Baltimore *Sun* at the end of the academic year, but Johnson refused to confirm or deny the report. Hamilton Owens, editor of the *Sun*, had attended the recent Newspaper Institute on campus, where he bragged to several people that Johnson would soon join his staff. Johnson's salary at the *Sun* was reported to be $6,000 per year, compared to his university salary of $4,000, and he had supposedly turned down an offer from a Virginia newspaper for $6,000. The *Tar Heel* said Johnson's departure would be a big loss for the university and the state. It said he had filled the difficult position of department chairman to everyone's satisfaction and concluded, "The university campus hopes that reports of his going are premature."[9] A week later, the *Tar Heel* reported that Nell Battle Lewis, a columnist for the Raleigh *News and Observer*, had said the state would "sorely miss" Johnson.[10] Two weeks later, the student newspaper reported that Oscar J. Coffin, editor of the *Raleigh Times*, was being considered as a replacement for Johnson, but that UNC president Harry Chase would neither confirm nor deny the report.[11] The rumors were true, and Johnson did go to Baltimore, where he became a well-known editorial writer for the *Sun*, a television commentator, and a novelist.

"Skipper" Coffin

Johnson was succeeded by one of the legendary figures in journalism at the University of North Carolina: 39-year-old Oscar Jackson Coffin, known as "O. J." or "Skipper." He had been editor of the *Tar Heel* and a typesetter for the University Press and had graduated in 1909, so he could not have taken a journalism course at UNC. In the 1909 *Yackety Yack*, Coffin's senior class listing has his original or selected quotation: "Here's to those who love us well, those that don't can go to hell." He had worked

7. "A Journalist of the Old School Drops In," *Tar Heel*, Nov. 15, 1924, 2.
8. "State High School Journalism Contest," *Tar Heel*, April 1, 1925, 3.
9. "Gerald Johnson Resigns Position," *Tar Heel*, Feb. 11, 1926, 1.
10. "Johnson Lauded by Miss Lewis," *Tar Heel*, Feb. 18, 1926, 1.
11. "Coffin May Replace Gerald Johnson Here," *Tar Heel*, April 1, 1926, 1.

Oscar "Skipper" Coffin, chairman of the Department of Journalism, 1926–50, and dean of the School of Journalism, 1950–53, ca. 1930. *(North Carolina Collection, University of North Carolina at Chapel Hill Library. Reprinted with permission.)*

for the Asheboro *Courier* and the *Charlotte Observer* and was editor of the *Raleigh Times* when he came to Chapel Hill to become chairman of the Department of Journalism. Coffin may have contemplated teaching at UNC as early as 1916, when he was at the *Observer.* In a 1916 letter to President Edward Kidder Graham, he expressed doubts about his future in Charlotte and said he hoped to go to the *Greensboro Daily News.* He also suggested another option: "If I get fired—and I'd take it as a compliment from Cowles—I'll be down to talk things over." In the same letter, he said his infant son (also named O. J.) had died after living only two days.[12] Coffin's only preparation for teaching journalism was one month spent "observing" teachers at Columbia University's School of Journalism, and he recalled that most of what he learned there was how not to teach newspapering.[13] Stuart Sechriest, whom Coffin hired as a faculty member in 1946, said that when people asked Coffin why he became head of the Department of Journalism, he said, "Only God knows!"[14]

Coffin did not have News Bureau responsibilities because Robert Madry had returned to his former position as director of the bureau after working as a journalist in New York and Paris. Madry taught two courses in educational publicity, the first public relations courses taught at UNC, and Coffin taught the other journalism courses. The department moved to

12. Coffin to Graham, April 12, 1916, Oscar Coffin Papers #3907, Southern Historical Collection, University of North Carolina at Chapel Hill Library.

13. Jack Riley, "Tar Heel of the Week: O. J. 'Skipper' Coffin," Raleigh *News and Observer,* May 14, 1950, IV-3.

14. Sechriest, interview with the author, May 21, 2007.

two rooms on the south side of Alumni Building and offered new courses, including the two public relations courses and two specifically for *Tar Heel* staff members:

5–6. EDUCATIONAL PUBLICITY. Junior and senior elective. "A course designed to give instruction in the writing of public school and college events for newspapers. Not to be given unless there is a registration of at least four students. (Not open to general A.B. students.) Three hours a week, fall and winter quarters." Madry.

7–8. WEEKLY NEWSPAPER EDITING. Prerequisites, Journalism 1, 2, and 3. "A study of the functions of the weekly newspaper, with practical instruction in meeting the problems of the neighborhood news medium. Three hours a week, winter and spring quarters." Coffin.

11. NEWS METHODS AND TREATMENTS. (Replaced PUBLIC OPINION AND THE NEWS.) "A study of contemporary newspapers and of prevailing methods of handling news. Three hours a week, winter quarter." Coffin.

30. COLLEGE REPORTING. Sophomore and junior elective. "A course in reporting for members of the staff of the university tri-weekly, "The Tar Heel." The work of the reporters is supervised and a maximum of one course credit is given for meritorious extra-curricular activity." Coffin.

31. COLLEGE EDITING. Junior and senior elective. "A companion course of Journalism 30, this being designed to aid editors and copy-readers of "The Tar Heel" in their head-writing, lay-out, and other editorial duties. Maximum credit of one course." Coffin.[15]

The two educational publicity courses were dropped in 1927, when Coffin was the only faculty member. Johnson's Journalism 10 course was changed to "Feature Writing," described as a course for advanced students in the production of feature stories, with a view to making the stories marketable. The title of Journalism 12 was changed to "Editorial Writing," which

15. *The University of North Carolina Catalog 1926–27* (Chapel Hill: University of North Carolina, 1926), 150–51.

was described as a comparative examination of newspapers' editorial policies and the relationship of newspapermen to the general public.[16]

The university's commencement speaker in 1927 was the noted journalist Walter Lippmann. University catalogs of that era included the printed commencement program, which included the names of all enrolled students. The program in 1927 identified students pursuing degrees in journalism (Arts-Jour) for the first time. Five were listed, including Holt McPherson of High Point, who claimed he was the first student to talk to Gerald Johnson in 1924 and therefore was the first student in the Department of Journalism. Later, as editor of the *High Point Enterprise,* he played an important role in starting the Journalism Foundation of North Carolina in 1949, changing the department to a school in 1950, and finding a new dean in 1953. The other students in 1927 were James Bruton Allen of Troy, N.C.; Ameel Fisher of Jacksonville, Fla.; Delbert Edley Livingston of Lakeland, Fla.; and William Henry Orrison of Anniston, Ala.

Alumni Building, ca. 1931. The Department of Journalism occupied offices and classrooms on the first floor from 1926 to 1935. *(North Carolina Collection, University of North Carolina at Chapel Hill Library. Reprinted with permission.)*

16. *The University of North Carolina Catalog 1927–28* (Chapel Hill: University of North Carolina, 1927), 151.

The department had only approximately 10 students in the late 1920s, prompting concern on the part of at least one editor in the state. John Park, editor of the *Raleigh Times*, had written to UNC president Chase about a report he had seen about the numbers of students in journalism programs around the United States; based on the report, he wondered if the sparsely enrolled UNC program should be abolished. Chase said he didn't know how to explain why UNC had so few journalism students, except to express doubt that journalism in North Carolina offered an attractive career field to college graduates.[17]

Chase forwarded a copy of Park's letter to Coffin and assured him that he had no "numerical ambitions" for the department and even less interest in the attempts of standardizing agencies to make departments conform to standards. He was not concerned, he said, about any ratings or numbers of students.[18] The comments about standardizing agencies probably referred to the emerging movement toward national accreditation of journalism programs. Coffin thus seemed to have had high-level administrative reinforcement for his disdain of accrediting organizations and accreditation standards, an issue that would plague him and the department 20 years later, when the university re-examined the issue and sought accreditation.

Park apparently thought Chase agreed that the department should be abolished because of its low enrollments.[19] Chase said he did not agree that the small number of students was an argument for eliminating the program, saying the department provided a valuable service, had a good influence on student writing and the student newspaper, and turned out men who had an idea what journalism was all about. He told Park, however, that the low numbers were a strong argument against any expansion of the department and that Coffin agreed with that assessment.[20]

Coffin was the only journalism instructor in 1930, but not all courses were offered every quarter. Course numbers changed for some courses as part of a universitywide revision, and Journalism 53, the number for the news writing course known to thousands of students until its number was changed to JOMC 153 in 2006, appeared for the first time:

17. Chase to Park, June 25, 1929, Chancellor's Records: R. B. House Series #40019, University Archives and Records Service, University of North Carolina at Chapel Hill Library.

18. Chase to Coffin, June 25, 1929, Chancellor's Records: House Series.

19. Park to Chase, June 27, 1929, Chancellor's Records: House Series.

20. Chase to Park, July 2, 1929, Chancellor's Records: House Series.

Coffin as Teacher and Mentor

Coffin was remembered as a teacher and friend by hundreds of former students. His collection of accumulated papers in the North Carolina Collection of the UNC–Chapel Hill Library contains hundreds of letters from former students as well as his replies to most of them. They wrote to tell him about marriages, births, and deaths; to report new jobs; to ask about changing jobs; and to seek career advice. Roland Giduz, a former student, recalled that Coffin insisted that students call him "Skipper,"[22] and many of them did that in their letters.

He was given that nickname by Edward Blodgett, a student who was called "Doc" by students and faculty members. Blodgett admitted that he was not a model student and that he used to go to Coffin's classes unprepared. Coffin did not put up with shoddy work and was quick to criticize Blodgett, who confessed he had no excuse for not doing the work and could answer only, "Aye, aye, Skipper." The name stuck.[23] Although Coffin was chairman of the Department of Journalism, he had an aversion to calling a newspaperman a journalist, saying: "A journalist is a man who comes into your office, claims to work on a newspaper in another town, and borrows five dollars from you. We train people to work on newspapers, not to be journalists."

Robert Ruark, who later achieved fame as a syndicated columnist and novelist, was one of Coffin's students in the early 1930s and made Coffin perhaps the only journalism administrator featured in a work of fiction. In Ruark's novel *The Honey Badger*, written nine years after Coffin's death,

---

21. *The University of North Carolina Catalog 1930–31* (Chapel Hill: University of North Carolina, 1930), 157.

22. Giduz, interview with the author, Oct. 10, 2007.

23. Robert Bartholomew, "O. J. Coffin is Rounding Out 25 Years as Journalism Dean," *Asheville Citizen*, Oct. 28, 1951, A7.

the protagonist, Alec Barr, attends college in Chapel Hill in 1933. He accompanies a journalism major to a gray-stoned building (Alumni Hall or Bynum Hall) to meet the dean of the journalism school, called "Skipper" Henry by "people he liked well enough to insult." Ruark described Henry in colorful terms that matched what others said about Coffin, calling him a "benevolent old sea-turtle, up to and including the barnacles. His eyes were hooded behind glasses that clung precariously to the end of a hooked nose." The fictional dean believed that the best way to clear a man's mind in the morning was whiskey, and his clothes smelled like "home-cooked corn liquor." Henry was a "fat, sloppy, ash-sprinkled, egg-speckled, tie-askewed, stringy-haired, liver-spotted Old Buddha."[24]

The fictional Dean Henry was in his sixties, had been a newspaperman most of his life, and wrote a column titled "Grits and Chitlins." Barr talks his way into Henry's journalism course although he is an economics major. Henry tells him about students in his course, saying most students took his course because he was supposed to be a "vulgar, cussin' old coot who tells dirty stories and don't hold any final exams." To test Barr's talent, Henry asks him to write a news story about the Biblical story of Esau selling his birthright for a mess of pottage. He gives Barr an admonition: "Don't try to improve too much on The Good Book. Them old Jew boys knew the value of a good hard verb, even if they did get a little muddled up on the facts." In the book, Henry assigned students to go to the police courts, the state capitol, sports events, insane asylums, and prisons, and to write reports on what they saw there. Instead of lecturing, he read and "dissected" the reports in class, "quite often cruelly."[25]

In one scene from the novel, Barr visits Dean Henry at his home, where Henry is sitting with his shoes off in a leather easy chair on his elm-shaded front porch. His glasses are on the end of his nose, and he has a half-filled glass of whiskey beside him. The fictional dean gives Barr advice about the few rules of the newspaper business: The writer should write only what he knows about and should not start writing until the story is clear in his head. He should not listen to anything off the record, reveal his sources, or take cheap gifts. Finally, he should "take it easy on the booze."[26]

Roy Wilder Jr., one of Coffin's former students and a classmate of Ruark's, thought Ruark exaggerated some of Coffin's characteristics and behavior in the Dean Henry character. Wilder said in 2007 that Coffin had a pot belly and his pants looked like they were going to fall down. He had to

24. Ruark, *The Honey Badger* (New York: McGraw-Hill, 1965), 148–57.
25. Ruark, 153.
26. Ruark, 157.

hitch them up when he talked, and his glasses did slide up and down his nose. He had a bad cough because of asthma. Coffin drank alcohol, Wilder conceded, but he never smelled it on Coffin or thought he was under the influence. He said Coffin was often rumpled, but he believed that his wife, "Miss Gertrude," would not have let him out of the house looking like the descriptions of Henry. Wilder recalled being invited to eat dinner in the Coffin home on many occasions and said the scene on the porch was over-blown because Mrs. Coffin would not permit drinking in the house or on the porch. The comment about Biblical writing was accurate, Wilder said, because Coffin often referred to the Bible as good, terse writing.[27]

In 2007, several of Coffin's former students talked respectfully about him. Walter Klein recalled that Coffin sent students to observe the local police court, much as Ruark's fictional Dean Henry did. When they came back to class, he grilled them about their stories.[28] Trudy Atkins recalled that students dreaded Coffin's class because he tore their stories apart.[29] Jo Pugh Woestendiek said she and other students enjoyed going to Cof-fin's house on Park Place and talking to Coffin and his wife on their front porch. She also recalled that Coffin could take a joke, even when it was at his expense. Students in her photography course took a picture of Cof-fin one day that appeared strange because he looked more like an animal than a human in it. When the students asked people what the creature in the picture looked like, some said it looked like an eel, and others said it looked like a donkey. Coffin laughed at Woestendiek's story about the pic-ture and helped her to get it published in the *Greensboro Daily News*—her first published story.[30]

A student who later became a famous bohemian poet also recalled Cof-fin with reverence. Lawrence Ferlinghetti graduated from the Department of Journalism in 1941, served in the Navy in World War II, and became owner of City Lights Bookstore and the associated City Lights Publishers in San Francisco in the 1950s. As the publisher of Allen Ginsberg's poem "Howl" in 1956, Ferlinghetti won an important freedom-of-expression court case. He was named the first poet laureate of San Francisco in 1998. Ferlinghetti remembered Coffin teaching a newsroom course in which students had to go out on campus and in the town, cover stories, and turn them in every day. He conducted the class as if he were a city editor and the students were reporters sitting around him at a rectangular table. In

27. Wilder, interview with the author, Oct. 31, 2007.
28. Klein, interview with the author, Oct. 5, 2007.
29. Atkins, interview with the author, Nov. 30, 2007.
30. Woestendiek, interview with the author, Feb. 20, 2008.

"Skipper" Coffin, Walter Spearman, and students gather around a famous alumnus—journalist and novelist Robert Ruark—who immortalized Coffin in a semiautobiographical novel, *The Honey Badger*, written nine years after Coffin's death in 1956. Ruark is seated in the center. Left to right are "Skipper" Coffin, Cecil Prince, Sam Summerlin, Sara Lee Gifford, Mary Elizabeth Pell, an unidentified student, Walter Spearman, Bill Rumfelt, and Clarence Whitefield. *(School of Journalism and Mass Communication, UNC–Chapel Hill. Reprinted with permission.)*

2008, as he imitated Coffin's classroom demeanor, Ferlinghetti's voice rose: "Now, when I say write a lead, I mean how, where, when, who, and why, in that order!"[31]

Lois Cranford, who received her journalism degree in 1945, had intended to major in mathematics but changed her mind after one term at UNC. She vividly remembered her introduction to Coffin and the department, saying she knocked on the door to the journalism office.

"Come in!" someone said in a rough voice.

"Doctor Coffin?" she asked tentatively as she stepped into the office.

"I'm O. J. Coffin!" he roared like a lion. "Ain't no doctor about it!"

That was Coffin, she said. "No pretense. He was an irascible, indomitable original, if ever there was one. Despite that gruff beginning, he was very kind to me, a lovable old codger, always chomping on a big cigar." He

31. Ferlinghetti, interview with the author, July 28, 2008.

welcomed her into the school and guided her—as he did countless other students—into courses in history, economics, and other fields.[32]

Alex Coffin, "Skipper's" great-nephew, entered the department as a student in 1955 and recalled that Coffin gave him the same advice about courses in other departments. He recalled from personal experience and from what faculty members told him that "Skipper" had been "irascible but dearly loved," especially by students. He often used his old car to drive students to see newspaper editors throughout the state, telling the editors that they had to hire the students.[33]

It was well-known that Coffin frequented a Chapel Hill tavern called the Shack. Giduz said Coffin was often there when it opened at 10 A.M. to smoke a cigar and drink a bottle of beer before going to his office. Coffin's wife called the Shack "Skipper's iron lung" because he could not live long outside of it, Giduz added.[34] Many students frequented the tavern to talk to Coffin and turn in their papers for his course. Woestendiek said she sometimes cut class to go there to drink beer with Coffin.[35] Cranford recalled that after classes ended in the afternoon, Coffin often "held court" at the Shack, downing a few beers and picking up grist for his folksy, humorous newspaper columns and his stimulating class lectures.[36]

Horace Carter remembered Coffin with great admiration and credited Coffin with inspiring him to be a crusading journalist because of a memorable event that occurred when Carter was editor of the *Tar Heel*. Carter had written an editorial that criticized university and state leaders for trying to pressure UNC president Frank Porter Graham into resigning from the national War Labor Board because, they felt, he was spending too much time in Washington, D.C. Within hours after the editorial appeared, state senator John Umstead called Carter and commanded him to meet Umstead at the Journalism Department immediately. When Carter arrived, Coffin met him and told him to hold his ground and not back down in the face of Umstead's pressure: "I don't give a damn what he said, but don't you back down one bit from what you wrote." Carter said Coffin's support that day inspired him to be a newspaper crusader, and Carter went on to win a Pulitzer Prize in 1956 for standing up to the Ku Klux Klan in Tabor City, N.C. He said Coffin was the "absolute replica of an old-time

32. Lois R. Cranford, "A '45 Carolina Coed Remembers," *JAFA News*, Spring 1987, 4–5, and interview with the author, Oct. 16, 2007.
33. Alex Coffin, interview with the author, Oct. 5, 2007.
34. Giduz, interview with the author, Oct. 10, 2007.
35. Woestendiek, interview with the author, Feb. 20, 2007.
36. Cranford, interview with the author, Oct. 16, 2007.

newspaperman" and a "tough old bird" who did not have a lot to do with people who didn't take him seriously. "He wanted you to learn something and go out and represent the University of North Carolina," Carter recalled. After Carter had achieved success and won his Pulitzer Prize, Coffin took pride in saying that Carter had been one of his students.[37]

Shortly after Coffin died in 1953, Joe Morrison, who was Coffin's student in the late 1930s and who joined the UNC faculty in 1940, submitted a manuscript about Coffin to *Reader's Digest* for its "Most Unforgettable Character" section. When the magazine rejected the article, Morrison got it published in the *Greensboro Daily News*. He said unabashedly in the article that he loved Coffin with all his heart and that he took Coffin's course because of his reputation for getting jobs for graduates of the department. Morrison said Coffin was "a softy trying to appear case-hardened, but was the kindest, warmest teacher I would ever know."

Coffin's guiding philosophy, Morrison said, was "a love of people—he preferred that they be 'folks'—and for his money nobody could be a decent newspaperman unless he enjoyed people." Morrison's description of Coffin at home resembled Ruark's description of the fictional Henry, saying Coffin sat in an easy chair by the fireplace, puffing away at a big cigar, "a solid granite block of a man." As Morrison read his news stories to Coffin, he nodded, "wheezing a little with the asthma that plagued him, growling out a correction now and then with Miss Gertrude quietly knitting on the sofa opposite." When Morrison graduated, Coffin hired him, first as a teaching assistant and later as a faculty member. Morrison suspected Coffin wanted to take advantage of Morrison's typing ability and use him as a secretary. After Morrison told Coffin his father had died when he was 11, Coffin took a special interest in him. Recalling Coffin teaching, Morrison said Coffin's voice "carried like a trench mortar, and he often rustled up old Willie Minor, the ancient Negro janitor, to sing a few revival hymns with him."[38]

Pete Ivey, another former student of Coffin's, later became head of the News Bureau at UNC. Writing about Coffin after his death, he said, "His wit was folksy. His criticism was swift and hard and fair, but it was softened by encouragement, a pat on the shoulder, and a hearty laugh." Ivey said Coffin pretended to hate pigeons, especially when they sat on a ledge outside his office in Alumni Building. "Coffin would sound off with blankety-blanks at the pigeons, and wish that they would leave for

---

37. Carter, interview with the author, Nov. 14, 2007.
38. Morrison, "'Skipper' Oscar Coffin—Late U.N.C. Journalism Teacher was Man of Plain Words," *Greensboro Daily News*, Jan. 19, 1958, D-1.

some other part of the campus." After he retired and moved to Raleigh in 1956, Coffin told people he did not plan to spend much time on the state capitol grounds there because there were too many pigeons. Ivey recalled that during the heat of Chapel Hill summers, Coffin slept on the porch of his house on Park Place and the newspaper carrier placed each morning's copy on top of him as he slept. Coffin's wife said she knew when his health had deteriorated because he stopped reading the newspaper.[39] The Coffin home, which was owned by the university, was located on Park Place in Chapel Hill. The site is now in a parking lot.

Coffin intimated on at least one occasion that he was sometimes frustrated with teaching. Writing to Henry Belk of the *Goldsboro News-Argus*, who had asked about the possibility of teaching advertising, Coffin said he had "no opening in the department that will enable any man, however wise, to get by by simply resting on the south end of his backbone and indulging in jargonistic conversation. Practically all of our work is lab work. I don't reckon you'd like it too well—sometimes I hate it—but if you think you would be interested, there would be no harm in talking it over.[40]

Phillips Russell and Walter Spearman

Two other men joined Coffin on the journalism faculty and became popular with students. Charles Phillips Russell returned to UNC (he had graduated in 1904) in 1931 at the request of UNC president Frank Porter Graham to teach in both the Department of English and the Department of Journalism. He was the great-nephew of Cornelia Phillips Spencer, who had achieved fame for ringing the bell in South Building on the UNC campus on March 20, 1875, to proclaim the reopening of the university after it had been closed during Reconstruction. In 1936, Russell decided to teach full time in the Department of Journalism, which he did until he retired in 1956. In addition to "Creative Writing" and "News Writing," Russell taught a new history course:

> 61. HISTORY OF JOURNALISM (3). "A study of the chief forces and personalities that have contributed to the development of American newspapers, particularly in modern times."[41]

39. Ivey, "Feet on the Desk," *Greensboro Daily News*, Nov. 4, 1956, 4-F.
40. Coffin to Belk, Aug. 5, 1946, Coffin papers. Coffin eventually hired Leon Pollander to teach advertising.
41. *The University of North Carolina Catalog 1937–38* (Chapel Hill: University of North Carolina, 1937), 185.

Phillips Russell in 1948. A journalism faculty member from 1931 to 1956, he often commented on student writing by saying, "Bring on the bear!" (Photograph by Stuart Sechriest. North Carolina Collection, University of North Carolina at Chapel Hill Library. Reprinted with permission.)

Horace Carter thought so much of Phillips Russell that he named his son Russell (who later became a UNC trustee and benefactor) after him. Carter also recalled that other people in the journalism department took care of him and encouraged him.[42] Trudy Atkins recalled Russell as having a big, bushy mustache, twinkling blue eyes, and bushy eyebrows. He sometimes invited her and fellow student Olive Ann Burns to have lunch at his house. Burns graduated in 1946 and wrote for the *Atlanta Journal and Constitution Magazine* before achieving fame with her novel, *Cold Sassy Tree*, in 1984.[43]

Ed Yoder, who was one of Russell's students in the 1950s, said the title of Russell's creative writing course was misleading, and he was contemptuous of the "hoity-toity" idea of creative writing, even though he had done a lot of it himself. He emphasized story structure and sometimes wrote on Yoder's papers: "I find wandering in your architecture." Russell was a stickler for organization and had useful ideas about how to structure writing. Yoder said that principle became riveted into his own writing, which eventually led him to be a columnist for the *Washington Post* and to win a Pulitzer Prize for editorial writing in 1979.

One of Russell's favorite sayings in class was "Bring on the bear." Yoder said it originated when Russell was reading "Goldilocks and the Three Bears" to his daughter. She knew the story by heart and grew impatient with his reading, saying, "Daddy, I thought this was a story about bears.

42. Carter, interview with the author, Nov. 14, 2007.
43. Atkins, interview with the author, Nov. 30, 2007.

Bring on the bear!" Applying that statement to writing, Russell said a writer should go one-third of the way down the first draft and mark it. That would be the place to "bring on the bear," and the writer should discard the first third. Russell also emphasized the importance of diction, and he sometimes asked students to write in the style of Japanese haiku or to write stories using only one-syllable words. Russell did a regular radio commentary on WUNC and had a way of punctuating an assertion by saying, "Yeah, um-hum."[44] Ferlinghetti credited Russell with inspiring him to be a writer. He said Russell was the one professor at UNC who made him love creative writing, especially because his course was often taught outdoors under the trees on campus.[45]

Enrollment data for the department are not available except for anecdotal reports, which showed eight students in 1924 and 10 in 1926. Data about the number of degrees awarded each year were printed in the university's annual commencement program and reflected growth in the number of students. The program listed five graduates in 1927, four in 1930, 11 in 1935, 25 in 1940, 23 in 1945, 28 in 1946, 52 in 1947, 78 in 1948, 79 in 1949, and 94 in 1950. The numbers dropped off after 1950, indicating the end of a postwar surge in graduates as men returned to campus after World War II and completed their degrees.

By 1935, enrollment had increased to the point that Coffin sought an additional faculty member and more space for the department. Robert B. House, the university's dean of administration (now called the chancellor), told A. W. Hobbs, dean of the College of Arts and Sciences and Coffin's superior, that he was troubled by Coffin's "restlessness" about the department. President Frank Porter Graham had said there was no money for new faculty positions and wondered if faculty members in the English department could teach some of the journalism department's writing courses. Nevertheless, Graham acceded to the request and approved the hiring of another man who became a legend in the department and the university.

Walter Spearman, who had been editor of the *Tar Heel* before graduating from UNC in 1929, wrote to Maryon "Spike" Saunders, head of the UNC General Alumni Association, in 1932 to say that he wanted to come back to the university to pursue an M.A. degree in English because he wanted to become an English professor in the future. He said his salary at the *Charlotte News* was sufficient to allow him to take a year off without pay, but he still wanted part-time employment on the *Carolina Alumni*

44. Yoder, interview with the author, Jan. 25, 2008.
45. Ferlinghetti, interview with the author, July 18, 2008.

Walter Spearman, beloved faculty member who taught journalism from 1935 to 1980, in a familiar pose in his Howell Hall office. *(North Carolina Collection, University of North Carolina at Chapel Hill Library. Reprinted with permission.)*

Review.[46] Saunders had no opening for Spearman at the time and told him the university's 1932 graduates were having trouble finding jobs during the bad economic times.[47] In 1935, Coffin and Graham called Spearman and asked him to join the faculty.[48] Spearman, who completed his M.A in drama instead of English, joined Coffin and Russell and taught a new course, Journalism 60, "Book Reviewing and Dramatic Criticism for Newspapers," as well as "News Writing" and "News Methods and Treatments," the editing course. The department had no secretarial staff, and Spearman and Russell at various times assumed additional responsibilities as the department's secretary for an annual stipend of $250.

Spearman worked part time for the *Alumni Review* while he was on the faculty before World War II. Shortly after reporting for military duty at Ft. Lee, Va., in 1942, he asked Saunders to reinstate him in the Alumni

46. Spearman to Saunders, April 5, 1932, Alumni Association records, UNC–Chapel Hill.

47. Saunders to Spearman, May 27, 1932, Alumni Association records.

48. Jim Jenkins, "It Started 5,000 Students Ago," *Greensboro Daily News*, Feb. 8, 1978, A6.

Association and said Saunders could take the $3 dues out of the money Saunders still owed Spearman for his work. Saunders replied with a check for $30 and promised a second check for $18, basing the amounts on Spearman's *Alumni Review* salary of $360 per year.[49]

Teaching was informal, Russell later recalled, and faculty members sometimes took the department's entire student body on field trips to newspapers. He said faculty members developed an esprit de corps, every man felt he had to keep up, and few graduates failed in their jobs. He and his colleagues could feel the pressure of growing enrollment and were uneasy about the possibility of the department changing to a school because they would have to abide by more rules in a school.[50]

Bynum Hall

The department moved to larger quarters in Bynum Hall (formerly known as Bynum Gymnasium) in 1935, after the university had used Works Progress Administration funding from the federal government to renovate it. Bynum had been completed in 1905, and it was paid for with a gift from Judge William P. Bynum to honor his grandson of the same name who had died in 1891 at the end of his sophomore year at the university.[51] The Department of Journalism was on the east side of the top floor (the News Bureau was on the west side), but Coffin's office was on the stairway landing of the west side of the first floor. Some faculty members had to walk through a classroom to access their offices. Courses with large numbers of students had to meet in other buildings, such as Gardner Hall. In 2007, Professor Donald Shaw—who was a student in the late 1950s—recalled that Bynum was a very small space and rather cluttered. When the department was there, he said it looked and sounded like an old newspaper office with chalk, dust, rulers, and clanking typewriters—similar to the newsrooms students would find when they went to work.[52] Dorothy Coble Helms, who graduated from the department in 1940, remembered that students sat around a table in a classroom and wrote their assignments.[53] Ken Sanford, who graduated in 1954, recalled that the department looked

49. Spearman to Saunders, June 28, 1942, and Saunders to Spearman, July 4, 1942, Alumni Association records.
50. Robin Denny, "School's Early Days Recalled," *UNC Journalist*, Nov. 9, 1974, 6.
51. Link, *History of the Buildings at the University of North Carolina*, 155.
52. Shaw, interview with the author, Oct. 19, 2007.
53. Helms, interview with the author, Sept. 24, 2007.

Bynum Hall, ca. 1934. Originally the university's gymnasium, it was the home of the Department and School of Journalism from 1935 to 1960. *(North Carolina Collection, University of North Carolina at Chapel Hill Library. Reprinted with permission.)*

like a classic newspaper newsroom when he arrived in 1952, including old typewriters.[54]

In anticipation of the move to Bynum, Coffin and other faculty members ordered reference books for the new reading room, including *Who's Who in America, North Carolina Yearbook, International Yearbook of Edi-*

54. Sanford, interview with the author, Oct. 5, 2007.

tor and Publisher, Daily Newspapers in America, Putnam's Book of Familiar Quotations, and foreign-language dictionaries for French, Latin, and German.

In 1938, House reported to Rogerson that he had reached four conclusions after a visit to the Department of Journalism: the university owed Walter Spearman $250 for secretarial services, the department needed two filing cabinets, House wanted to give the department one more classroom, and Coffin needed to know if the department was getting the full amount of money paid by students as course fees.[55] Rogerson replied that there was no money for equipment or classroom space. He also did not understand why Coffin had raised the issue of laboratory fees, saying Coffin had always complained that he could not be bothered with budgetary details, and Rogerson's office would continue to take care of Coffin's budgetary problems. He said he had made out Coffin's budget estimates and forms for him for several years.[56]

The country's entry into World War II meant a greater workload for remaining faculty members. Morrison went on military duty shortly after the Japanese attack on Pearl Harbor on Dec. 7, 1941, and served in Europe until the end of the war in 1945. Spearman left for military service in 1942 and returned after the war. J. Roy Parker was added to the faculty in 1941 to teach a new course in newspaper advertising and to change another course to "Country Newspaper Production."[57]

In 1943, the department created its first broadcast journalism course, Journalism 67, "Radio News and Features," taught at different times by Russell, Spearman, and Morrison. Students working with Russell reviewed the editorial opinions of North Carolina newspapers for a 15-minute radio program every Sunday on station WPTF in Raleigh.[58] A second advertising course, Journalism 63, "Newspaper Advertising II," was also added, and a note in the 1943–44 catalog said students in the V-12 Navy College Training Program on campus could enroll in "News Writing," "Feature Writing," "Editorial Writing," and "Advertising." In another accommodation to the V-12 program, the university switched from academic quarters to semesters in 1944.[59]

55. House to Rogerson, April 27, 1938, Chancellor's Records: House Series.

56. Rogerson to House, April 29, 1938, Chancellor's Records: House Series.

57. *The University of North Carolina Catalog 1941–42* (Chapel Hill: University of North Carolina, 1941), 222–23.

58. Coffin to House, Feb. 10, 1945, Chancellor's Records: House Series.

59. *The University of North Carolina Catalog 1943–44* (Chapel Hill: University of North Carolina, 1943), 212–13.

The war also affected student enrollment, especially for women. Under the university's restrictive policies at the time, women were admitted to the university in small numbers and primarily as transfer students in their junior year. Dorothy Coble Helms, one of the three women in the department in 1940, recalled that Coffin tried to talk two of them out of majoring in journalism because he said it was a hard career for women.[60] Despite those barriers, the percentage of women among journalism graduates each year was as high as 45 percent (five of 11) in 1935, 44 percent (eight of 18) in 1936, and 43 percent (10 of 23) in 1937. Russell recalled that the faculty had made a conscious decision about admitting more women: "There was kind of an agreement among the teachers that girls should be let in gradually. They were some of the smartest students I had."[61] With so many men in military service during the war, the percentages jumped to 75 percent women (21 of 28) in 1944, 83 percent (19 of 23) in 1945, and 82 percent (23 of 28) in 1946, as women were needed to replace men in newspaper offices. Female enrollment returned to its prewar levels in 1947, however.

Increasing enrollments and faculty losses due to the war took a toll on the department, prompting Coffin to complain to President Frank Porter Graham in early 1943: "No prophet or son of no prophet, I can make no predictions as to the future enrollment—it looks as if the increase in women students will keep the department hustling—and there is still more work than the present teaching force can adequately say grace over."[62] Coffin later complained several times about pressures caused by enrollment of veterans returning after war duty, and he anticipated that the veterans would be asking for more intensive and specialized skills instruction. "This is going to call for fresh instructional blood, and red. We have sought by our budget requests to approach this bridge; it will require the help of all hands to cross it."[63]

Coffin's pleas apparently paid off. After Spearman and Morrison returned from war duty in 1945, Louis H. Edmondson, who stayed only one year, joined the faculty to teach four new radio courses:

70. INTRODUCTION TO RADIO JOURNALISM

72. CONTINUITY WRITING

60. Helms, interview with the author, Sept. 24, 2007. She later married Jesse Helms, who represented North Carolina in the U.S. Senate from 1973 to 2003. The two met when they were both reporters on the Raleigh *News and Observer*.

61. Robin Denny, "School's Early Days."

62. Coffin to Graham, Jan. 6, 1943, Chancellor's Records: House Series.

63. Coffin to House, Feb. 10, 1945, Chancellor's Records: House Series.

Department of Journalism faculty, ca. 1948. Seated, left to right: Walter Spearman, Lola Lee Mustard, "Skipper" Coffin, Phillips Russell, Leon Pollander. Standing, left to right: Stuart Sechriest, Tom Lassiter, Joe Morrison. *(School of Journalism and Mass Communication, UNC–Chapel Hill. Reprinted with permission.)*

> 73. RADIO NEWS
> 77. PROGRAM PLANNING[64]

Three faculty members were added in 1946: Stuart W. Sechriest, John W. McReynolds (who stayed only one year), and Leon M. Pollander, who taught advertising. Sechriest added a new course: Journalism 80, "News Photography." The first woman faculty member, Lola Lee Mustard, started teaching advertising courses in 1948, and Thomas J. Lassiter taught Parker's courses while he was on leave.[65]

64. *The University of North Carolina Catalog 1945–46* (Chapel Hill: University of North Carolina, 1945), 139–40.

65. *The University of North Carolina Catalog 1948–49* (Chapel Hill: University of North Carolina, 1948), 256–57.

> "Administration is perhaps just about
> what this department has least of.
> I am a plough-pulling horse that in-
> tends to break no new ground
> until I get a fresh supply of
> fodder."—*"Skipper" Coffin*[1]

4. Pressures for Change

While he may have been ambivalent about teaching, Coffin made no pretense about his dislike for administrative duties, and he faced a number
of administrative challenges. As was true for other departments in the
university, the Department of Journalism had scarce resources during the
Depression, suffered faculty absences during World War II, and had to
deal with an influx of returning veterans after the war. Coffin had little use
for national associations of journalism educators, including accrediting
bodies, and that provincialism put him at odds with other professors on
campus and some members of the state press. That attitude would eventually color his leadership of the Department of Journalism and fuel demands by alumni and state newspaper leaders for improvements. Those
pressures for change, especially for accreditation, brought changes to the
department, leading to higher status as a separate school with a dean.

Coffin as Administrator

Stuart Sechriest said Coffin wanted students to take only a few journalism
courses without majoring in journalism so that the College of Arts and
Sciences—and not the Department of Journalism—would have to keep

1. Coffin to P. I. Reed, July 31, 1944, Oscar Coffin Papers #3907, Southern Historical
Collection, University of North Carolina at Chapel Hill Library.

records on them.[2] Coffin expressed his feelings about academic administration to the director of the School of Business Administration at the University of Tennessee, which was organizing a department of journalism in its School of Business and wanted a suggestion for someone to head the department. Coffin said a journalism department belonged in a college of liberal arts—not in a school of business—and that a department was "more serviceable" than a school. He added, however, that campus journalists did not always see eye to eye with him. Revealing how he felt about teaching as a profession, Coffin said his own faculty was composed of experienced newspapermen who would "hardly know how to assimilate a professional teacher."

Admitting that he was not open-minded, Coffin said student enrollment in the department had grown from 10 when he started teaching in 1926 to more than 150 in 1946. The faculty had no trouble finding jobs for the department's graduates, he said, but that was more the result of close ties with newspapermen in North Carolina, South Carolina, and Virginia than the department's academic reputation. "I don't think we have much of that," he said of the department's reputation, "and of the eight or nine journalism fraternities in existence we have refused to sponsor one." (That was apparently a reference to academic and professional societies for students, which Coffin adamantly opposed.) He warned that even if the University of Tennessee were to follow the UNC model, it would be "apt to incur considerable criticism from the journalistic Ph.D.s, M.A.s and the like, with an occasional expression of wonderment from the Southern Newspaper Publishers Association [SNPA] why you haven't been accredited after the fashion of Oklahoma, Missouri, Nebraska, Idaho, or any other schools farther to the west."[3]

The university had no African-American students in the late 1940s, but Coffin acknowledged a need to educate black journalists. In 1948, an official of Lincoln University, a historically black college in Jefferson City, Mo., sent Coffin a survey asking for the number of Negro graduates of the UNC journalism program. Coffin told him the university system was still segregated by race and he could not help him with the questionnaire.[4] In 1950, the president of North Carolina College (N.C.C.) at Durham (now N.C. Central University) asked Coffin about financial aid for Negro students at N.C.C. who wanted to major in journalism at UNC. Coffin outlined the requirements for the department and assured the president that he would

2. Gregg Davis, "Coffin Founded J-School," *UNC Journalist*, Nov. 9, 1974, 6.
3. Coffin to Theodore W. Glocker, Nov. 11, 1946, Coffin Papers.
4. Coffin to Edward Clements, March 29, 1948, Coffin Papers.

cheerfully give any assistance he could to the education of Negro journalists. He said some of the larger newspapers in the state would benefit from a Negro reporter, but the newspapers had to take the initiative.[5]

Coffin was clearly unimpressed with advanced academic degrees for journalism teachers, and none of his faculty members had an advanced degree in journalism. Spearman received an M.A. in dramatic art from UNC in 1937, and Morrison did not earn his master's degree from Columbia until 1958 and his doctorate from Duke University in 1961, after Coffin had died. Coffin had the same attitude toward starting a graduate program in the department. Roy Thompson, a former Coffin student, said Coffin had an explosive reaction when someone suggested that the department should grant master's degrees in journalism: "He showered sparks through his cigar, scorching the earth in his wrath and said, 'A newspaperman needs a master's the way a hog needs spats.'"[6]

Thompson also said Coffin rarely held faculty meetings and did not attend meetings of other deans on campus until he was forced to do so. When he heard of a desire to establish a chapter of Sigma Delta Chi, the national journalism fraternity, in the department, he said it would be done "over his dead and defenseless body." Coffin did not believe women should be in his classes, Thompson recalled. When a woman showed up, Coffin asked her, "Why don't you go back home and find yourself a good provider?"[7] (That contrasts with what other women, namely Dorothy Coble Helms, Trudy Atkins, and Lois Cranfield, later said about Coffin.)

Disdain for National Organizations

National journalism education associations did not mean much to Coffin, either. He had joined the American Association of Teachers of Journalism (AATJ) but probably never attended any meetings. His attitudes about such organizations were revealed in his reactions to an invitation from Perley Issac Reed, director of the School of Journalism at West Virginia University, to join the newly formed American Society of Journalism School Administrators (ASJSA) in 1945. Coffin's response indicated he did not have the inclination or time to worry about administration, which he said was scarce in the department.

5. Coffin to A. Elder, Sept. 12, 1950, Coffin Papers.

6. Bebo Edmunds, "School of Journalism Celebrates 50 Years," *Chapel Hill Newspaper*, Nov. 10, 1974, 1C.

7. Thompson, "'Skipper' Wanted Craftsmen for Newspapers," *Winston-Salem Journal and Sunday Sentinel*, Sept. 22, 1974, C-1.

He wondered why "an aging reporter-editor who was his own secretary" would want to join such an association. Acknowledging that the end of World War II would bring difficulties to the department, he said the faculty would still focus on "trying to help undergraduates learn to order their thoughts, if they had any." He said he had recently told another UNC administrator about the department's postwar plans: "To keep on trying to teach 'em to read and write, I reckon; nobody else seems interested in the dirty work."

Coffin told Reed that faculty members could not afford to travel to professional meetings even if they knew where the meetings were. He said he belonged to AATJ because he was a "union man," but he was too busy with "copyreading, cross-examination of would-be craftsmen, and operating the vacuum-cleaner and plumber's friend" to attend a meeting of a professional association or to look on himself as a professional man. He thought there were enough societies and associations and added that he wanted students "who appreciated and were ready to attempt to execute some of the niceties of self-expression and some teachers who conceived of teaching as being more nearly reading students' papers than efforts at their own at lodge-meetings."

Coffin was not trying to justify his attitude, he said, though he admitted it was limited and provincial, but he simply wanted to explain why the administration of the department was in the hands of a "lone wolf blowing little noses, washing backs of ears and sometimes wishing he could take his academic self more seriously and his classroom work less so." He closed with another jab at advanced degrees: "I didn't set out to write a confession of faith—for God knows I am tired of listening to sleeve-worn hearts throb overtime even though they be attached to Ph.D. gowns."[8]

Reed was persistent and repeated his invitation. Coffin was just as adamant in his second refusal and said he could not attend an ASJSA conference in Reno, Nev., because the university would not pay his expenses and his wife would insist on going with him: "I mark the twain of enthusiasm and solidarity which you suggest now exists among your members. I wish you well and if I thought it would do any good would remember you in my prayers. But I am as unregenerate as when I wrote you last. I might make heads, I make tails of what you are attempting; I 'low it doesn't make sense."

Coffin reiterated that while it might be possible for him to join ASJSA, accept a committee appointment, and carry on "extensive and futile" correspondence, he was too busy reading student papers to have time to read

8. Coffin to Reed, July 31, 1944, Coffin Papers.

a paper before a "society, association, conference, classis, or presbytery." Any benefit he got from a professional group would be "taken under false pretense." He said he was so busy that he seldom attended meetings of the university faculty and had never joined the faculty club. Instead of thinking of himself as antisocial, however, he said he was a "plough-pulling horse that intends to break no new ground until I get a fresh supply of fodder."[9] Coffin later said no to yet another Reed plea, and he added a forceful response to Reed's offer to aid the department in moving towards sounder standards: "Hell, there's nothing wrong with our standards now except the difficulty we experience in living up to them."[10]

In a 1946 exchange of letters with SNPA's Walter Johnson, Coffin revealed more of his attitude toward educational administration and frustration about the large number of veterans returning to campus after the war. SNPA had asked him to report the number of students majoring in journalism, and Coffin replied that he had 150 candidates for journalism degrees, too many for the physical equipment and instructional staff. "We could have easily doubled this number had not admission been denied to some 8 to 9 thousand G.I.'s. . . . We are handling more students, especially G.I.'s, than anybody has the right to ask us to do."[11] Data that Coffin submitted to *Journalism Quarterly*, a publication for journalism educators, reported 158 journalism majors in 1947 and 180 in 1948.

Coffin responded to another SNPA request for information in 1946 by saying he had neither the records nor the facilities to keep them. He said it would take twice as much physical space and three times as many faculty members to handle all of the applicants for admission. He admitted that UNC, like other schools, had not been prepared for the influx of returning soldiers. He said he had only 25 typewriters but needed 75 and had never had a new one. The department's growing pains were caused, he said, by the need to supply advertising men and country editors and the pressure of students from the metropolitan areas, especially young women of the deeper South. He said the state legislature had not listened to his pleas, and other academicians on campus were not enthusiastic about promoting "trade schools" such as journalism. The problem was compounded by the poor language skills of high school graduates and college freshmen and sophomores, Coffin complained. He did not blame anybody else and admitted he had done little as a department head to anticipate and avert the problems. The state press was trying to help, he said, and the depart-

9. Coffin to Reed, July 23, 1945, Coffin Papers.
10. Coffin to Reed, July 30, 1945, Coffin Papers.
11. Coffin to Walter Johnson, Nov. 25, 1946, Coffin Papers.

ment was near the top in university priorities for its own building. Coffin seemed to be confused about ASJSA, the journalism administrators' organization, mistakenly calling it an accrediting organization in his correspondence with Johnson.[12]

Accreditation was becoming important, however. It was a system that established standards for journalism programs and evaluated them at the invitation of university presidents. The origins of such accreditation efforts in journalism education can be traced to the formation of the American Association of Schools and Departments of Journalism in 1917. Although its activities were not formally called accreditation, it established standards for membership based on facilities that were available to journalism students and called the approved programs "Class A" schools. A joint committee of journalism educators and newspaper industry leaders was formed in the early 1930s but was inactive during the Depression, and the National Council on Professional Education for Journalism was formed in 1939. That eventually led a group of journalism school administrators and representatives of media organizations (mostly newspapers) to create the American Council on Education for Journalism (ACEJ), the first true accrediting body in journalism education, in 1945. ACEJ's Accrediting Committee (five educators and three newspaper representatives) sent evaluation teams to schools and departments and used the teams' findings to make recommendations to ACEJ's Accrediting Council (five educators and five newspaper representatives), which decided about accreditation. Accreditation was voluntary, and the initiative for seeking accreditation was supposed to come from journalism departments or universities. Programs were supposed to be evaluated in their own situations and against their own objectives, not national standards.[13]

ASJSA was not an accrediting organization and did not have standards about equipment, facilities, or faculty. Coffin said he could have joined the association earlier, but the university administration was unwilling to provide the staff and equipment needed to meet the accreditation standards, and he would not go about the "fourflushing" that existed in journalism programs at Washington and Lee and the universities of Georgia,

12. Coffin to Johnson, Dec. 7, 1946, Coffin Papers.
13. For a history of the accreditation movement in journalism education, see Earl L. Conn, "The American Council on Education for Journalism: An Accrediting History" (PhD diss., Indiana University, 1970). The organization's name was changed in 1981 to the Accrediting Council on Education in Journalism and Mass Communications.

Alabama, and Florida.[14] Johnson opined in response that the state was neglecting the university and speculated that the new accrediting organization, ACEJ, might be able to help Coffin and the department.[15] Coffin responded defensively, saying that while the university administration believed in the journalism program, he had to take his turn among other departments on budgetary matters. He made no apology for the department, saying that while it might not be doing enough, it was good as any in the South or elsewhere.[16]

On several occasions, Coffin said the department could have done better if it had had more faculty members and more space—improvements that would have required additional funds from the university. Coffin did request those items, but according to archived correspondence, he does not seem to have been especially persistent in his requests—and an important principle of academic administration is that persistent administrators eventually get additional resources. In fairness to Coffin, the financial situation at the university—especially during the Depression—may have been so severe that he could not have gotten what he wanted and knew it would have been a waste of time to try.

Embarrassment on Campus

In the 1940s, the Department of Journalism had become an embarrassment on campus for its lack of academic rigor. Many courses had no exams and were known as "slides."[17] Coffin, for one, was casual about assigning grades for student work in his courses. Thompson said Coffin gave grades only because the university required him to, and he sometimes returned papers with a cryptic comment: "Why?" When students asked what that meant, he said, "Why did you hand it in?" Another note he sometimes wrote on papers: "Not worth a damn."

Coffin gave Thompson an A in an editorial-writing course, but Thompson never attended class or wrote an editorial. Coffin explained that he gave him the grade because of the outside work Thompson had done for newspapers. Thompson worked extra-hard on the next course he took from Coffin, and Coffin praised him for his efforts. Thompson was surprised to get a grade of F in the course, and when he asked for an explana-

14. Coffin to Johnson, Dec. 7, 1946, Coffin Papers.
15. Johnson to Coffin, Dec. 12, 1946, Coffin Papers.
16. Coffin to Johnson, Dec. 16, 1946, Coffin Papers.
17. Robert Peterson, "Luxon Fought for Expansion," UNC Journalist, Nov. 9, 1974, 6.

tion, Coffin told him newspapering was like that: "You'll get a good story dropped in your lap one time and then again you'll work yourself to death for nothing." When Thompson arrived at Coffin's class late one day, Coffin asked him sarcastically if he had a motion to put before the class. Thompson said, "I move that the class dismiss and reconvene at Jeff's [a bar on Franklin Street] for a beer." Coffin asked for discussion from the class, got none, and said, "Class is dismissed and will reconvene at Jeff's in 10 minutes." Students who did not go to Jeff's that day had their grades lowered, according to Thompson.[18]

Jim Shumaker was in Coffin's editorial writing course and did not write any editorials all term. Coffin confronted him at the end of the course and said Shumaker owed him 10 editorials. Shumaker sat down that night and wrote the editorials and tied them in a bundle with a piece of twine. He described Coffin's reaction when he dropped the bundle on Coffin's desk the next day: "He stared balefully at the bundle, puffing furiously on a cigar, wheezing, eyes bulging, and said if he didn't have to read them he'd give me an A for the course." Shumaker accepted the offer, threw the bundle in the wastebasket, and got his A.[19]

Although he would have been the last person to predict it when he was a student, Shumaker returned to the School of Journalism in 1973 as a faculty member and taught until his death in 2000. He became a legend in his own right, somewhat in the curmudgeonly mode of Coffin, and earned the admiration of scores of students. He had left school without a degree because he had not completed the university's required hygiene course. Before he was allowed to join the faculty in 1973, he had to complete his bachelor's degree, which required him to complete the hygiene course. At a faculty luncheon in Shumaker's honor at the Pines Restaurant, Dean Jack Adams held up a bar of soap and asked Shumaker to identify it. When he did, Adams pronounced that Shumaker had completed the hygiene course and earned his degree.

Before he joined the faculty, Shumaker was a teacher of sorts while serving as editor of the *Chapel Hill Weekly*, where he mentored scores of journalism students and graduates. Jock Lauterer, who was a student in the 1960s and later a faculty member, worked as a photographer for Shumaker at the *Weekly* while he was a high school student. He credited Shumaker with teaching him the "So What and Who Cares" rule. Lauterer sometimes got involved in the stories he was photographing—a no-no

18. Thompson, "'Skipper' Wanted Craftsmen for Newspapers."
19. Shumaker, quoted in Wint Capel, *Shucks and Nubbins: The Wit and Wisdom of O. J. Skipper Coffin*, (Chapel Hill, N.C.: CapeCorp Press, 2000), 24.

Jim "Shu" Shumaker was a graduate of the School of Journalism and a faculty member from 1973 to 2000. He was the inspiration for the P. Martin Shoemaker character in Jeff MacNelly's "Shoe" comic strip. *(Kathy Norcross, School of Journalism and Mass Communication, UNC–Chapel Hill. Reprinted with permission.)*

for journalists—as when he took photographs of a civil-rights demonstration in front of the Colonial Drugstore on Franklin Street. When he finished, he put down his camera, picked up a sign, and started demonstrating himself—later drawing harsh criticism from Shumaker in the newsroom.[20]

Jim Wallace, another student photographer in the 1960s, also said he learned a lot from Jim Shumaker at the *Chapel Hill Weekly* when Wallace worked at the *Tar Heel* and took the newspaper to the *Weekly* each night to have it printed. Wallace said Shumaker was hampered by Orville Campbell, the newspaper's owner, who would not let him publish all the things he wanted to. In one instance, Wallace claimed, Shumaker wrote an editorial and gave it to Gary Blanchard, editor of the *Tar Heel*, to be published because Campbell would not let Shumaker print it.[21]

Shumaker became the inspiration for a character in a nationally syndicated comic strip. In the late 1960s and early 1970s, Jeff MacNelly worked for Shumaker as the editorial cartoonist for the *Chapel Hill Weekly*. When

20. Lauterer, interview with the author, March 24, 2008.
21. Wallace, interview with the author, Nov. 9, 2007.

MacNelly later created his nationally syndicated comic strip, "Shoe," his main character, a bird named P. Martin Shoemaker, was editor of the *Treetop Tattler-Tribune* in the strip and was modeled after Shumaker. MacNelly also won three Pulitzer Prizes for editorial cartooning.

Roland Giduz took Coffin's editorial writing course in his senior year, while he was also writing editorials for the *Tar Heel*, and Coffin told him he could simply turn in those editorials for the course. Giduz was enrolled for that course and—with Coffin's blessing—Professor J. P. Harlan's archeology course that met at the same time and on the same days. He did no work for Coffin's class and got an A in both courses.[22]

Clarence Whitefield, a student from the mid-1940s, recalled that Coffin smoked cigars or cigarettes—despite his chronic asthma—in class and liked to engage the class in dialogue. At the end of class, he often said, "Well, today, we have been chasing rabbits," meaning they had not accomplished anything. Coffin required students to have feature stories published in newspapers, and they often submitted the same story to more than one paper.[23]

Not all students were pleased with their journalism courses. The university's Committee on Instruction conducted a poll of university students at the end of May 1947 to assess students' attitudes about their teachers and courses. Of the 79 journalism students who responded, only 23 percent rated their courses as excellent. The other ratings were 38 percent good, 23 percent fair, 10 percent poor, and 6 percent very poor.[24] Coffin left no record of his reaction to the student ratings.

Professors in other departments on campus had negative attitudes toward the department because of its lack of rigor and the dearth of faculty research activity. Jack Adams recalled being told when he joined the faculty in 1958 that other professors on campus had questioned why "trade school" departments such as Journalism or Radio, Television, and Motion Pictures belonged in a university. Many thought of the journalism faculty as "whiskey-drinking, cigar-smoking newspapermen" who were turning out people just like themselves, Adams recounted.[25] Ken Sanford, a student at the time, also recalled that Coffin was held in low esteem by other academic administrators on campus.[26]

22. Giduz, interview with the author, Oct. 10, 2007.

23. Whitefield, interview with the author, Oct. 11, 2007.

24. UNC's Committee on Instruction to Department Heads, July 15, 1947, Coffin Papers.

25. Adams, interview with the author, Aug. 21, 2007.

26. Sanford, interview with the author, Oct. 5, 2007.

Pressure for Accreditation

Journalism education was changing in significant ways at other universities, and negative attitudes in the Department of Journalism about those changes kept the program out of the national mainstream. Other journalism educators formed national associations and met regularly to discuss common issues, but Coffin did not participate. At other schools, scholars with advanced degrees joined journalism faculties, collaborated with scholars from other disciplines, and conducted social science research in the new academic disciplines of communication and mass communication, but Coffin saw little value in advanced degrees or faculty research. That attitude eventually paved the way for outside pressure to change the department and its leadership.

Some newspaper people saw accreditation of university journalism programs as a way to ensure high quality and considered accreditation a badge of honor. The persistent efforts of one of those newspaper editors in North Carolina had a profound impact on the UNC program. After graduating from the Department of Journalism in 1928, Holt McPherson taught a journalism course at Gardner-Webb College while working at the *Shelby Daily Star*, and he said he learned more as a teacher than he ever did as a student. Because of his teaching experience, he served on SNPA's Schools of Journalism Committee, which he represented on the Accrediting Council for 28 years.[27]

McPherson was managing editor of the *Daily Star* and an influential member of the NCPA. His

Holt McPherson, a 1928 graduate of the Department of Journalism, became an influential newspaper editor at the *High Point Enterprise*. He led efforts to get the department to seek accreditation, influenced the selection of Dean Neil Luxon to head the School of Journalism, and was instrumental in creating the School of Journalism Foundation. *(School of Journalism and Mass Communication, UNC–Chapel Hill. Reprinted with permission.)*

27. Interview with Holt McPherson by E. P. Douglass, April 9, 1975, Southern Oral History Program Collection, Southern Historical Collection, University of North Carolina at Chapel Hill Library.

membership on the Accrediting Council indicated his strong support for the accreditation process, and his work with the council exposed him to practices and conditions that characterized accredited schools and departments. McPherson was deeply troubled by the fact that UNC was not one of those programs, and it was the height of his ambition for the UNC program to gain accreditation.

The initiative for accreditation of the department came not from the department or university leaders but from the NCPA. At a meeting of the NCPA's Associated Dailies section at the Langren Hotel in Asheville on Sept. 13, 1946, McPherson proposed a plan "to lift the standards of journalism schools in North Carolina." He said several schools around the country were receiving financial support from foundations and were becoming accredited. He said the UNC program was not accredited and that "proper appropriations and legislative measures should be made in order for the publishers of North Carolina to benefit by the school [*sic*] of journalism."

At the NCPA business meeting the next day, McPherson introduced a resolution, "For Accreditation of the UNC Department of Journalism," which he said reflected discussions at meetings of daily and weekly newspaper editors the previous day. It cited ACEJ's program of accreditation and minimum standards and said NCPA wanted to cooperate with the department to produce useful newspaper staff people. The resolution called for the university "to bring the Department of Journalism to a standard that will win for it accreditation." A motion to that effect made by Josh Horne and seconded by Lester Gifford was unanimously approved, and a School of Journalism committee was named and directed to report to NCPA at its January meeting. In addition to McPherson, the committee included Bob Thompson, editor of the *High Point Enterprise*; Nady M. Cates, editor of the *Twin City Sentinel*; Ed Anderson, publisher of the *Transylvania Times*; Leslie Thompson, editor of the *News Reporter* in Whiteville; and W. E. Horner, publisher of the *Sanford Herald*. The resolution also pledged that the association would do whatever it could to help the department.[28] McPherson said later—with the perspective of almost 30 years of hindsight—that Coffin, whom he described as "a bit of an iconoclast," didn't think accreditation was of any value, but was sure that the department could pass, so the university applied for accreditation.[29]

McPherson wasted no time and reported NCPA's action to UNC presi-

28. Minutes of the annual business meeting of the North Carolina Press Association, Sept. 14, 1946.
29. McPherson, interview with Douglass, April 9, 1975.

dent Frank Porter Graham two days later, on Sept. 16. He suggested that someone at the university should obtain the checklist of requirements for accreditation and that the NCPA committee should meet with Graham and others. (The checklist was ACEJ's 16-page "Factual Data Report" that asked about facilities, budgets, library resources, curriculum, and faculty members.) McPherson expressed appreciation for the work of the department and said he hoped NCPA could work cooperatively with Graham to improve the department. McPherson also sent a copy of the letter to Coffin and to UNC comptroller William D. Carmichael Jr., because McPherson thought Carmichael understood the financial aspects of the department's problem.[30]

It was significant that NCPA felt it had to go directly to the university and President Graham on the matter of accreditation. NCPA records indicate that Coffin and his faculty members rarely attended NCPA summer meetings, and no one from the Department of Journalism was registered for the 1946 convention or mentioned in the convention proceedings. Records show that Coffin had attended the 1936 and 1941 NCPA summer meetings, and he and others from the department probably attended the annual winter institutes in Chapel Hill. Nothing in Coffin's nor Chancellor Robert House's files indicates any communication about accreditation before the NCPA action. It appears that Coffin was not going to do anything about the issue until forced to do so.

President Graham was no stranger to journalism. As a student, he had been editor-in-chief of the *Tar Heel* in the fall of 1908, just before Coffin became editor in January 1909. He was on vacation when McPherson notified him of the NCPA action, and Chancellor House responded to McPherson, saying Graham would respond when he returned.[31] Five days later, Graham's secretary wrote to McPherson and told him Graham had been in the hospital for almost three weeks. He had been discharged with the understanding that he was to take complete rest, and he would respond as soon as he could.[32]

Graham finally responded to McPherson on Oct. 15 and said he deeply appreciated his interest and that of the NCPA. He said that he, House, and Carmichael were "deeply interested" in his proposal and were determined

30. McPherson to Graham, Sept. 16, 1946, Chancellor's Records: R. B. House Series #40019, University Archives and Records Service, University of North Carolina at Chapel Hill Library.

31. House to McPherson, Sept. 20, 1946, Frank Porter Graham Files #40007, University Archives, University of North Carolina at Chapel Hill Library.

32. Graham's secretary to McPherson, Sept. 25, 1946, Frank Porter Graham files.

to do something about it. He invited the committee to come to a dinner meeting at 6:30 on Oct. 24 at the Carolina Inn to discuss the issue. A handwritten note at the bottom was apparently written by Graham's secretary, who had called McPherson and read him the letter. McPherson suggested a meeting during the NCPA institute in Chapel Hill in January, as long as that would not be too late to seek a legislative appropriation.[33]

McPherson responded the next day, saying committee members had been pressing him about meeting with Graham. One committee member had been particularly adamant: "One of them has suggested that Duke University may be interested in putting in a journalism school that will meet accreditation standards and he suggests that since the university apparently isn't interested that we turn our efforts to Duke; I do not yet feel the university is not interested in this project designed to develop the newspaper men and women who will have the task of seeking out and presenting truth through an enlightened and effective press." He said he did not want to press Graham, but the newspaper people were earnest about wanting the university's Department of Journalism to measure up to accreditation standards. He said they all wanted to get the discussion under way in time to seek legislative support.[34] That would not be the last time that McPherson would mention a threat about supporting accreditation at Duke instead of UNC.[35]

McPherson wrote back on Oct. 19 to say that he had asked Earl English, executive secretary of ACEJ, for a copy of the checklist, but English said he could not provide it until after ACEJ met in Chicago on Nov. 23. McPherson interjected that attending the ACEJ meeting would cause him personal hardship: "How I hate to miss that Carolina-Duke football game!" English had told him that the department's budget would be the most significant item and by itself could predict a school's overall rank "with 75 percent effectiveness."

McPherson acknowledged that the state had made a large investment in the journalism department, but it was unlikely that the department would meet accreditation requirements. He said NCPA's discussions at Asheville had focused on a long-range plan to "bring the journalism school, backed by the press of the state in every way, to greater usefulness to the press and the state." The existence of the plan was not meant as a criticism of the school, whose past usefulness was appreciated, but it was intended to

33. Graham to McPherson, Oct. 15, 1946, Frank Porter Graham files.

34. McPherson to Graham, Oct. 16, 1946, Frank Porter Graham files.

35. McPherson later mentioned the Duke threat in 1953 when he was impatient and unhappy with the search committee that was looking for a successor to Coffin.

"gear it to the functional needs of the state in a way that the return on investment will be greater and waste will be lessened if there is such."[36]

The committee met with Graham in Chapel Hill on the afternoon of Jan. 23, 1947. After the meeting, Graham wrote to committee members and thanked them for their "fine and helpful interest" in the Department of Journalism. "Your interest is a tonic to us all. You had many valuable suggestions and we hope you will continue to give us the benefit of such suggestions. With your help, we will be able to make a strong Department of Journalism which, if we are wise, may become a school of journalism." He said university officials were thinking of a three-step plan: get a legislative appropriation for the department, erect an adequate building for the department, and establish a foundation to supplement state appropriations. "The initiative and enthusiasm of your chairman [McPherson] is contagious and, I believe, will be unabated in carrying out the program for the Department of Journalism."[37]

Shortly after that meeting, Coffin, in what appears to be his first official act with regard to accreditation (and perhaps under a mandate from Graham), wrote to Earl English, executive secretary of the ACEJ, to ask for the questionnaire that schools and departments had to submit before seeking accreditation. His letter offered an excuse for why the department had previously been lukewarm about accreditation and revealed his attitudes about accreditation, saying that newspaper and radio station executives had already "accredited" the department. His comments were defensive and provincial (by his admission), especially concerning the role of educators with doctorates in the accreditation process. The letter also exemplified Coffin's circumlocution and seemed to suggest that the move toward accreditation was only a trial:

> We members of this department, who have pretty generally
> stopped at membership in the association of teachers of journal-
> ism, have been slow to move in the matter of accreditation. Not
> that we have anything to hide, but perhaps because we have always
> had more applications for admission than we could accept. Too, in
> our twenty-odd years of existence we have had no alumni whom
> we were willing to recommend as journeymen reporters or desk
> men who remained unemployed beyond a reasonable length of
> time. Because we do not think we have approached all the answers

36. McPherson to Graham, Oct. 19, 1946, Frank Porter Graham files.
37. Graham to members of the NCPA committee, Feb. 1, 1947, Frank Porter Graham files.

and because we like to work with others in our field, we are willing
to try to play ball in this matter of accreditation. But the common-
est sort of candor and a modicum of self-respect demand that we
assert that we have been for years accredited by the newspaper and
radio executives in the area to which we have addressed our efforts.

Sounds provincial, doesn't it? It is. But with well over 150 years
of active newspaper experience represented in the faculty—and
meantime we have accumulated other men experienced in radio
and all forms of advertising save personal ballyhoo—we have
been loath to accept a rating conferred by Ph.D.s and assistants to
publishers.

We would welcome any sort of committee on accreditation
or whatever, but would like to see how far we can go with a
questionnaire—which did not place too much emphasis on equipment and projects contemplated—before making application. In
short, we have either done a good job or we haven't. We would like
to do a better one, but would still prefer to continue to show results
before accepting a curtain call.[38]

Later that year, McPherson had to dispel rumors that he was interested
in becoming head of the journalism department. He sent Graham a brochure about Emory University's journalism program and said he definitely
did not want to be chairman of the department. He also said Dr. Daniel
Marsh of Boston University had asked him to be chairman of its journalism program, but he had said he was not available.[39]

The state press continued to apply pressure for accreditation. John Park
of the *Raleigh Times* pushed the department toward accreditation as well
as academic designation as a school, which he thought would give UNC
journalism more prestige and independence. He told McPherson that he
shared the "embarrassment" that the only journalism program in North
Carolina was still a department when the university deserved a school. Park
conceded that the department was "functioning fairly well," but he said he
wanted to see "an outstanding School of Journalism in North Carolina—at
Chapel Hill, Raleigh, Duke or elsewhere—with thoroughly able and fully
recognized leadership to which every newspaper in the South can point
with pride and extend full cooperation." It is worth noting that he mentioned departmental leadership without naming Coffin and that he also
raised the threat about Duke University. Park sent a confidential copy of

38. Coffin to English, Feb. 10, 1947, Chancellor's Records: House Series.
39. McPherson to Graham, July 19, 1947, Frank Porter Graham files.

his letter to House, who forwarded it to Coffin with a handwritten comment: "For your information. Preserve confidence and return to me."[40]

McPherson continued to lobby UNC officials, writing to House on Nov. 5, apparently without sending a copy to Coffin. He reaffirmed his desire to improve the Department of Journalism, and he said his accrediting visits to Emory University and the University of Georgia had made him feel even more strongly that the state was not meeting its challenge and opportunity. He alluded to being dissatisfied with the January meeting between Graham and the committee, saying he was frustrated that he was not able to get that same point across at the meeting. The fault was not with the university, he said, and the press and radio of the state needed to back the project, as they had done in Georgia. "Until that is done," he said, "I don't believe you'll be on the ball as I know you want to be."

He expressed optimism about the outcome of the accreditation visit scheduled for UNC's Department of Journalism in February 1948. McPherson thought the data that the department had submitted would place the department at the national median or a little below in most categories. (Accreditation standards at the time were highly quantitative.) Achieving accreditation would not be enough, however, and McPherson hoped the state press would continue to strengthen the department and the market for its graduates. He implied that part of the problem may have been the department's failure to publicize its work. He closed with a plea: "This thing is too close to my heart and I appreciate so fully the work of the Council, in which I've worked these past several years, that I'm jealous for the university to make its honor list."[41] House responded with a short note saying only that he was helping Coffin to get ready for the accreditation visit.[42]

The department and university were indeed preparing for the visit. House told Coffin that he and Graham would be available to talk to the site-visit team and said the university would pay ACEJ's $100 investigation fee.[43] Coffin thanked House for his availability to meet with the accreditation team, whom he called "our inquisitors." He also asked House for $150 to print a separate catalog for the department. While he promised that it would not include pictures of the department chairman or the chancellor, it would "serve in part to fend off such helpful people as alumni Ed An-

40. Park to McPherson, Aug. 30, 1947, Chancellor's Records: House Series.

41. McPherson to House, Nov. 10, 1947, Chancellor's Records: House Series.

42. House to McPherson, Nov. 15, 1947, Chancellor's Records: House Series.

43. House to Coffin, Oct. 14, 1947, Chancellor's Records: House Series.

derson and Holt McPherson."[44] Anderson, from Forest City, was another early graduate of the department and a North Carolina editor active in the national accreditation movement. House agreed to pay for the catalog.

The "Inquisition"

The ACEJ site-visit team came to Chapel Hill on Wednesday and Thursday, Feb. 18–19, 1948. The team included two educators (Earl English, University of Missouri and executive secretary of ACEJ, and James E. Pollard, Ohio State University) and two newspaper executives (Alexander F. Jones, assistant to the publisher of the *Washington Post*, and Leon S. Dure, whose newspaper was not identified.) When the team expressed disappointment at not finding an ethics course in the curriculum, Coffin answered by saying he gave such a course in one sentence: "Remember that you were a gentleman before you became a newspaperman." At that point, Coffin invited members of the team to join him for a beer at a local tavern.[45] It is unlikely that they joined him because accreditation teams were supposed to avoid social contacts with representatives of the department.

The department had submitted a detailed "Factual Data Report" several months before the visit. Based on those data, ACEJ produced a quantitative profile of the department that compared it with other schools in a variety of areas. For example, each member of the Accrediting Committee evaluated UNC's entrance requirements on a 5-point scale (5 was the highest), and those were averaged (UNC's score was between 2.3 and 2.6). Similarly, its score on maintenance of standards was below 2.3, or in the "low" category compared with other schools. A library-adequacy rating (between 46 and 64, a median-low rating) was determined by calculating the percentage of books and periodicals in the department's library compared with a list of 473 titles compiled by 52 experts in 26 fields. Scores on individual items were aggregated to give the department net scores of -5 on budget, -4 on facilities, -1 on curriculum, +2 on press relationships, and 0 on students and on faculty. Its overall score was -9. The system was so quantified that ACEJ calculated statistical measures (correlation coefficients) that compared individual items for all schools.

The team's report included several items on which visitors rated the department on a scale of high, median high, median, median low, and low. These ratings were qualitative and were meant to provide continuity from school to school, not to provide statistical data. The department

44. Coffin to House, Oct. 18, 1947, Chancellor's Records: House Series.
45. Capel, *Shucks and Nubbins*, 62.

scored "high" on regional validity, financial support (reliable but inadequate), student-faculty relations, credit requirements, faculty teamwork, and graduate placement and alumni relations (see Table 4.1). It scored "low" or "median low" on laboratory equipment (especially for photography), library facilities, utilization of off-campus facilities, student accomplishment, and student morale. Among other things, the team learned that teachers did not have course outlines (syllabi) and that textbooks were outdated. The team criticized the lack of opportunities for students to get their work published, and it said the department should assume a leadership role in newspaper research. Upon completion of its visit, the team recommended that the department not be accredited.

The Accrediting Committee reviewed the recommendation on May 13–14, 1948, in Cleveland, Ohio, and chose to affirm the recommendation before passing it along to the Accrediting Council. The committee's decision was based on comparisons with other schools, although ACEJ professed to evaluate schools against their own objectives and not against other schools. The Accrediting Council officially conveyed its accreditation decision in a letter to Coffin on June 1, which said accreditation was being withheld at that time and that the department could apply for a reexamination as early as Sept. 30, 1948.[46]

Frustrated about the accreditation decision, McPherson revealed his feelings on July 29 to Carmichael, the university's comptroller and a perceived ally. He had been pleased to hear that Carmichael had expressed support for a printing trade school at UNC, which McPherson said would fit well with his vision of an expanded journalism school. McPherson proposed that the school be named for Josephus Daniels, publisher of the Raleigh *News and Observer* and U.S. Secretary of the Navy in 1913–21, who had died six months earlier, on Jan. 15, 1948. McPherson thought the Daniels family would support the idea, perhaps with money.

McPherson complained that he had been telling university officials for years that they were missing a golden opportunity to have a distinguished journalism school, but until "ACEJ flunked it on a petition for accreditation, I found no one but myself concerned about it." Things had recently changed, he said, and he found an "aroused purpose to get something moving there." He blamed the "superannuated" Coffin for the problems, saying he had "bucked at every proposal and not fought hard enough for the money he needed to do the job right." McPherson believed that a distinguished journalism school at UNC would pay off for future generations

46. English to Coffin, June 1, 1948, Chancellor's Records: House Series.

Table 4.1. Summary of Accrediting Team Ratings for UNC
Department of Journalism, February 18–19, 1948

Evaluation Item	Rating	Remarks
Administrative setup: layers of control between department and president	Median high	
Effectiveness of administrative setup for policies, curriculum, faculty appointments and promotion, entrance requirements, and budget	Median high	Responsibility was with department chair, who enjoyed confidence of higher administrators.
Regional validity: duplication of programs	High	
Reliability of financial support	High	Reliable but inadequate.
Facilities (general)	Median	Needs additional classroom and faculty space.
Laboratory equipment	Low	No work in typography, no projector or audio playback, little evidence of reference books, photography equipment quite limited—one Speed Graphic camera.
Library facilities	Low	Practically nonexistent, university library excellent, no essential trade publications.
Utilization of institution's courses in other departments	Median high	Good use of Arts and Sciences but not Commerce School. Students should be able to take courses outside Arts and Sciences.
Utilization of off-campus facilities	Median low	Very few opportunities for practical newspaper experience. Student publication controlled by student body. Need to coordinate outside speakers.
Student accomplishment	Median low	Little evidence except for some freelance features.
Student morale	Median low	Good individually but lacks focus. No student organizations.

Evaluation Item	Rating	Remarks
Student-faculty relations	High	
Curricula	Median	Amount of journalism courses offered (16 percent) was lowest of the schools examined. Department needs to be brought abreast of modern developments such as readership studies. Needs an outlet for student writing. Needs up-to-date textbooks, periodicals, and related materials. Department should assume leadership in the field of newspaper research to serve North Carolina newspapers.
Effectiveness of standards for entrance and graduation	Median high	
Credit requirements	High	Average student earned 32 credits in journalism.
Other curriculum matters		Committee could not evaluate because course outlines were not normally prepared. This is needed.
Competence of teachers	Median	
Teaching methods	Median	
Faculty teamwork	High	
Faculty personality, vitality, and achievement	Median high	
Graduate placement and alumni records	High	

in improved public relations and service to the state. He also wanted to see more support from the NCPA, which he said was "largely a social affair."

McPherson then offered a brash proposal. The university could lease or buy Louis Graves' *Chapel Hill Weekly* and hire Graves to head the journalism and printing school. No one could do a better job or engender more confidence from the state press than Graves, McPherson claimed. He admitted it would take a lot of persuading on Carmichael's part to get Graves to do it, but it would be worth it and would constitute "the finest day's work you or any other would have done for the university in many a day."

Not even Graham could escape McPherson's scorn. He said Carmichael was the first man he had met who had any enthusiasm for the improvement of the journalism department and that others were only paying him lip service. "I've been 'yessed' right out by all the others from Frank Graham down," he charged, "but I don't stop that easily when I'm on a trail as strong as this one." The letter was in Graham's file, which means Carmichael forwarded it to him.[47]

Carmichael replied that he was enthusiastic about both the School of Journalism and a printing trade school, but he believed the latter ought to be at N.C. State University. He suggested that Graham and others had discussed other, more grandiose plans for journalism at Chapel Hill. Graham wanted to create a Communications Center that would include the Department of Journalism, the University Press, a new school of advertising, a Department of Radio, Television, and Moving Pictures, and a graphic arts department. "There is a wonderful opportunity in this area for some university with vision and ingenuity," Carmichael said. He praised McPherson for being a tower of strength and a good "cocklebur" in the matter, and he implored him to "continue his hypodermics." "God bless you," he concluded."[48]

McPherson thanked Carmichael for the compliments and countered with proof of how strongly he felt about improving the journalism school at Carolina. He said he had made out his will several years earlier, and it would bequeath his estate to the university trustees to use as they saw fit to improve the training of journalists. "I'm hoping it will—by the time of my death—be a large sum and that you'll be a whale of a long time getting that money!" he joked. He confessed that the idea of a communications center was too big for him to comprehend, and he feared that a school of journalism would get lost in it. "There is great danger that we are getting a structure at Carolina that is top-heavy, and I fear trouble lies ahead in building it larger but not in building better what we have and are doing there. It's too big for me to grasp, but I fear bigness for bigness' sake!"[49]

At the same time that ACEJ had refused to accredit the UNC department, it accredited 35 of the 41 other institutions that were evaluated in 1947–48. The list of accredited programs was publicized throughout the

47. Graham to Carmichael, July 29, 1948, Frank Porter Graham files.
48. Carmichael to McPherson, July 30, 1948, Frank Porter Graham files.
49. McPherson to Carmichael, Aug. 6, 1948, Frank Porter Graham files.

newspaper trade press. McPherson, as chairman of SNPA's Schools of Journalism committee, presented a lengthy report to member newspapers at its 1948 meeting. He noted that UNC's program had not been accredited but that NCPA had named a committee to work with the university to help the "School [*sic*] of Journalism" achieve accreditation.[50]

Reactions to the Accreditation Decision

The first reaction came on June 17. A document in Chancellor House's files consists of notes or minutes titled "Staff Meeting, Journalism Department, on Accreditation Low Points." Authorship of the document is not certain; it may have been House's report, or it may have been a report someone prepared for him. The notes indicate a serious effort on the part of the department and university to correct the deficiencies that had led to the denial.

Someone suggested that all of Bynum Hall be assigned to the department, including a reading room with trade periodicals and new books, a typography lab, a playback recorder for radio, and increased office space. Another suggested that the *Tar Heel* or another local newspaper, the *News of Orange County,* be used as a publication outlet for students, with the department assuming responsibility for everything but the editorial page. Someone raised a question about student organizations and the possibility of starting a chapter of the American Newspaper Guild trade union. The notes indicated general agreement on an eight-course major and on hiring additional faculty members, including someone with a doctorate to teach "lecture courses." The notes suggested a new course in sports writing and directed all instructors to have course outlines ready by the end of the summer. Sechriest proposed that the existing NCPA committee be invited to visit the department and report its findings first to the administration and then to the department. Someone else suggested getting course catalogs from all accredited programs. Coffin thought the department could make its case to NCPA at its next Press Institute in Chapel Hill.[51]

ACEJ's decision did not change Coffin's attitudes about accreditation, though. In a letter to John Park of the *Raleigh Times* a few months later, he was unapologetic and said the decision was due to a lack of space and facilities. ACEJ, he said, was leaning more toward "formulaism" than the

50. "Reports on Schools of Journalism," presented to the annual meeting of the Southern Newspaper Publishers Association, St. Petersburg, Fla., Nov. 8–10, 1948.

51. "Staff Meeting, Journalism Department, on Accreditation Low Points," June 17, 1948, Chancellor's Records : House Series.

department wanted to go, and it also wanted the department to be more involved with student publications. He expressed regret for "not having found favor in the eyes of those who have perhaps found more of the answers than we." He said he still did not feel a need to apologize to the department's alumni because its graduates were "more soundly educated than if more attention had been paid to trade techniques." The problems of space and equipment stemmed from a lack of money, he said, and he asked the press association and other friends of the department to provide any assistance they could.[52]

Coffin made another dig at accreditation and faculty members with doctorates when he wrote to Bill Horner of the *Sanford Herald* to see if he would consider teaching for a year, saying the department was more interested in providing people for community newspapers than for big-city dailies. He said he was not troubled by the fact that metropolitan publishers and persons with doctorates had not accredited the department, because the quality of the department's alumni proved the quality of the program. He repeated the plea for assistance from the legislature and the state press.[53]

Coffin told Frank Daniels, publisher of the Raleigh *News and Observer* and president of the NCPA, that the university administration had included a budget request for money to improve working space and other physical requirements to meet accreditation standards. Once again, he claimed the department had more than met the standards for teaching and placement of graduates. He could brag about the work of the department, he said, because he had done so little of the work himself, and he asked again for the NCPA's help: "If the press of North Carolina thinks there is anything to this accreditation, it can certainly help hold the budget makers' feet to the fire."[54]

Three years later, Coffin was still critical of the accrediting process and the decision to withhold accreditation from UNC's department. Perley Reed, with whom Coffin had exchanged letters about national journalism education organizations, had written an article in the *New York Times* that criticized the accrediting process because, he claimed, it restrained freedom of the press. Coffin said he agreed with Reed's statements about accreditation and claimed that the department's graduates held their own against those from accredited programs.[55]

52. Coffin to Park, June 19, 1948, Coffin Papers.
53. Coffin to Horner, July 21, 1948, Coffin Papers.
54. Coffin to Daniels, Nov. 9, 1948, Coffin Papers.
55. Coffin to Reed, Jan. 31, 1951, Coffin Papers.

Coffin was especially critical of the accrediting council's recommendation that the department should forge closer relationships with the *Tar Heel* or start its own student publication. In 1951, he responded to a survey about relationships between journalism departments and campus newspapers by saying the *Tar Heel* was run by students. He had served five years on the Publications Board that ran the student newspaper and had asked to be released from that obligation because a paid employee of the paper had failed to discharge his responsibilities and claimed censorship when he was reprimanded. Coffin explained that he, Spearman, and Russell had been *Tar Heel* editors when they were students, but "the less the School of Journalism has to do with a student publication in an institution such as ours, the better." He added a personal reason: "I've sworn never to help handle student funds again when three 18-year-old youngsters are permitted to out-vote two adults with something of a sense of responsibility."[56]

NCPA Review

The NCPA's journalism-school committee continued its work, and House wrote to McPherson in December 1948, thanking him for chairing the committee, suggesting that the NCPA expand the work of the committee, and promising the cooperation of the university and the department. He proposed that the committee conduct an on-site study to develop material for an "authoritative report and definite recommendations" for possible changes. President Graham would welcome such an approach, he said, if it were "made in a spirit of cooperation and good will, to the end that the Department of Journalism might be second to none." He said the department had a good faculty and was graduating some good people. At the same time, the failure to secure accreditation was a "matter of concern to the university and offered a problem it could help to solve."[57]

Daniels wrote to House about McPherson's work, and he implied that Coffin was not cooperating fully: "Holt feels that he has done just about all he can do and is presently butting his head into a stone wall. I have not sent a copy of this letter to Oscar Coffin, but if you think it is advisable, I will be happy to do so."[58] House did ask Daniels to forward a copy of the letter to Coffin, saying he needed all the help he could get and that he relied on Coffin to advise him. The university desired accreditation and was working toward it, House said, but he had not been aware that it would

56. Coffin to Laurence Campbell, March 8, 1951, Coffin Papers.
57. House to McPherson, Dec. 23, 1948, Chancellor's Records: House Series.
58. Daniels to House, Dec. 28, 1948, Chancellor's Records: House Series.

be a problem. He said he could not move quickly to improve the situation because of lack of money.[59]

The NCPA committee visited the department May 5–6, 1949. They attended classes and talked with university officials, faculty members, and students. They found a cooperative spirit in the department that they said was good for both the department and newspapers. They were impressed with the quality of the department, despite its obviously inadequate facilities. Conditions were crowded, and there was a need for more space, including a typography laboratory. University officials assured the committee that the department was next on the list for its own building, but that would be three to five years in the future. Prior to the visit, the committee had surveyed newspapers and learned that a major criticism of college journalism programs was lack of attention to country journalism. They were pleased to see expansion of that program, especially with the hiring of Tom Lassiter.

The committee criticized the department's lack of experience in the practical production problems of a modern newspaper and the lack of internships, and it suggested a summer-internship program. One of its most significant actions was to recommend that the NCPA activate the foundation it had first discussed in 1946 and establish an endowment goal of $100,000.[60]

McPherson mentioned the visit in an editorial column in his newspaper on May 9. He said the department had been turning out remarkable graduates but had never had time to "shout the glories of its own accomplishment, being content to let its product speak in its own eloquence for it." Despite inadequate space and finances, he said the department was doing good work but needed greater cooperation and support from the state press. He admitted that the department had not done enough self-commendation, but it could become one of the distinguishing features of an already great university. McPherson included a copy of the editorial in a letter to House and said he was ready to help provide "well-rounded journalism training from which accreditation would come as a matter of course and which will distinguish the university as it merits."[61]

59. House to Daniels, Jan. 10, 1949, Chancellor's Records: House Series.

60. "Report of Special Committee from the North Carolina Press Association to the University of North Carolina Seeking Effective Gearing of the Department of Journalism to Present-Day Needs of the Press of the Area and Seeking Ways in which the Press Can Cooperate Best to Attain That," July 9, 1949, Chancellor's Records: House Series.

61. McPherson to House, May 9, 1949, Chancellor's Records: House Series.

Coffin, perhaps responding to criticism that he had not done enough to publicize the department's accomplishments, sent House an annual report in May 1949. He said the department had approximately 80 graduates in 1948 and expected the same in 1949. (According to data from the university registrar's office, the department had 68 graduates in 1948.) All graduates who wanted jobs got them, and most were working in the media. The accreditation issue still chafed him, however:

> The department, we think, has retained its recognition long since achieved with the press of the state and area, and while there has been some agitation for national accreditation, it now appears that the more vocative (or shall we say demanding?) of our critics have decided we are doing well-nigh as much as our facilities will permit. What to do about expanding these facilities and further challenging the department to lengthen, widen, and deepen its usefulness is something we shall be delighted to pray over with you and the legislature, from whence cometh our help—not neglecting to state our willingness to accept any string-free thing proffered by the publishers or the council on accreditation.[62]

62. Coffin to House, May 9, 1949, Chancellor's Records: House Series.

"This is not much of a school and
I'm no dean to write home about."
—"Skipper" Coffin[1]

5. A School Begins and an Era Ends

The failed accreditation bid stimulated the state press and the university to initiate actions that pointed the department toward changes in its name, status, leadership, and facilities in the early 1950s. The state's newspapers created a foundation that became an extremely important resource. "Skipper" Coffin resigned in 1953, and a national search for a successor involved Holt McPherson and the state's newspapers. Journalism at UNC would never be the same.

Coffin and his faculty colleagues had been lukewarm to the idea of changing the department to a school of journalism, but university leaders announced the change on Sept. 1, 1950, and named Coffin as dean.[2] A school had more autonomy than a department because Coffin reported directly to the provost and not to the dean of the College of Liberal Arts. In addition, being a dean was more prestigious than being a department chairman, although Coffin did not seem to care about that. The new school had eight faculty members. Coffin, Roy Parker (emeritus), and Walter Spearman were full professors; Stuart Sechriest and J. R. Riley were

1. Coffin to J. Albert Dear, Feb. 10, 1950, Oscar Coffin Papers #3907, Southern Historical Collection, University of North Carolina at Chapel Hill Library.

2. House to Coffin, Jan. 23, 1950, Chancellor's Records: R. B. House Series #40019, University Archives and Records Service, University of North Carolina at Chapel Hill Library.

associate professors; Joe Morrison was an assistant professor; Lola Mustard was an instructor; and Leon Pollander was a lecturer.

School of Journalism Foundation

The state's newspapers took a significant step when they fulfilled their pledge to help the school by incorporating the School of Journalism Foundation of North Carolina, Inc., on Nov. 16, 1949. The idea had arisen in 1946 when the NCPA urged the university to seek accreditation for the department, and it arose again after the school's failed accreditation attempt in 1948. McPherson led other editors in the state to create the foundation to collect money to "advance the field of journalism at or through the School (or Department) of Journalism," including student financial aid, chaired professorships, and equipment. The charter included the names of 118 foundation members.[3]

The foundation's board of directors met for the first time on Jan. 20, 1950, in Chapel Hill. Present were McPherson, John W. Harden, William E. Horner, and Leslie S. Thompson. William C. Lassiter, the NCPA's legal counsel, attended to assist the foundation with legal matters. The NCPA had paid all fees and expenses associated with the incorporation of the foundation. McPherson was elected president, a post he held until his death on Aug. 10, 1979, when he was succeeded by C. A. "Pete" McKnight of the *Charlotte Observer*. The foundation's bylaws adopted at the first meeting authorized the board to hire an executive vice president to "stimulate financial support" and run the foundation office, but no one was ever appointed to that position. From the earliest years, the foundation's board of directors held its annual meeting in conjunction with the NCPA winter institute in Chapel Hill in January or February. That practice ended when the foundation changed its accounting system from a calendar year to a fiscal year in 2007, and meetings are now held in October.

At the board's 1951 meeting, McPherson reported that first-year contributions had totaled $12,405 (including $1,000 from McPherson himself). By the end of 1951, major gifts of $1,000 or more had been received from Ernest H. Abernethy of Atlanta, Ga.; Jefferson Standard Life Insurance Co.; Carolina Power and Light; the Raleigh *News and Observer*; Burlington Mills Foundation; the NCPA; Gifford Publishing Co.; the *Charlotte Observer*; and Piedmont Publishing Co. Mr. and Mrs. L. C. Gifford of the *Hickory Daily Record* gave an early gift of $1,000 in memory of their daugh-

---

3. Certificate of Incorporation of the School of Journalism Foundation of North Carolina, Inc., Oct. 1, 1949, Chancellor's Records: House Series.

ter, Sara Lee Gifford, a school alumna who had been killed in an automobile accident on Nov. 5, 1949. They eventually gave an additional $25,000 to create the Sara Lee Gifford Courtyard next to Howell Hall and a garden behind Carroll Hall. (In a 1975 interview, McPherson claimed that it had been his idea to fund the Sara Gifford courtyard but that he had deferred to the Giffords.)[4] The foundation gave the school $500 in 1951—$416.66 to supplement the salary of Professor Jack Riley, and $83.34 to start a travel fund for faculty members. The foundation's remaining funds were split between cash and investments in U.S. Treasury notes. The minutes of the meeting showed that two anonymous gifts of $1,000 to honor Phillips Russell and Oscar Coffin had been received after the end of the report period.

The foundation gave the school no money in 1951 but gave it $400 in 1952, including $150 for a visual education project in advertising and $250 for faculty travel, and $500 each in 1953 and in 1954.[5] Minutes of foundation meetings do not show that Coffin or anyone else from the school attended meetings in 1950 or 1951. Coffin and Russell attended on Jan. 25, 1952, and Coffin and Spearman on Jan. 23, 1953.

"No dean to write home about"

Jim Shumaker, one of Coffin's students and later a faculty member in the School of Journalism and Mass Communication, said Coffin's deanship fit him as naturally as "an ascot tie fit a plow hand."[6] Coffin did not believe the new status as the School of Journalism would make much difference. He expected only limited growth of the school because it would get no additional funding, but he said the school would add a course in industrial journalism—mostly about trade journals—and the faculty wanted to add more courses in advertising and radio. He wanted to adhere to the six-course requirement in journalism but said he would ask for a maximum of eight, saying the faculty wanted to "cling as closely to a well-rounded bachelor's degree" as it could. (That change was in response to a criticism from the accrediting team.) He acknowledged that a more flexible curriculum would please the foundation and help it to apply pressure to the

4. Interview with Holt McPherson by E. P. Douglass, April 9, 1975, Southern Oral History Program Collection, Southern Historical Collection, University of North Carolina at Chapel Hill Library.

5. Except where otherwise noted, information about the foundation is from minutes of its meetings, which are in the archives of the School of Journalism and Mass Communication at UNC–Chapel Hill.

6. Shumaker, "Deanship Fit 'Skipper' Well," *JAFA News*, Spring 1994, 6.

state legislature for more funds.[7] Replying to a former student at the *Atlanta Journal* who had congratulated him on his new title, Coffin said that until the school got money from the legislature for classrooms, a photography darkroom, an assembly room, and laboratory space, "This is not much of a school and I am no dean to write home about."[8]

Coffin retained his longstanding resistance to national organizations, and even the chance to try to stem the rising tide of accreditation was not enough of an incentive for him to join the American Society of Journalism School Administrators (ASJSA). Perley Reed of West Virginia University again asked Coffin to join ASJSA, saying that Cloyd H. Marvin, president of George Washington University and secretary of the National Commission on Accrediting (NCAC), had lauded ASJSA because it represented the interests of both nonaccredited and accredited schools. Reed noted that the NCAC had refused to recognize journalism's accrediting organization, the American Council on Education for Journalism (ACEJ). Marvin was opposed to the "so-called accrediting agencies that had been cracking the whip over the heads of college presidents and others for many years."[9] Coffin responded with a hint of the health problems that would eventually force him to step down from the deanship, saying he would not be an administrator for more than another year and would leave the administration of the school to his younger colleagues. "If this sounds like I have wearied of well-doing, just let it go at that. I am damned tired of holding on to the plow. Not that I would take a bandwagon ride—altitudes make me dizzy and I think I rate foam rubber."[10]

Still, ASJSA leaders did not give up easily on Coffin. Its president joined the effort to get him to join, saying ASJSA was part of the newly created Association for Education in Journalism, along with the Association of Accredited Schools and Departments of Journalism. ASJSA, he said, was not an accrediting organization and included representatives of both accredited and nonaccredited programs.[11] Coffin's response echoed his earlier complaints about his health, saying a siege of asthmatic bronchitis had convinced him that he was "no longer a fit subject for organization or affiliation." The new organizations certainly had no appeal to him: "As a one-time somewhat rugged individualist—admittedly deteriorated well nigh to depletion—I am inclined to the view that the world, flesh and devil

7. Coffin to J. Albert Dear, Feb. 10, 1950, Coffin Papers.
8. Coffin to John Mebane, April 25, 1950, Coffin Papers.
9. Reed to Coffin, Feb. 5, 1951, Coffin Papers.
10.Coffin to Reed, Feb. 12, 1951, Coffin Papers.
11. E. C. Trotzig to Coffin, April 27, 1951, Coffin Papers.

are all over organized. I think well of your outfit, especially those who look askance at accreditation, but I could perform no service and hence am forced to decline membership therein."[12]

Chancellor Robert House had to explain to McPherson why neither Coffin nor anyone else from the faculty had attended the 1950 NCPA meeting in Asheville. He said Coffin had asthmatic bronchitis, he and his car were too old for such trips, other faculty members had legitimate reasons that kept them from going, and the department had no money for travel. Coffin had spent only $25 on travel for himself in his 24 years on the faculty, and Spearman and Phillips only occasionally got money to attend national meetings. House reacted favorably to McPherson's suggestion that the foundation might provide travel funds to help faculty members attend meetings of the NCPA and other associations.[13]

On campus, the school took steps to improve its standing by creating an administrative board that included faculty members from the school (Pollander, Russell, and Spearman) and other departments: Clarence Heer from the Department of Economics, Hugh Lefler from History, Charles Robson from Political Science, Harry K. Russell from English, Albert I. Suskin from Latin, and Earl Wynn, professor of radio and communication and director of the Communication Center. Administrative boards were largely advisory but occasionally did perform official functions, such as approving requests for grade changes. Coffin also pledged that the new school would maintain its close affiliation with the College of Arts and Sciences.[14]

New Mission

Coffin and the faculty set about changing the curriculum and focus of the school, which were reflected in a new mission statement that the school adopted in 1950: "The School prepares young men and women for careers in journalism by offering an academic program which provides a basic liberal education, an understanding of the responsibilities of a free press in a democratic society, and a fundamental knowledge of journalistic techniques." The statement is significant because it ranked journalistic skills third behind a liberal education and an understanding of the

12. Coffin to Trotzig, May 14, 1951, Coffin Papers.
13. House to McPherson, July 13, 1950, Chancellor's Records: House Series.
14. Coffin to House, June 24, 1950, Chancellor's Records: House Series. The College of Arts and Sciences had been created in 1935 from the College of Liberal Arts and the College of Applied Science.

role of the press. Two courses were devoted to college newspapers, while "News Writing" was divided into three courses (53, 54, and 55), and 54 and 55 were later changed to two reporting courses. Sechriest taught "News Methods and Treatments," which later became "News Editing," and Russell taught two creative writing courses that were not cross-listed with the Department of English. Two courses were devoted to newspaper advertising and one to advertising copywriting. Morrison taught a radio journalism course that was cross-listed in the Department of Radio, which had been created in 1947. All the courses except one, "History of Journalism," involved practical aspects of journalism.

Requirements outside the school in the first two years were the same as those for students pursuing other B.A. degrees at the university: two courses in English; four in social science; one in hygiene; three in physical education; four in natural science; one in math, Greek, or Latin; four in the humanities; and two in different foreign languages. Requirements in the junior and senior years included one course in economics, two in history, two in political science, and six to eight in journalism and electives. Students were advised they had to be able to type with reasonable skill.

Coffin frequently complained that faculty members had heavy workloads, but a 1952 report of teaching assignments and course enrollments (Table 5.1) indicates that the workload was not onerous compared to faculty duties in the early 21st century. Coffin taught only one course with six students, Pollander taught two with a total of 12, and Spearman taught two with a total of 14. At the upper end, Lassiter taught three courses with a total of 40 students, and Morrison taught three with 39.

Coffin and the university continued their efforts to raise the public profile of the school. Coffin wrote an article for the *Durham Morning Herald* in which he said converting to a school would not mean major changes. He explained that a new course in business journalism was a first step toward instruction in public relations, but he maintained that the best preparation for working in public relations was newspaper work. Friends of the school would not have to worry that the journalism program would focus only on techniques that graduates could learn in the field, he said; the school would also provide the information content that would help them.[15] Starting in 1951, either the chancellor's office or the school hired the Carolina Clipping Service in Raleigh to collect newspaper stories about the school (and possibly the entire university). That seems to be evidence of greater efforts to publicize the school, perhaps in reaction to suggestions that it had not done enough publicity. One story that the clipping service found

15. Coffin, "Before They Draw Wages," *Durham Morning Herald*, Oct. 7, 1950, II-26.

Table 5.1 Teaching Assignments and Course Enrollments,
School of Journalism, Fall Semester 1952

Course	Teacher	Enrollment
53. News Writing I	Lassiter	17
53	Morrison	16
53	Sechriest	10
54. News Writing II	Spearman	8
55. News Writing III	Spearman	6
56. Feature Writing	Lassiter	10
57. News Methods and Treatments	Sechriest	10
58. Editorial Writing	Coffin	6
59. Country Newspaper Production	Lassiter	13
62. Newspaper Advertising I	Mustard	15
62	Mustard	8
62	Pollander	8
63. Newspaper Advertising II	Pollander	4
63	Mustard	4
64. Creative Writing	Russell	13
73. Radio Journalism	Morrison	17
74. Business Journalism	Morrison	6
80. News Photography	Sechriest	11

Source: Class Census Enrollment Blanks, Report to the Consolidated University of North Carolina, Oct. 3, 1952, in Chancellor's Records: House Series.

said graduates of the school had won 14 awards for excellence in newspaper work, prompting Coffin to remark, "Poets are born, not made, but I am convinced that a bit of collegiate furbishing often makes 'em more fitten. And don't we get a swell bunch of students!"[16]

16. "UNC Grads Receive 14 '50 Press Awards," *Charlotte Observer*, Feb. 1, 1951. (Although the name of the newspaper and the date were written on a clipping in Coffin's

Coffin Steps Down as Dean

Early in 1951, Coffin was coming under fire, at least from McPherson. In a letter marked "Personal and Confidential," House wrote to McPherson, defending Coffin in an apparent response to something McPherson had said or written. House affirmed that Louis Graves and Gerald Johnson had been "tops as creative artists," but that they had concluded they did not want to teach. House said Coffin had been forced to "organize and develop journalism from an inspiring classroom experience (for he, too, quickly became an inspiring teacher) on through the practical training, placing and guiding newspaper men and women." He said Coffin was "drafted into a national scope of newspaper training because of the excellence of his work." The university's financial crisis brought about by the Depression prevented Coffin from increasing the size of the faculty, House said, and he admitted that Coffin did not have as many resources as other department heads had been given. Coffin was so modest and unassuming that some people thought he was an obstructionist, House noted, but he was a good administrator with an open mind. House concluded with a strong statement of support: "No dean in the University of North Carolina has a better or more human conception of the values in cultural education a professional man should have as a part of his profession."[17]

A year later, Logan Wilson, academic vice president for the Consolidated University of North Carolina, asked House about the situation at the School of Journalism. Given that the chancellor of the Chapel Hill campus reported to the president of the consolidated statewide university system, a letter from Wilson to House would carry some weight. Wilson had seen a local newspaper story that listed 40 accredited schools of journalism but pointedly said the UNC school was not accredited. He had read the 1948 accreditation report and said he assumed that appreciable improvements had been made since then, but he wanted evidence of those improvements. He suggested that Coffin and his colleagues be asked to give an item-by-item self-evaluation of the school, compared to the specific points in the 1948 report.

Officials of the Consolidated University were not interested in accreditation just for the sake of accreditation, Wilson said, but the school should

---

files, the story could not be located in the *Charlotte News* or the *Charlotte Observer* on that date.)

17. House to McPherson, Jan. 4, 1951, Holt McPherson Papers #4222, Southern Historical Collection, University of North Carolina at Chapel Hill Library.

be accredited if it deserved it. If not, he continued, "We should know specifically in what respects we are still below standard." Wilson attached a handwritten note to the letter that gave House an opportunity to ignore the request for Coffin's self-evaluation: "Will this thing build a fire without giving anybody third-degree burns? If you think it will do more harm than good, I'll hold back." House responded with his own handwritten comment: "Let this come on. It's just another item we did not get to first base on."[18] Wilson's suggestion for the self-evaluation could be interpreted as a criticism of Coffin's lack of any response to the failure to achieve accreditation, and House's comment could be read as acknowledgement of a problem with Coffin. However, there are no documents in any of the principals' files to indicate that the matter went beyond this exchange between Wilson and House.

Coffin's chronic asthmatic bronchitis was getting worse, but he managed to stay in the dean's office two more years before abruptly telling House in April 1953 that he had to step down from the deanship effective immediately. The letter was characteristically Coffin:

In the name of God, Amen!

I, Oscar Jackson Coffin, born threescore and six years ago in this section of the briar-patch designated North Carolina, United States of America, having entered without fear, albeit with appreciable trepidation, upon my second childhood, in the interest of our common objective, the preservation, broadening and deepening of a people's University, am constrained to ask you to relieve me of my responsibilities as Dean of the School of Journalism. My spirit is willing, but there are others available whose flesh is stronger and whose vision of the bigger business which the State's higher education has become is indubitably clearer. I confess without expectation of any sort of attempted contradiction that I have rather consistently deferred contemplation of a forest to serve as would-be surgeon of the trees. . . .

I can't say I have adored every minute of being dean. I have frequently faltered in the University's good fight; but I have, as lay in me, kept the faith. Let us hope I have not done violence to our common idea; and over against my academic shortcomings I would ask only for the placing of the fact that with your help and

18. Wilson to House, Jan. 21, 1952, Gordon Gray Records #40008, University Archives, University of North Carolina at Chapel Hill Library.

that of South Building . . . I have secured and retained the services of a teaching staff who have both the capacity and the will to do a better job than I can hope ever to blueprint for them.

True, I hope to be missed—for affection and trust are not dismissed in a moment in this community—but the deaning of this school will be greatly improved and I'll still be around for some years yet as, I hope, a non-dogmatic co-laborer in the vineyard.[19]

In an editorial response to Coffin's decision, McPherson praised him as a teacher but implied that he had not been forceful enough in asking for more resources for the school. "He will continue to teach, which is his forte anyhow, and he is a great teacher in modern exemplification of that teaching principle of Mark Hopkins on one end of a log and his student on the other, with development of that student being his aim." Ignoring his own role in the accreditation controversy, McPherson implied that the school had produced good graduates while not adhering to the superficialities required by accreditation. He said that under Coffin's leadership, Carolina's journalism school had a distinctive flavor, and its graduates had spoken eloquently for it even while its well-meaning friends would have placed more emphasis on "superficialities with which national accreditation might have [been] attained." He said Coffin was not orthodox or acquisitive and had taken what he had been provided, even though he was entitled to more.

"Filling Oscar Coffin's shoes isn't going to be easy," McPherson said. "We sincerely hope that his successor will retain the flavor and spirit of teaching he has exemplified, that he will fight for, and get, that which Oscar Coffin has managed without because of his own modesty and willingness to make the best of what was available to him." McPherson alluded to the loss of the journalism program at Emory University and said UNC might help to fill the void of that loss. He also hinted that Duke University or Wake Forest University might start journalism programs, but if the UNC school got the facilities it needed and a dean who could carry on Coffin's teaching tradition, there would not be a need for another journalism school in the state. "This one will continue to feed a quality of inspired young men and women into a business which draws heavily upon enthusiasm of youth for its usefulness," he said, "and most hands will agree we need better, if not more, newspapermen."[20]

19. Coffin to House, undated, Coffin Papers.
20. McPherson, "Journalism Challenge," *High Point Enterprise*, June 10, 1953.

Searching for a New Dean

House immediately reported the news of Coffin's decision to Gordon Gray, a newspaper publisher and radio station owner from Winston-Salem who had become UNC's president in 1950. House suggested the appointment of a university committee with a mission to make recommendations about the school and search for a new dean. House suggested four newspapermen who might be solicited for advice: Al Resch of the *Sanford Herald*, W. K. Hoyt of the *Winston-Salem Journal,* Thomas Robinson of the *Charlotte News,* and Frank Daniels of the Raleigh *News and Observer*.[21] Gray agreed with the search committee idea and said that contributions to Journalism Foundation funds might increase with the appointment of the new dean and could be used to supplement the dean's salary. He said he would personally help to raise such money to get a first-class dean as "measured by a national yardstick."[22]

Although Gray did not tell committee members what he meant by a "national yardstick," he did reveal his meaning to George Stephens, owner of a printing company in Asheville, who had suggested to Gray that the new dean should come from the existing journalism faculty. Gray reiterated his national yardstick comment and said if that yardstick produced two men of equal ability, one from outside the faculty and one from inside it, the choice would be the man who was already on the faculty. He hedged his statement, however: "I have not given sufficient thought to the matter nor am I sufficiently informed to know whether we have a person equal to anyone we could bring in. Therefore, I have no prejudices or convictions." Then, in a revealing admission, he said the long-range morale of the faculty could not be worsened by bringing in someone from outside. "Sometimes I ask the question whether the University at Chapel Hill isn't too ingrown," he added.[23] These statements imply that Gray may have been inclined from the start to bring in someone from outside.

Coffin had his own ideas about the search committee and suggested the addition of what he called "working" newspapermen, specifically Miles Wolff of the *Greensboro Daily News*, Sam Ragan of the Raleigh *News and Observer*, and Don Shoemaker or Claude Ramsey of the *Asheville Citizen*. He also suggested Phillips Russell and Roy Parker as faculty members for the committee. Two days later, he suggested more faculty names:

21. House to Gray, April 20, 1953, Chancellor's Records: House Series.
22. Gray to House, April 22, 1953, Chancellor's Records: House Series.
23. Gray to Stephens, June 2, 1953, Gordon Gray Records #40008, University Archives, University of North Carolina at Chapel Hill Library.

W. W. Pierson of the Graduate School as chairman, and professors Albert Coates, Hugh Lefler, B. L. Ullman, Harry Russell, and Harriet Herring, if House "needed a woman." He suggested Weimar Jones as an additional newspaperman.[24]

Significantly, neither House nor Coffin suggested McPherson. Coffin had revealed his animosity toward McPherson in a 1947 letter to House about printing a school brochure, saying it would "fend off critics like McPherson." House may have had similar thoughts or may have been sensitive to Coffin's feelings. By May 1, however, when House announced the final list of committee members, McPherson was on the list of seven newspaper representatives and seven faculty members. The chairman was Whatley W. Pierson, dean of the Graduate School, and several faculty members were named: Phillips Russell, School of Journalism; Albert Coates, director of the Institute of Government; Hugh Lefler, Department of History; Berthold Ullman, Department of Classical Languages; Harry Russell, Department of English; and Harriett Herring, Department of Sociology. Lefler and Harry Russell were also members of the school's administrative board.

In addition to McPherson, newspaper representatives were W. K. Hoyt of the *Winston-Salem Journal*, Thomas Robinson of the *Charlotte News*, Weimar Jones of the *Franklin Press and the Highlands Maconian* and president of the NCPA, Roy Parker (a former faculty member in the school and owner of several newspapers in Ahoskie), Miles Wolff of the *Greensboro Daily News*, and Sam Ragan, president of the Eastern Carolina Press Association and executive director of the *News and Observer*. By today's university practices, the even balance between faculty members and newspaper representatives from outside the university was unusual. Given what House and Gray certainly knew about the opinions of some North Carolina newspaper people, they (or at least Gray) may have structured the committee in an attempt to give an advantage to or to equalize the chances of a candidate from outside the school. House instructed the committee to consider current members of the faculty for the deanship as well as others and to measure the person they recommended by Gray's "national yardstick." He said that if the committee recommended a current member of the faculty, that person would "want his standing protected by having him measured with the best available in the nation." He repeated Gray's keen interest in and thoughts about foundation funds.[25]

Because Coffin was leaving the deanship immediately, House had to

---

24. Coffin to House, April 28 and 30, 1953, Chancellor's Records: House Series.
25. House to Pierson, May 1, 1953, Chancellor's Records: House Series.

Unable to choose between Walter Spearman and Neil Luxon, the 1953 search com-
mittee forwarded both names to Chancellor Robert House. Seated, left to right: Holt
McPherson, Harriet Herring, Whatley Pierson, Roy Parker, W. K. Hoyt. Standing,
left to right: Berthold Ullman, Harry Russell, Hugh Lefler, Thomas Robinson, Miles
Wolff, Sam Ragan, Phillips Russell. Not pictured: Albert Coates, Weimar Jones.
*(North Carolina Collection, University of North Carolina at Chapel Hill Library.
Reprinted with permission.)*

name someone to run the school. He did not expect the search committee to have a recommendation until September, and because Spearman
had indicated he would be a candidate for the deanship, House appointed
Phillips Russell to be "executive officer" of the school until a new dean
could be selected. He said such an appointment would meet the immediate practical requirements of the school, leave the committee free, and not
embarrass anyone.[26] Russell received an added administrative stipend of
$91.66 per month.

The committee went to work immediately, meeting on May 16 and June
6. Pierson wrote to deans and directors of journalism programs at five
universities—Missouri, Illinois, Columbia, Northwestern, and Indiana—
to invite them to suggest names. The committee did not use advertising
or other means to publicize the vacancy. It wrestled with the issue of the
"national yardstick" and the relative importance of a background in newspaper work versus an educational background with an advanced degree.

26. House to Gray, June 10, 1953, Chancellor's Records: House Series.

Students and the State Press React

Speculation about Coffin's successor centered quickly on Professor Walter Spearman, a UNC graduate who had been on the faculty since 1935. A biographical sketch prepared for the University News Bureau in August 1953 said he was "chief assistant to Coffin." That document—which apparently was not published—seems to have been prepared in advance in case Spearman was named dean.[27]

The *Daily Tar Heel* wasted no time in expressing its thoughts and preferences regarding the deanship. On May 13, Editor Rolfe Neill wrote an editorial advocating the choice of Spearman because he "backed the current curriculum" and because he had worked with Coffin and knew the routine duties of the school. Neill praised Spearman for knowing publishers and editors in the state and for being popular with students and faculty colleagues. In closing, he said, "Soon, we may meet Dean Spearman."[28] That was not to be the last word on selection of the dean from Neill, who later became a prominent journalist and editor and publisher of the *Charlotte Observer*.

Louis Graves, who had headed the journalism program in the early 1920s (when it was still in the Department of English) and who was owner and editor of the *Chapel Hill Weekly*, chimed in on the accreditation issue but did not mention names. He took the occasion of Coffin's departure from the deanship to criticize the idea of accrediting journalism programs, saying he had heard that some NCPA members were pressing the university for accreditation. He charged that accreditation was largely a matter of "keeping up with the Joneses" and had "more to do with show than reality, more to do with the pride of belonging—like a college boy with a fraternity pin—than it had to do with the training of young men and young women to do good newspaper work."

Graves said he wanted UNC to have good journalism teachers and good facilities, but people should not get excited about whether the program was on a list of accredited schools or not. A journalism school was important to a university, he said, but it had greater value if it did not fit the academic pattern. It was good, he said, that the old-time "traditional vagabond journalist, the drinker and wastrel" was disappearing and being replaced with respectful, well-trained men and women. Journalists, however, because of the nature of their occupation, ought to be mavericks. A

27. "Biographical Sketch of Walter Spearman," August 1953, Alumni Association records, UNC–Chapel Hill.

28. Rolfe Neill, "Home Grown and A-1," *Daily Tar Heel*, May 13, 1953, 2.

journalism school should also be somewhat of a maverick, too, he said, and the paramount value of a journalism school was in its standing with newspapers that were searching for talent. When the university chose a new journalism dean, Graves hoped the primary criterion would be competence in the day-to-day job of training young people for newspaper work. He hoped the university would not be too eager to get a "celebrity whose principal function would be to serve as a front at conferences, conventions, and banquets."[29]

Other newspaper people in the state also made their opinions known. Jones told Gray the deanship was one of the most important positions in the state because that person would have an impact on many newspapers in North Carolina. It was also important because newspapers faced the challenge of shifting their emphasis "from techniques and mere cleverness of expression to a deeper sense of the responsibility of the press," he said. He did not know if Gray's reference to a national yardstick meant stature or reputation, but he hoped it was stature because he thought a "big name" dean would have nothing to prove, be too timid to protect his reputation, and continue to work in the same pattern that had made him successful. He said a relatively unknown person would be a gamble but would be the best bet.[30] Jones later distinguished himself on the search committee by missing only one meeting despite living in western North Carolina.

Parker said in an editorial in the *Hertford County Herald* that the new dean could be a "big name" or a "big-minded, big-hearted, broad-based classroom teacher." Henry Belk of the *Goldsboro News-Argus* told Parker he agreed with him: "We do want, certainly, a man who is able and interested in developing, inspiring and challenging young men and women; not one particularly concerned with promoting himself."[31] Both men seemed to be talking about Spearman without naming him. Ragan told Pierson the school's curriculum was generally good but that it should constantly be examined to see what needed to be changed. He said the *Daily Tar Heel* should be put under the school's control so students could get more newspaper experience. Ragan agreed with the recommendation that the new dean should have practical newspaper experience, but he questioned the value of magazine experience.[32]

McPherson, who had become editor of the *High Point Enterprise*, assured House by letter that foundation funds would be available to supple-

29. Graves, "Accreditation," *Chapel Hill Weekly*, May 15, 1953, 2.
30. Jones to Gray, June 10, 1953, Chancellor's Records: House Series.
31. Belk to Parker, June 19, 1953, Chancellor's Records: House Series.
32. Ragan to Pierson, July 17, 1953, Chancellor's Records: House Series.

ment the new dean's salary. He hoped the UNC school could fill the gap created in the South when Emory University lost its journalism school. McPherson reminded House that his accrediting work with ACEJ had acquainted him with outstanding journalism educators and implied that some of them might be considered for the deanship.[33] He did not tell House this at the time, but McPherson had a particular person in mind.

Norval Neil Luxon

In his accrediting work, McPherson had become good friends with Norval Neil Luxon, 54, an assistant to the president of Ohio State University who had responsibilities for the university's budget. He had an undergraduate degree in journalism and a master's degree in history from Ohio State and a doctorate in history from the University of California at Los Angeles. He had been editor of the *Lantern,* Ohio State's student newspaper, while he was an undergraduate there, and he had worked for newspapers for three years. He was on the journalism faculty at Ohio State from 1928 to 1942, when he stopped teaching to serve in a variety of administrative posts on campus. He had been president of the American Association of Schools and Departments of Journalism and was one of the original educator members (and chairman) of ACEJ's Accrediting Committee at the time of UNC's failed accreditation bid.

McPherson happened to be attending an Accrediting Council meeting at the Waldorf-Astoria hotel in New York on April 20, 1953, when he had an encounter that would have a great impact on the selection of a new dean and the future of the school. Luxon, who was also at the meeting, walked up to McPherson at a luncheon and initiated a conversation.

"When in the hell are you going to get a decent journalism school at Chapel Hill?" Luxon asked pointedly.

"Why in the hell don't you come down there and help us?" McPherson replied with equal bluntness.

"I'm available," Luxon responded.[34]

Two weeks later, his availability became pertinent when Coffin announced his plans to retire. A news item about Coffin's resignation appeared in the May 30 issue of *Editor and Publisher,* a trade magazine widely read by journalism educators and people in the newspaper industry.[35] In Columbus, Ohio, Luxon saw the announcement and immediately

33. McPherson to House, May 4, 1953, Chancellor's Records: House Series.
34. Interview with McPherson by E. P. Douglass, April 9, 1975.
35. "Skipper Coffin Steps Down," *Editor and Publisher,* May 30, 1953, 42.

started a letter-writing campaign to put his name before the committee as an interested candidate. He did not apply directly, however, because he feared such a move would hurt his chances. He explained to McPherson that applying for an academic position was different from applying for a position in the private sector, and the quickest way to kill one's chances was to appear too eager for the job or to apply for it. Instead, he asked his friends to suggest his name.[36]

Luxon launched his letter-writing campaign on June 2 by sending letters to Ralph Casey, director of the School of Journalism of the University of Minnesota; Earl English, dean of the School of Journalism of the University of Missouri; Jefferson Fordham, dean of the law school of the University of Pennsylvania and a UNC alumnus; Frank Luther Mott, dean emeritus of the School of Journalism of the University of Missouri; and A. H. Kirchhofer, managing editor of the *Buffalo Evening News*. Kirchhoffer was a longtime friend who had been president of the Accrediting Council in 1952 when Luxon was chairman of the Accrediting Committee. In essentially the same letter to each man, Luxon asked them to tell pertinent people about his interest in being dean at North Carolina.

In one of the letters, for example (marked "Confidential and Urgent"), Luxon asked Casey to tell the search committee (if he were to be asked) that he was "deeply and sincerely" interested in returning to journalism education. He said he had been willing to take a $3,500 salary cut when he applied for the deanship at the University of Washington the previous year, but someone else had been hired. He suggested that Casey write to McPherson in case the committee did not contact Casey. "Confidentially," Luxon emphasized, "I would like very much to head a journalism school with an opportunity to develop it." Luxon worried, however, that McPherson would think he was making too much money at Ohio State to consider a move to North Carolina. Luxon was also concerned about the perception that he had not been teaching for nine years.

A week later, Luxon told Casey he had become pessimistic about the search process, saying English had told him the search committee was not insisting that candidates be journalism educators.[37] In another letter, Luxon told Casey he would try another angle. A close friend of his, Harvey Davis, the provost at Iowa State University, was going to talk with Edward K. Graham Jr., the son of the man who taught the first journalism course at UNC, who was then chancellor of the Women's College of North

36. Luxon to McPherson, June 17, 1953, Norval Neil Luxon Papers #4585, Southern Historical Collection, University of North Carolina at Chapel Hill Library.
37. Luxon to Casey, June 9, 1953, Luxon Papers.

Carolina in Greensboro. Luxon hoped Graham might have some influence with House and Gray.

Casey followed Luxon's wishes and wrote to McPherson on June 5, nominating Luxon and saying he was willing to return to journalism teaching and administration.[38] McPherson forwarded Casey's letter to Pierson and said Casey's strong recommendation of Luxon was significant: "This may be just the break we're looking for to get that national figure President Gray wishes."[39] Casey had worked with McPherson and Luxon on ACEJ's Accrediting Council and Committee, and the three of them had probably discussed the North Carolina situation and Luxon's interest before Coffin resigned.

Kirchhofer also responded quickly to Luxon's request and wrote to McPherson, who forwarded that letter to Pierson and again referred to Luxon as "a fortunate break" who measured up to Gray's ideal for a national figure and who would make the school even more "distinctive and useful."[40] In an example of how complicated Luxon's efforts eventually became, Casey told him on June 14 he did not think he could write directly to Pierson because he did not know him. Casey suggested that Luxon ask English to give Luxon's name to Pierson and ask Pierson to write to Luxon to see if he were interested.[41] English responded to Luxon's request on June 6, saying he had already sent a list of names, including Luxon's, to UNC. He was worried, however, because UNC administrators were not stipulating that the next dean be a journalism educator, saying, "They may wind up no better off than they were." On the other hand, he said, "It is quite possible that they will give a man a free hand down there, in view of the years they have struggled along with little or nothing."[42]

McPherson wrote to Luxon in confidence on June 15 and affirmed how strongly he felt about him. He hoped Luxon would see the challenge in the position and "press as vigorously as you ethically can the realization of it. Nothing would please me more than to see a man of your dynamic nature and broad spirit leading the school." He also revealed some of the thinking of members of the committee, telling Luxon he would fill Gray's desire for a man of national stature but warning that some people wanted "the man second to Coffin" to be dean. Without mentioning him by name, he said Spearman was "an excellent fellow," but several committee members

---

38. Casey to McPherson, June 5, 1953, Chancellor's Records: House Series.
39. McPherson to Pierson, June 9, 1953, Chancellor's Records: House Series.
40. McPherson to Pierson, June 24, 1953, Chancellor's Records: House Series.
41. Casey to Luxon, June 14, 1953, Luxon Papers.
42. English to Luxon, June 6, 1953, Luxon Papers.

felt he did not possess "the drive to carry the school forward as quickly as it should." Spearman would be an excellent number-two man, McPherson said. He added that as a newspaperman on the committee, he did not want to "press unduly a selection in the academic field," but he wanted a man of Luxon's drive and nature. "Nothing would please me more than to be able to support your bid," he assured Luxon, "assuming you are the best man for the place." McPherson wanted to keep his active role in the process a secret, and he asked Luxon to refrain from telling anyone he had contacted him.[43]

By the second week of July, the committee had received 35 applications and nominations. A subcommittee (not identified) reviewed the names and recommended five persons for a priority list: Spearman; Luxon; James Markham, a faculty member in the School of Journalism of the University of Missouri; Henry Ladd Smith, a faculty member in the School of Journalism of the University of Wisconsin; and Raymond Nixon, a faculty member in the School of Journalism of the University of Minnesota. Authorized by House to invite two applicants from outside the university to come to Chapel Hill for interviews, the committee chose Luxon and Markham but dropped Markham from consideration after he told Pierson he had taken a position at Pennsylvania State University. Thus, the field was narrowed to Spearman and Luxon.

Pierson informed Luxon on July 15 that he was a finalist, mentioning an enlargement of the school and the possibility of a new building.[44] Luxon responded immediately with a definite expression of interest: "With the right kind of an opportunity and the assurance of the support of the University Administration in building a truly professional School of Journalism, I would give serious consideration to returning to active participation in the field of journalism education."[45] That was Luxon's first official written contact with a UNC official regarding the new deanship.

Luxon assembled extensive materials to prepare for an interview at Chapel Hill.[46] He analyzed data from the school's rankings on the ACEJ questionnaire and identified 12 areas of concern: library, teacher salaries, faculty work space, total budget, teaching budget, publications, teaching loads, laboratory equipment, membership in professional societies (ranked 48th out of 48), percent of faculty members who belonged to the American Association of Teachers of Journalism, maintenance of stated

43. McPherson to Luxon, June 15, 1953, Luxon Papers.
44. Pierson to Luxon, July 15, 1953, Chancellor's Records: House Series.
45. Luxon to Pierson, July 18, 1953, Chancellor's Records: House Series.
46. These undated notes are in the Luxon Papers.

standards, and conditions of service for the faculty. He also prepared a detailed outline of his remarks to the search committee, including his experience and educational philosophy, which focused on the importance of state schools; the value of teaching, research, and public service; and his thoughts about the professional status of journalism education. He asserted that journalism education should be professional and should meet high standards; students should meet the basic requirements of the College of Arts and Sciences and should take no more than 25 percent of their courses in journalism; and the school should offer graduate work at the master's degree level.

Under a heading of "Situation at North Carolina," he surprisingly indicated that he would not be qualified to speak about the 1953 situation regarding accreditation, but he listed the problems he found in the ACEJ data. He would prepare five-year and 10-year plans on the basis of his observations, his analysis of the school's relations with other academic departments, and newspaper visits. Finally, he listed reasons why he would leave a top-echelon post at Ohio State, noting he did not see much future for a 54-year-old man as an assistant to a university president, and saying he would welcome a challenge to build a truly professional school. He cited the example of Frank Luther Mott, who had left the University of Iowa at age 55 to face a similar challenge when he became dean of the School of Journalism at the University of Missouri. "I feel much the same way," Luxon wrote.

McPherson told Luxon on July 24 that he wanted to meet with him when he came to Chapel Hill for an interview.[47] After Luxon arranged to visit Chapel Hill, McPherson wrote again on Aug. 6 to say he would meet with him and would bring along Miles Wolff, executive editor of the *Greensboro Daily News*, who was also interested in improving the school. He assured Luxon that he could speak freely in Wolff's presence.[48] Because Luxon traveled from Columbus to Chapel Hill on Aug. 7, he may not have received the letter before he arrived.

Luxon had a busy weekend in Chapel Hill, starting with a meeting with the search committee on Saturday, Aug. 8, 1953. McPherson, meanwhile, had concluded from earlier search committee sessions that a majority of people on the committee "had a favoritism for a man who was then connected with the school [Spearman]." He took Luxon back to the hotel after his interview and told him that they were "whipped because I had counted

47. McPherson to Luxon, July 24, 1953, Luxon Papers.
48. McPherson to Luxon, Aug. 6, 1953, Luxon Papers.

noses and that he was not going to be chosen. He took it very well and said that he understood how those things worked."[49]

Search Committee Action

The committee had already interviewed Spearman, and it met immediately after Luxon's interview on Aug. 8 to evaluate the two candidates.[50] The committee began its deliberations by discussing several qualifications the new dean would need:

- He should have practical newspaper experience and teaching experience in journalism.
- He should endorse the idea that journalism students needed a sound liberal arts education and that professional courses in journalism should not exceed 40 to 45 credit hours of a student's total course work.
- He should develop close ties with leading newspapers in the South and consult with them about the quality of the school's graduates.
- He should be able to administer a "small fund" to bring in prominent guest lecturers. (Nothing was said about fundraising.)
- He should work closely with other academic departments.
- He should anticipate a new building and the problems associated with it.
- It would be an asset if he participated in the affairs of the university and in outside organizations, but duties inside the school were paramount.
- Given that the school had experienced "noteworthy" growth in students and faculty, the new dean would have to conserve the strengths of the school, "with sympathy and appreciation," while developing new strengths.

Pierson's report then compared Spearman's and Luxon's qualifications:

- Luxon was deemed stronger in academic preparation because of his Ph.D. and M.A. degrees. Spearman had an M.A. in theater.
- The report was inconclusive about newspaper and academic experience, saying neither man had been head of an

49. McPherson, interview with Douglass, April 9, 1975.
50. The search committee report was conveyed from Pierson to House in a letter dated Aug. 12, 1953. Chancellor's Records: House Series.

academic unit. Luxon had "more significant" administrative experience—especially being assistant to the president of Ohio State—and Spearman had somewhat more teaching experience, although both had more than 14 years' teaching experience, and Luxon had not taught since 1944. Pierson did not take a stand on the issue of newspaper experience and pointed out that Spearman had been editor of the *Tar Heel* and had worked for the *Charlotte News,* while Luxon had "considerable" experience on newspapers in Ohio and Texas and had edited an Army newspaper when he was at Oteen Veteran's Hospital in Asheville, N.C., after World War I.

- Pierson said the evidence showed an advantage for Luxon in writing and research because of his published dissertation and several other publications about journalism education.
- Luxon got the nod with regard to contacts with national organizations and other schools of journalism because he had attended many meetings of journalism administrators, had served as president of the American Association of Schools and Departments of Journalism, and was familiar with the accreditation process. Spearman had only lately developed contacts with other journalism programs, Pierson added.
- Spearman "clearly" had a stronger acquaintanceship with the local situation, and Pierson cited 20 or more letters of support for Spearman, emphasizing his familiarity with journalism in the state, his teaching experience, and his support from students. Some letters said it would be a good idea to promote a man from within the school.
- The committee had little evidence of Luxon's capacity to deal with job placement of graduates but said it had "very considerable evidence of Spearman's sustained interest" in that activity.
- The committee concluded that both men enjoyed good health and were vigorous. Luxon was 54 and Spearman was in his early forties. The report said Luxon seemed to be "in excellent health and a man of physical vigor" who apparently was cured of a tubercular infection he suffered while at Oteen Hospital.

The committee wrestled with the potential financial problem resulting from the fact that Coffin wanted to continue to teach, meaning the school would not have a vacant faculty position or additional money allocated for a new dean. It decided to make its report without regard to finances, leaving that issue to the administration. After the committee considered the various factors, Spearman and Luxon were both nominated, and each received "strong support" from members of the committee, according to Pierson. It was an apparent stalemate, however, so instead of ranking them or indicating a preference, the committee agreed unanimously to send both names to House with an objective appraisal of their qualifications. Other than saying that both men had received strong support, Pierson did not report a committee vote. The committee authorized Pierson to write the appraisal of the candidates without the rest of them seeing or approving it, and he sent the committee's report to House on Aug. 12, ten weeks after the committee was appointed.

Pierson said in his report to House that Luxon was highly recommended as a man of "force and integrity of character, vigor in intellect, capacity for administration, and proven interest in scholarship" who was definitely interested in returning to teaching and administration in journalism. He said Luxon would be willing to come to UNC at a financial sacrifice, relating his willingness to take the job for $10,000. He was receiving a salary of $13,500 at the time and would probably soon be given an increase to $15,000 by Ohio State.

Spearman, on the other hand, had the support of colleagues, many students, and newspapermen in and out of North Carolina. He was commended for "his energy, his devotion to the institution and to the school, his interest in students, his success as a teacher, and his participation in general community and faculty affairs." Pierson then turned to what was perhaps the overriding concern about Spearman—that he had been so long and so closely associated with Coffin that he would be "prone to continue existing policies unchanged." Some supporters, however, had said Spearman "had integrity and independence, and, given the opportunity would, as resources are provided, lead the school to new growth and usefulness, while at the same time conserving the elements of strength which have already been developed."

Pierson said his report was as fair and objective as he knew how to make it from the committee discussions. He said, however, that if he were speaking on his own, he might add some details. There is no record if he ever had such a private discussion with House or Gray, although it is likely that he did.[51] The decision was then in the hands of Gray and House.

51. Pierson to House, Aug. 12, 1953, Chancellor's Records: House Series.

6. A Dean Is Named

For Luxon, McPherson, and Spearman, the decision about the new dean
must have seemed to take an eternity, but it was only a few weeks. The
anxiety over the decision revived a threat about asking Duke University
to start a journalism program. The eventual decision about the new dean
would engender critical reactions and entail a dramatic change in the
school.

McPherson was upset when he left the Aug. 8 search committee meeting in Chapel Hill because of the committee's failure to reach a decision
about a candidate—and especially because the committee had not recommended Luxon. He conveyed his doubts to Luxon at the Carolina Inn after
Luxon's interview and before the committee's final meeting. After driving
back to High Point, he immediately wrote an impassioned letter to UNC
president Gordon Gray. He apologized for any typographical errors in his
letter, saying he had typed it himself. (He managed to make a two-sided
carbon copy of the letter, which he sent to Luxon.) McPherson said in
blunt terms that Gray would soon have to make a decision that would be
of the greatest importance to the university, "whether it is to step up its
Journalism School to one that will be a credit or whether it is to remain in
the mediocrity that too long has characterized it." McPherson told Gray

1. McPherson to Gordon Gray, Aug. 8, 1953, Norval Neil Luxon Papers #4585,
Southern Historical Collection, University of North Carolina at Chapel Hill Library.

the committee had split almost evenly between Luxon (favored by the newspaper people) and Spearman (favored by the faculty members).

McPherson's letter indicated that he and other newspaper people in the state had complained earlier about Coffin to university leaders, who had assured the editors that the selection of the next dean would be the opportunity to change the school. Lamenting the inadequacies of the journalism program, he said former UNC president Frank Porter Graham and Chancellor Robert House had earlier urged the newspaper people "not to make a fight on Oscar Coffin, that he was near the end of his run and to get ourselves in readiness to help supplement what the university could offer and thus commend as Coffin's successor the best available man." He said the newspaper representatives on the search committee thought the search process had been "a discouraging, frustrating and almost shocking experience to see the clannishness, the jealousies and selfishness, the inbreeding tendency and absolute fear of bringing in a strong outside man as evidenced by some of the faculty folks on the committee."

Luxon, he said, was a recognized leader in journalism education, but faculty members on the committee would not allow the committee to endorse anyone but Spearman, "a man handpicked by Coffin as his successor and who lacks the drive and experience necessary to break out and develop a great school. He has been the acting dean to all practical effects and his 18 years of association just haven't evidenced the type of leadership or promise you need there." McPherson told Gray that his desire to have an outstanding journalism school was so important to him that he was directing his appeal "to advance the school rather than leave it in the mediocrity in which it too long has operated and from which we thought we had definite assurances of relief with this development."[2]

Reasons for Optimism

Despite McPherson's pessimism, the remainder of Luxon's visit to Chapel Hill had given Luxon reason to be optimistic. Back in Columbus on Aug. 10, he wrote McPherson and described the details of his activities in Chapel Hill, asking him not to reveal the source of the information. After the search committee meeting, Luxon had spent considerable time with Pierson. They met again at the Carolina Inn on Sunday morning and were joined by Cliff Lyons, dean of the College of Arts and Sciences, to discuss academic aspects of the journalism program and the attitude of other university faculty members about the School of Journalism. At 2:30, Pier-

2. McPherson to Gray, Aug. 8, 1953, Luxon Papers.

son took Luxon on a tour of Chapel Hill neighborhoods (Country Club, Greenwood, and Mt. Bolus) to give him an idea of housing possibilities. (John Foushee, a Chapel Hill real estate agent, gave Luxon another tour of neighborhoods on Monday.) Responding to an impromptu invitation, Luxon went to Coffin's house for watermelon Sunday afternoon, followed by cocktails with Lyons and his wife and dinner at the Piersons' home. Later Sunday evening, Louis Round Wilson, the university librarian, visited the Piersons, and he and Luxon discovered they had many mutual friends.[3] Describing the Chapel Hill visit to his friend Harvey Davis a few months later, Luxon said he had also met informally with seven of the eight faculty members in the journalism school—presumably everyone but Coffin—and they had told him they favored Spearman.[4]

Luxon expressed confusion about McPherson's pessimistic observation on Saturday after the interview and told him about his subsequent conversations with Pierson. "I gave him no inkling that I had seen you after the meeting," Luxon reported. "His attitude was in marked contrast to yours and he talked about what I could do when I came and so on." They had talked about issues regarding the deanship, Luxon said, and those conversations led him to believe the job was his. He said they had gotten "down to brass tacks" about salary issues. Luxon told Pierson he would take the job for $10,000, although he hated to take such a drastic cut in salary, and he told Pierson about salaries of other journalism deans.

Luxon also met with Comptroller William Carmichael Jr. on Monday, and that meeting gave him another reason to be optimistic: "Carmichael told me that Pierson had told him that the committee was unanimously in favor of my appointment. And as a matter of fact, Pierson practically told me that, too, or at least implied it so strongly that had I not had your previous report, I would have had no doubts." (If Pierson told Carmichael that the committee unanimously favored Luxon, he contradicted what Pierson's committee report told Gray about the decision—that the committee had reached a stalemate.)

Luxon had a luncheon meeting with Gray at the Carolina Inn cafeteria on Monday. Luxon told McPherson he was enthusiastic about the possibilities of the deanship and would enjoy working for Gray, a man he could respect and who understood "the objectives we would be trying to attain in the journalism school." He said Gray had impressed him with his understanding of journalism and his ideas about what a school of journalism should do. Luxon thought Gray's comments showed insight and

3. Luxon to McPherson, Aug. 11, 1953, Luxon Papers.
4. Luxon to Davis, Oct. 2, 1953, Luxon Papers.

judgment on problems of the press in general and in no way resembled "generalities voiced too often by university presidents and many newspaper publishers." Luxon said Gray told him he did not know what the committee would recommend but asked if he would take the job if it were offered. "I was frank with him," Luxon recounted, "gave him the facts, told him I would come for $10,000 but hoped it could be higher, expressed my disappointment at the delay in getting new quarters. I said that if I had the backing of the administration in making staff appointments, I would concentrate the first few years in revising the curriculum and in building a good staff."

Luxon thanked McPherson for his efforts and said the credit would go to him if Luxon got the job. He also asked if the Journalism Foundation could supplement the $10,000 salary. In closing, he told McPherson he hoped he would "soon be on the ground working closely with you to build a real school of journalism at your Alma Mater."[5]

Having gotten his own copy of the Aug. 8 report, Gray directed Pierson on Aug. 20 to tell Luxon and Spearman that the matter had not been resolved. One problem was the money issue occasioned by Coffin's desire to continue teaching. That meant the school would not have a vacant faculty position and hence no money to pay Luxon if he were offered the job. (Academic units typically have a limited number of faculty positions and can hire faculty members only to fill existing positions. To hire Luxon while Coffin continued in his position would have required the university to allocate an additional faculty position and salary money to the school.) Gray said, however, that the decision about a dean should not be based on availability of funds and that he was looking to the Journalism Foundation and other sources for additional money.[6]

Luxon and McPherson Wait and Worry

For the next three weeks, Luxon and McPherson exchanged several letters that revealed their anxiety about the uncertainty surrounding the decision about the next dean. Luxon received a letter from Chilton Bush, director of the Institute for Journalistic Studies at Stanford University, who said he hadn't heard any news about a decision at UNC. He reported that a

5. Luxon to McPherson, Aug. 11, 1953, Luxon Papers.
6. Gray to Pierson, Aug. 20, 1953, Chancellor's Records: R. B. House Series #40019, University Archives and Records Service, University of North Carolina at Chapel Hill Library.

graduate student at Stanford who had graduated from UNC told him that the school, "although it was trade schoolish, had a good reputation among the editors of the state." Bush said the university was of "high grade" and Luxon could build the school to distinction.[7]

McPherson apparently received Luxon's Aug. 11 letter (recounting his experiences in Chapel Hill) on the 12th and immediately replied, saying Luxon's letter was good news because he had been despondent about the chances "at getting things broken out at Chapel Hill and into the open." He enclosed a copy of the Aug. 8 letter he had sent to Gray, and he said he had subsequently called Gray on Aug. 10 and was told that Gray had not yet received the committee report. Gray also told him there was a problem of finding money if Luxon were to be hired. McPherson told Luxon he wasn't too hopeful at hearing that news, although Gray had said he had been impressed with Luxon. McPherson advised Luxon that it might be best to stop pressing the salary issue because it appeared "the sale is made." He said he wanted Luxon at Chapel Hill because Luxon recognized the job that needed to be done and was "the one man who can break that Journalism School out of its mediocrity."[8]

Luxon told McPherson on Aug. 15 that he was "considerably puzzled" by the situation but thought it would be best for both of them to sit tight. He said Pierson had repeatedly assured him that a decision would be made by Sept. 1. He expressed his own theory about the contradictory reports on the committee's votes. He believed Pierson had taken matters into his own hands, even though Pierson had told Luxon on the Monday of Luxon's visit that he was writing a report to circulate among the faculty members on the committee prior to giving it to the chancellor. Pierson contradicted that statement in his letter to House on Aug. 12, in which he indicated that he had written the report about the recommendation without the committee members seeing it.[9]

Exuding optimism but asking that his letter be treated in strict confidence, Luxon told A. H. Kirchhofer, his journalist friend in Buffalo, N.Y., on Aug. 18 that he had had a good interview in Chapel Hill. He said he was "keenly interested" in the job and would take a salary cut—but not a large one—to go to UNC. He said McPherson was in his corner and that newspaper members of the committee unanimously wanted him to come. He seemed confident that he would be offered the job because he said he

7. Bush to Luxon, Aug. 11, 1953, Luxon Papers.
8. McPherson to Luxon, Aug. 12, 1953, Luxon Papers.
9. Luxon to McPherson, Aug. 15, 1953, Luxon Papers.

and his wife planned to spend their upcoming vacation in the Chapel Hill area and that he would "probably make the shift January 1."[10]

On Aug. 22, McPherson wrote to Luxon at Michigan State University, where Luxon was attending the convention of the Association for Education in Journalism (AEJ). McPherson reported "a slightly encouraging development at Chapel Hill in which President Gray has suggested I 'relax and by no means assume the worst.' Aside from that there is only ominous silence."[11] Gray was apparently responding to McPherson's pessimistic Aug. 8 letter.

Reviving the Duke University Threat

Saying he was still hopeful that the Luxon appointment would work out, McPherson revealed a surprising alternative if anything were to get in the way of that appointment. That alternative was revealed in a document McPherson included in his letter to Luxon: a carbon copy of a letter McPherson had written on Aug. 22 to J. L. Horne Jr., publisher of the Rocky Mount *Evening Telegram*, who had surprisingly nominated McPherson to be dean. McPherson had told Horne that there were a number of reasons why he could not be dean, primarily because he was not qualified. He said rumors had surfaced in 1947 that he was a candidate for the deanship, and those rumors implied that he had started the Journalism Foundation to create an advantage for himself. He said he had written to President Frank Porter Graham at that time to say he was not a candidate then and would not be in the future. He then referred to Luxon, saying, "I have a hope this thing is going to work out to bring to the deanship one of the ablest men in the business in the nation. Keep your fingers crossed and wish me luck."

Then he raised the threat: "Confidentially, if it doesn't work out, some of us are going to be coming to you and other influential Duke leaders, asking you to get into the journalism school business and pledging you our support." McPherson typed a note to Luxon at the top of the carbon copy and signed it "HM." He identified Horne as a director of the Associated Press and a trustee of Duke University, "where we'll set up a journalism school if Chapel Hill fails to take this opportunity really to get on the ball. That is confidential, although Duke has long flirted with the idea. I don't want to appear to make any threats or have anything I say or do twisted into such."[12] McPherson had raised the Duke threat in 1946 when

10. Luxon to Kirchhofer, Aug. 18, 1953, Luxon Papers.
11. McPherson to Luxon, Aug. 22, 1953, Luxon Papers.
12. McPherson to Luxon, Aug. 22, 1953, Luxon Papers.

he was trying to get UNC officials to improve the Department of Journalism and seek accreditation for it.

When Luxon returned from the AEJ convention, he found a letter from Pierson dated Aug. 24—the letter that arose from Gray's instructions to tell Spearman and Luxon the matter had not been settled. Luxon wrote to Pierson on Aug. 30 and said he had had a "long chat" with Spearman at the convention. During that conversation, Luxon said, Spearman told him the committee had reached a stalemate and recommended both of them.[13]

On the surface at least, Spearman and McPherson had a cordial relationship. Spearman had written to McPherson in 1952 to congratulate him on his new post as editor of the *High Point Enterprise* and to suggest that they might be able to get together more often to talk about the school and the state press. He enclosed a copy of a report he had written as executive secretary of the Journalism Foundation in October 1952, which reported how the school had spent the $400 it received from the foundation the previous year—equipment money to purchase a movie screen and travel money to send faculty members to conferences. He mentioned the possibility of the school's move to Howell Hall and said it would require cooperation and financial support from the foundation. He also said the school wanted to start sending a newsletter to alumni.[14]

Luxon told McPherson on Aug. 29 that Gray would not return to his office until Sept. 7, when Gray expected that the journalism school matters would be settled. Luxon said that had been Spearman's understanding, too, revealed in their conversation at the AEJ meeting at Michigan State. Luxon again speculated on the apparent confusion about the search committee's vote regarding him and Spearman, saying Pierson told him he was confident that the committee's recommendations (Luxon called attention to the plural) would be seriously considered. Warning that he was speculating, Luxon concluded that if Spearman had correctly reported the situation to him, Luxon interpreted the situation as follows: The committee could not agree, the newspapermen wanted Luxon, the faculty wanted Spearman, Pierson personally favored Luxon, and the administration had to make the decision.[15]

McPherson told Luxon on Sept. 1 he had a "heartening" development to report. There had been some talk in "responsible circles" that the search committee should abandon Luxon and Spearman and choose McPherson

13. Luxon to Pierson, Aug. 30, 1953, Chancellor's Records: House Series.

14. Spearman to McPherson, Oct. 16, 1952, Holt McPherson Papers #4222, Southern Historical Collection, University of North Carolina at Chapel Hill Library.

15. Luxon to McPherson, Aug. 29, 1953, Luxon Papers.

instead. "It has gotten around so much," McPherson added, "I felt it necessary to get my position clarified without stirring the situation unduly at Chapel Hill." He said he had called Carmichael and made it clear he was not available under any circumstances. Carmichael had led him to believe that "if there is no rocking of the boat now, this thing is going to work out the way you and I want it."[16]

Luxon assured McPherson on Sept. 3 that he could support him as dean: "I want you to know, Holt, and I write this with all the sincerity I can muster, that if you will take the deanship I will at once write Dean Pierson and Gordon Gray and withdraw my name from consideration." He noted that McPherson was an alumnus, had an interest in building a great school, and had years of experience in North Carolina journalism. Luxon then made a startling suggestion: McPherson could take the deanship, raise money for an endowed professorship, and try to hire Luxon to fill that professorship.[17] McPherson reassured Luxon on Sept. 5, "There is just one man for the job at Chapel Hill, as I see it, and that is you." He said he was not the man for the job and wanted to support Luxon. "I am still for Luxon and will continue to be."[18]

Moving to a Decision

By Sept. 3, House seemed to be favoring Luxon and wrote to Gray after discussing the committee report with Pierson and Spearman. He told Gray that if finances were available, the addition of Luxon "would be good for all concerned since it would add to the resources of the school and in no sense impair the prestige of Mr. Spearman." He said Spearman had told him he would accept the deanship if it were offered to him or would "gladly go on about his regular business" if it were not. House alluded to the money problem, saying it would not be a good idea to bring Luxon to the university unless he could be paid a regular salary without relying on foundation funds.[19]

On Sept. 4, Spearman, apparently believing that a decision had not been reached, thanked House for their "frank and confidential" discussion that week. He expressed appreciation for the trust that House had expressed in him and asked him to forward letters of support from former students on to Gray, saying he had not solicited the letters. He also alluded to Rolfe

16. McPherson to Luxon, Sept. 1, 1953, Luxon Papers.
17. Luxon to McPherson, Sept. 3, 1953, Luxon Papers.
18. McPherson to Luxon, Sept. 5, 1953, Luxon Papers.
19. House to Gray, Sept. 3, 1953, Chancellor's Records: House Series.

Neill's editorial in the *Daily Tar Heel* and expressed resentment toward the role McPherson was playing in the search process: "Seeing some of these letters might give Mr. Gray a picture of the situation different from the impression he would get from Mr. Holt McPherson."[20] House forwarded the letters about Spearman to Gray and said Spearman was no "small-time man in the field." He had told Spearman it would be good for the school if he could get $10,000 to pay Luxon, and he told Gray that Spearman seemed to agree. House again expressed concern to Gray about the issue of a faculty position and finding money to play Luxon.[21]

As Luxon had reported to McPherson, he and House had discussed the salary issue during his visit to Chapel Hill. House's files in the university archives contain a handwritten note on Carolina Inn stationery, but with no indication of who wrote it (Table 6.1). The note included what seemed to be 1952–53 data about budgets, enrollments, deans' salaries, and enrollments at other journalism schools. Luxon would have had access to such data from accreditation reports, and he stayed at the Carolina Inn during his visit to Chapel Hill, so he was almost certainly the author. The average of the salaries he reported was $9,980, almost exactly the salary figure he had mentioned.

By Sept. 11, House (probably with Gray's concurrence) had chosen Luxon and asked Carmichael to find a way to pay him, "the top man recommended" by the search committee. (He said that despite the fact the search committee's written report had given him the two names without

Table 6.1 Data on Budgets, Deans' Salaries and Terms, and Enrollments for Journalism Schools at Representative Universities

Institution	JOUR Budget	Dean's Salary	Dean's Term (months)	Enrollment
Illinois	$141,226	$11,550	12	276
Michigan	$56,310	$8,920	9	94
Minnesota	$102,897	$10,250	9	252
Ohio State	$47,436	$8,628	9	109
Wisconsin	$86,768	$10,550	9	167

Source: Anonymous, undated note, Chancellor's Records: House Series.

20. Spearman to House, Sept. 4, 1953, Chancellor's Records: House Series.
21. House to Gray, Sept. 9, 1953, Chancellor's Records: House Series.

expressing a preference.) House said he and the committee believed the school urgently needed such an "accession of teaching strength and administrative ability." He wanted to keep Coffin on the faculty, citing him as "one of the most helpful and active members in the entire university, a man who is really the power behind the weekly, and to a large extent, the daily press of North Carolina." He cited the recent Pulitzer Prize won by Horace Carter of Tabor City (a graduate of the school) and Willard Cole of Whiteville, and he called Coffin a "superb teacher, a wise counselor and a practical, responsible man" who knew how to get his students to work." Keeping Coffin and hiring Luxon would also increase the teaching staff of the school, which needed doing, he said.[22]

Gray told House the next day that he could have the needed money to hire Luxon.[23] Pierson telegraphed and wrote to Luxon on Sept. 14, offering him the deanship at a salary of $10,000 per year and telling him that House wanted him to assume the office as soon as possible.[24] Shortly after that, McPherson and Luxon had a chance encounter in Ohio and talked about Pierson's telegram. McPherson had been in Dayton on church business and was walking out of his hotel room with his luggage when the telephone rang. He put his suitcase down and went back to answer it. The caller was Luxon, who had tracked him down. Luxon said, "You said that I wasn't going to get that job, but I have a telegram from Pierson, offering it to me. What do you know about it?" McPherson admitted that he didn't understand it.

McPherson had intended to fly to Charlotte and drive home to High Point, but Luxon asked him to change his plans and come to Columbus that night so they could talk about the job. McPherson changed his plans, drove a rental car to Columbus, and spent the night with the Luxons. The next morning, Luxon drove him around the Ohio State campus as they talked about the UNC offer. Luxon finally said he would take the job if McPherson could go back to North Carolina and raise $100,000 to create a foundation to fund student scholarships and professors but not to pay Luxon. McPherson said he would gladly undertake to do it and believed that it could be done. "And that's how this school fought its way out of being just a local regional school into one of the five, possibly one of the four, recognized greatest schools in this country," McPherson later recalled.[25]

Luxon wanted his wife, Ermina, to see Chapel Hill before he made a

22. House to Carmichael, Sept. 11, 1953, Chancellor's Records: House Series.

23. Gray to House, Sept. 12, 1953, Chancellor's Records: House Series.

24. Pierson to Luxon, Sept. 14, 1953, Chancellor's Records: House Series.

25. McPherson, interview with Douglass, April 9, 1975.

decision, so they drove from Columbus for a visit on Sept. 21–22. The visit was apparently a success, because Pierson told Luxon after the visit that people at UNC had been "captivated by Mrs. Luxon."[26] On the drive back to Columbus, the Luxons celebrated their 25th wedding anniversary on Sept. 22 with the McPhersons and W. K. Hoyt (of the *Winston-Salem Journal*) and his wife at a dinner at the High Point Country Club. Luxon told McPherson on Sept. 28 that he had informed Ohio State's president that he was resigning and had written Gray and House to say he could start at Chapel Hill on Dec. 1.[27] He wrote to Pierson on Sept. 29 to say he was accepting the offer and had submitted his resignation at Ohio State. It would be effective Nov. 30, and he could start at UNC on Dec. 1.[28] McPherson told Gray about the success of the Luxons' visit to Chapel Hill and congratulated him on the "courageous and forward-looking step" of hiring Luxon, saying it would lift the school "out of a mediocrity that too long has plagued it." He also said Luxon had been impressed with Gray's forthrightness and understanding of the problems facing the school.[29]

House made the appointment official with a letter to Luxon on Oct. 5, saying the $10,000 salary was for both the deanship and the faculty position and did not include an additional stipend for being dean. He explained that was advantageous to Luxon because it meant he would keep his entire salary even when he was no longer dean. House made no mention of any additional money from the Journalism Foundation. He addressed the school's space problems that had been an issue for Luxon, saying they were drastic and would remain so for the immediate future. He told Luxon he had assigned additional space for the school in the Caldwell Annex building and was trying to get an extra office in Bynum Hall. He closed by asking for Luxon's leadership in an effort to get the School of Pharmacy building (Howell Hall) for the School of Journalism.[30] By Oct. 23, the Luxons had purchased a vacant lot at 27 Mt. Bolus Road, north of downtown Chapel Hill.[31]

The idea that Pierson may have influenced Gray in Luxon's selection is buttressed by a letter McPherson wrote seven years later, when he thanked Pierson for his role in bringing Luxon to UNC. He said Pierson

26. Pierson to Luxon, Sept. 23, 1953, Chancellor's Records: House Series.

27. Luxon to McPherson, Sept. 28, 1953, Luxon Papers.

28. Luxon to Pierson, Sept. 29, 1953, Chancellor's Records: House Series.

29. McPherson to Gray, Sept. 24, 1953, Gordon Gray Records #40008, University Archives, University of North Carolina at Chapel Hill Library.

30. House to Luxon, Oct. 5, 1953, Chancellor's Records: House Series.

31. Luxon to the president of the University of Michigan, Oct. 23, 1953, Luxon Papers.

Norval Neil Luxon, dean of the School of Journalism from 1953 to 1964, was a marked contrast to "Skipper" Coffin in dress and style. *(North Carolina Collection, University of North Carolina at Chapel Hill Library. Reprinted with permission.)*

had permanent status as the "elder statesman" who had shaped the School of Journalism, and added, "All of us shall be forever grateful to you for the statesmanly way you plotted that development, for without your keen perception it could never have been done."[32] The statement about Pierson's plotting the development suggests that he may have taken personal initiative in the way he presented the search committee's report to the chancellor and the president.

In a letter to Luxon in 1960, McPherson took credit for his role in Luxon's appointment in 1953. "I caught a lot of hell for bringing you in," he told Luxon, "but those who were most critical are now the most praiseful and thinking it was their project to get you here."[33] Luxon returned the compliment in 1963 and acknowledged the roles of McPherson and Pierson in bringing him to Chapel Hill: "It was you who projected me into the picture and it was your backing of Whatley Pierson and your working on Gordon Gray that had much to do with the offer to come to the university."[34]

32. McPherson to Pierson, Oct. 13, 1960, Luxon Papers.

33. McPherson to Luxon, Dec. 26, 1960, Luxon Papers.

34. Luxon to McPherson, Jan. 21, 1963, Provost's Records #40039, University Archives, University of North Carolina at Chapel Hill Library.

William Friday had been Gray's assistant in the president's office in 1951 before becoming president himself in 1956. He confirmed in 2008 that McPherson had considerable influence during the transition from Coffin to Luxon. McPherson and Gray were fellow newspaper people who talked the same language, Friday said. "If you knew Gordon Gray at all," Friday added, "you knew he was for the Neil Luxon type of personality. He saw Luxon as a necessary type of transition and one he would be very supportive of. McPherson and others like him found a very ready audience and a very willing president. I have no doubt about that."[35]

Reactions to Luxon's Appointment

Luxon's appointment was announced in the student newspaper on Oct. 4, and it took only five days for Rolfe Neill, the editor, to blast the appointment with an editorial entitled "What Price Accreditation?" He said that in choosing a new dean, the university had "fumbled and never recovered." He charged that using a "hybrid" committee of faculty and nonfaculty members to pick a dean was unprecedented and had not been done in the case of other dean searches on campus. (That gives some credence to the possibility that House and Gray might have structured the committee to give considerable influence to the state's newspapermen.) The editorial said that although the committee had lined up 8 to 6, possibly even 9 to 5, in favor of Spearman, a vote was never taken. (Such information must have come from a Spearman supporter on the committee, because such preferences were not cited in the committee report or any correspondence. McPherson's Aug. 8 letter to Gray implied that the faculty members had lined up behind Spearman and the newspaper people behind Luxon. That would have been a 7-7 split if Pierson had indicated a preference, although Pierson could have sided with Luxon.) The committee had fallen short, Neill charged, by presenting Spearman's and Luxon's names without a recommendation and allowing House and Gray to make the decision. (It is now common practice for search committees to present two or three names to the chancellor without a ranking or preference.)

Neill strongly criticized the decision and charged it had been overly influenced by the university's desire for accreditation. He said the committee had overlooked Spearman's knowledge of the state's newspapers and had ignored his demonstrated success with students and newspaper experience. "It was an affront (and a scare, no doubt, to promotion-minded faculty members in other areas here) to the excellent job Spearman has

---

35. Friday, interview with the author, June 18, 2008.

done," Neill charged. He said the arrival of a "Ph.D. with a string of imposing titles and administrative duties, an author of journalism textbooks (and, incidentally, a man rather bare of practical newspaper experience)" was evidence of things to come and the "signal flare of the impending battle of journalism accreditation." The price to get accreditation had been too high, Neill concluded.[36]

Gray responded to the charges about accreditation a month later, saying he was not impressed by accreditation and that accredited standing was not important for the School of Journalism. He said he questioned the worth of accreditation in general and said some accredited schools of journalism did not match the quality of the UNC program. Gray denied specifically that the issue of accreditation for the school had influenced his decision to hire Luxon over Spearman.[37] Gray had already told Luxon that some people at UNC and in the state had questioned the wisdom of bringing in someone from outside the school, but Gray reassured Luxon, saying he was not concerned about the situation because he was convinced that Luxon would quickly overcome any apprehensions.[38]

Luxon kept a file of editorials that were written about his appointment, including Neill's from the *Daily Tar Heel*. He answered each editor with essentially the same letter, saying it was a positive thing that the newspaper was sufficiently interested in the school and the new dean to devote news and editorial space to them. (There is no evidence that he responded to Neill, at least in writing, but Neill said almost 50 years later that he and Luxon eventually became good friends.[39]) He acknowledged the problems he would face and said the first obligation of a state university was to the people of the state, and the first objective of the School of Journalism would be to the state's newspapers. He said he hoped to have the cooperation of the faculty and the state's newspapermen and hoped they would soon be calling him "Neil" or "Lux" instead of "Doctor Luxon," as many did in their editorials.

In some letters, he acknowledged Coffin's contributions to the school and the state and said he had trained under a similar man. In fact, he said, he had respected that man so much that he and his wife had just driven 100 miles to attend his funeral. In other letters, he said change in any institution was bound to be accompanied by disappointment, and he hoped any concern about his appointment would soon disappear. Depending on

36. "What Price Accreditation?" *Daily Tar Heel*, Oct. 9, 1953, 2.
37. "Gray Not Impressed by Merit of Accreditation," *Daily Tar Heel*, Nov. 7, 1953, 1.
38. Gray to Luxon, Oct. 26, 1953, Luxon Papers.
39. Neill, interview with the author, Oct. 5, 2007.

what the editorial had said, Luxon sometimes said his graduate degrees in history did not disqualify him as a newspaperman.

Henry A. Dennis, president and editor of the *Henderson Daily Dispatch*, said Luxon's appointment was a milestone. While he respected Luxon's eminence and ability, he was disappointed that someone from North Carolina was not chosen. He acknowledged "an unmistakable atmosphere of provinciality about North Carolina," and he said its journalism was no exception. That had been changing as people from outside North Carolina were acquiring newspapers in the state, which had effected a distancing between publisher and public. Dennis lauded the school for seeking national prominence, but he had hoped it could have been done while still retaining the flavor that Coffin and his colleagues had created. He was confident that North Carolina newspaper people would welcome Luxon and cooperate with him. He wished him well and hoped he could build a journalism school that would be among the best in the country.[40]

The *Goldsboro News-Argus* said the main job of the school was to train men and women to work on newspapers, magazines, or radio or television stations, and they needed to be grounded in a solid general education. The editorial said North Carolina newspapers had long insisted on (and actually had) a "standard" school of journalism, except for facilities and personnel. The writer lauded Coffin and his staff for doing a "great job in kindling young minds and giving them inspiration and sound training." The editorial said that if the school did not get more money, it would continue to operate as it had and would not have a chance of being accredited. Luxon would step into Coffin's shoes, but he would need more money.[41]

The *Greensboro Daily News* said Luxon's appointment marked a turning point in the school because of his many degrees, publications, and wide administrative experience. As an Ohioan entering what had been an exclusively North Carolina situation, he would need intelligence, diplomacy, and judgment to blend the school's distinctive North Carolina flavor with an emphasis on national accreditation and big-time status. It warned that "few institutions move to the big time without lessening their down home atmosphere." Because the school was concerned with turning out newspapermen for North Carolina, the dean and faculty needed to know about North Carolina newspapers and the men and women who ran them. "All the accrediting and certification in the world will not substitute for knowledge and understanding of the North Carolina scene. . . . North Carolina journalism, like all things, must move on. But in the moving on

40. Dennis, "With an Outside Flavor," *Henderson Daily Dispatch*, Oct. 10, 1953, 4.
41. "UNC Journalism," *Goldsboro News-Argus*, Oct. 12, 1953, 4.

we trust the movers will not leave behind what was good of the old."[42] That somewhat critical editorial would seem warm and embracing when contrasted to an editorial column in the same newspaper about the naming of Luxon's successor in 1964.

An editorial in the *Kinston Daily Free Press* described Luxon's background and said he had taken a considerable cut in salary to accept the job. It said friends of the school and former students were disappointed that Spearman was not selected, but they were not surprised, "because it had been common knowledge since late summer that there were strong differences of opinion relative to the future of the school." The editorial said if Luxon embraced the vision of the practical exponents of North Carolina journalism and added his own varied and useful experience, there was no reason why the School of Journalism "should not move forward to its rightful place among the nation's leaders."[43]

Robert Mason's critical editorial in the *Sanford Daily Herald* said many newspapermen probably had mixed emotions when they learned that "a longtime educator just past the apprentice stage in practical experience" had been named dean. He said Luxon, who had graduate degrees in history, would succeed Coffin, "who holds no doctorate and envies none who does." Coffin had stressed practical aspects, handling classes as workshops and choosing his associates on "knowledge of their ability as craftsmen as well as his estimate of their teaching ability." There was little doubt that Coffin had expected one of his associates to succeed him, Mason said, "but another thought prevailed and the School of Journalism, which is not now accredited because of its dearth of advanced degrees, will be taken over by an academician who can be expected to strive to place it on all the scholastic honor lists." Only time would tell, Mason said, if Luxon would emphasize the theoretical over the practical. "One thing is certain. It will be a long time before the School of Journalism at the University of North Carolina is absent the shadow of O. J. Coffin, made greater by inheritances from Gerald Johnson and Louis Graves, the master journalists who preceded him for brief terms, and greater yet by the newsmen-teachers with whom he surrounded himself."[44] Luxon sent his standard reply to W. E. Horner, Mason's publisher. Horner passed the letter to Mason, who attempted to reassure Luxon: "I am certain that you are quite qualified for the position and it was not my intention to infer that you are not."[45]

42. "Dr. Luxon's Problem," *Greensboro Daily News*, Oct. 8, 1953, I-8.
43. "New Journalism Dean," *Kinston Daily Free Press*, Oct. 5, 1953, 6.
44. Mason, "The Old Order Changeth," *Sanford Daily Herald*, Oct. 7, 1953.
45. Mason to Luxon, Nov. 5, 1953, Luxon Papers,

The Coffin Era Ends

Coffin continued to teach until May 1956, when he wrote to Chancellor House and asked to be relieved of his teaching duties:

> I am going out as I came in, a used newspaperman, A.B., UNC, 1909. In parting I would like to thank Alma Mater for letting me stay around so long in association with colleagues for the most part consecrated to the common good as affected by communication of thought and with students who while not all of them wanted to know anything, generally have been purposeful, honest and companionable.[46]

He died just five months later, at age 69, on Oct. 29. His death prompted many editorials in state newspapers, several of which were quoted in the school's *Journalism Newsletter*. The Raleigh *News and Observer* said he had a barbed wit but was without malice and admired decency in human beings. The *Daily Tar Heel* said he believed in good writing and in being homey, and he drank beer with students because he enjoyed it. The *Smithfield Herald* said Coffin loved honesty, truth, and accuracy and hated hypocrisy and pretension. In *Byways of the News*, Charles Craven listed adjectives that described Coffin: "ornery, quick-witted, ironic, warm, caustic, down-to-earth, garrulous, skilled, experienced, prominent, respected, kind, profane, beloved." The *Sanford Daily Herald* described Coffin's front porch as the most sociable hiring hall that ever existed. It said students had taken to Coffin's way of "cussing one minute and citing the Book of Job as an example of polished-down writing the next, of deflating campus stuffed-shirts with a colorful phrase or two, and of applying country terms to urbane subjects and characters."

Robert Ruark memorialized Coffin in his syndicated column, using words that sounded like his description of the Skipper Henry character in *The Honey Badger*: "a humorously irascible gentleman whose hooked nose and craggy chin gave him the appearance of a truculent turtle. He had a pair of piercing blue eyes behind frosty glasses and a laugh that could be reminiscent of the croaking of ravens." He said Coffin's death meant that a light in his life had been extinguished. Coffin, he said, had little use for ineptitude, and if Coffin had now gone someplace where he could read obituaries, he was probably editing those written about him.[47]

46. Coffin to House, May 15, 1956, Oscar Coffin Papers, Southern Historical Collection, University of North Carolina at Chapel Hill Library.

47. *Journalism Newsletter*, February 1957, 2.

Oscar "Skipper" Coffin, ca. 1950, in a familiar pose with a cigar. *(Photograph by Wint Capel. North Carolina Collection, University of North Carolina at Chapel Hill Library. Reprinted with permission.)*

Even McPherson found good things to say about Coffin. Just as he had claimed he was Gerald Johnson's first student in 1924, McPherson said he had been Coffin's first student when Coffin arrived at UNC in 1926. McPherson said he had developed an affection for Coffin that survived "a lot of buffeting" for 30 years and was glad to be part of the effort to create a scholarship to honor him. He said people were wrong when they thought that the Journalism Foundation was created to get rid of Coffin. They were wrong, too, when they thought McPherson wanted Coffin's job. The foundation created the scholarship before Coffin died, and the knowledge of it "was like medicine to him," McPherson said. He noted that he never enjoyed anything as much as seeing Coffin's reaction to the honor.[48]

Luxon had paid homage to Coffin in his annual report to the provost for 1955–56. He said space limitations in the report prevented him from giving a full assessment of Coffin's impact on newspapers and newspapermen in the state, acknowledging that the 46 daily and 150 nondaily newspapers in North Carolina were staffed largely by Coffin's former students. Many journalists in Washington, D.C., were former students, too, as were wire service correspondents in the United States and abroad. Luxon said in closing, "The tenets of the profession, the respect for careful craftsman-

48. McPherson, "Good Afternoon," *High Point Enterprise*, Nov. 6, 1956, 4A.

ship, the thorough grounding in the humanities, and the fact that journalism plays a significant role in the contemporary scene—all these and much more—were emphasized by Professor Coffin in his informally conducted classes and at other still less formal meetings with his students in his home and elsewhere. The school's graduates, his former students, will long remember and long be influenced by his precept and example."[49]

Despite what Luxon said about Coffin in such public documents, he privately believed that Coffin and his wife remained bitter about McPherson and how things had changed in the school. In 1962, McPherson told Luxon he had received a "resentful" letter from Gertrude Coffin and wanted Luxon's advice about responding to her, saying, "I'd like to be straight with her before anything happens."[50] Luxon responded with a letter he had marked "Personal and Confidential, Better Destroy after Reading," but he kept a copy in his files. He advised McPherson against corresponding with Mrs. Coffin: "She has been extremely bitter since Skipper's retirement and death. The dedicatory exercises [for Howell Hall in October 1960] made her extremely unhappy and she was caustic in remarks made to friends while here then and when she has been here since that date." Luxon related what he believed had been Coffin's feelings about McPherson:

> As a matter of fact, Skipper never had a good word for you (and he
> had many, many, bad ones) after my appointment was announced.
> Whenever he could get in a nasty crack at you in conversation,
> he did. . . . Skipper ridiculed everything I did with the School of
> Journalism as long as he lived and would still be doing it if he
> were still alive. He never lost an opportunity to make slurring and
> dirty remarks about Ph.D.s. His ideal for the school (if he ever
> had one) was long outmoded before he was eased out of his job.
> But he (naturally) resented being eased out and was bitter over my
> appointment and what I set out to do with the school. . . . Just between
> the two of us, I can't quite understand the number of persons
> in North Carolina who publicly praise him in print and privately
> decry what he did the last eight or ten years on campus.[51]

49. Luxon, "Annual Report of the School of Journalism, 1955–1956," Provost Records.

50. McPherson to Luxon, May 29, 1962, Luxon Papers.

51. Luxon to McPherson, May 31, 1962, Luxon Papers.

"We are going to go places on this campus."—*Neil Luxon*[1]

7. A Break with the Past

And so the torch passed from Oscar Jackson Coffin to Norval Neil Luxon. Luxon was 54 years old when he became dean of the School of Journalism on Dec. 1, 1953. He was a contrast to Coffin in both philosophy and style. Courtly in style and mannerisms, he had two graduate degrees, believed a university journalism program should have a strong academic foundation, and thought teachers should also be scholars in the field of journalism and mass communication. He was attuned to national accrediting standards for journalism programs, and he came to UNC with the goal of improving its school to meet those standards and become accredited. He knew he would have only 10 years to accomplish his goals because of the university's policy that forced faculty members to relinquish their administrative posts when they reached age 65. Thus, he wasted no time and worked tirelessly to change the school. By the time he stepped down, he had led the school in a new direction, changed the curriculum, created a graduate program, given the school national prestige, and established the basis for its eventual reputation as one of the best journalism schools in the world.

Luxon was part of a new generation of journalism educators who valued a more scholarly approach to the field, taught courses about issues in journalism (in addition to practical, skills courses), and showed a greater

1. Luxon to Ralph Casey, Feb. 1, 1954, Norval Neil Luxon Papers #4585, Southern Historical Collection, University of North Carolina at Chapel Hill Library.

appreciation for research. Some of those educators favored quantitative research and became known in journalism education as "chi-squares," in contrast to those who favored qualitative research (or no research at all), and were called "green eyeshades."[2] Journalism was establishing itself as a legitimate academic field of study as well as a preparation for professional careers.

Luxon differed from Coffin in appearance and almost always wore a suit with a flower in his lapel. In a 2007 interview with the author, Donald Shaw said he and other students of the late 1950s sometimes wondered if Luxon got his flowers from the rose garden at the Morehead Planetarium. That was not true because Luxon and his wife were accomplished gardeners who grew many flowers at their home at 27 Mt. Bolus Road in Chapel Hill.[3] Jack Adams recalled that Luxon also sometimes purchased his lapel flowers from a Chapel Hill florist.[4]

While Coffin was often described as being very approachable, former students were more likely to describe Luxon as tough and even aloof. Wayne King said Luxon was not the kind of person whom students liked because he was a bit distant, even while being friendly: "His sense of drama was missing; he was like an aspiring actor who could not act." King also used to wonder if Luxon wore a plastic shirt collar.[5] Ken Sanford said Luxon earned the respect of other deans on campus, but students thought he was somewhat stuffy and pompous.[6] Jim Wallace recalled that Luxon was always the "big guy at the top and not the friendliest person he ever met. He was a bit standoffish, but you didn't mess around with him. If he said you needed to do something, you did it."[7] Coffin wanted students to call him "Skipper" and admonished them not to call him "Dean Coffin" or "Doctor Coffin." It is unlikely that any student addressed Luxon as anything other than "Dean Luxon" or "Doctor Luxon."

Wayne Danielson, who was one of Luxon's first faculty hires and later his successor, said Luxon was a powerful administrator who built the program the way he wanted it. Luxon had an old-fashioned notion of what a dean should be, Danielson said, and he made the UNC deanship important and largely independent. Luxon believed in the notion of a "circle of

2. Chi-square is a statistical test of relationships among variables, and "green eye-shades" refers to the visor that newspaper people wore to reduce the glare of harsh newsroom lights.

3. Shaw, interview with the author, Oct. 19, 2007.

4. Adams, interview with the author, April 2, 2008.

5. King, interview with the author, Feb. 20, 2008.

6. Sanford, interview with the author, Oct. 5, 2007.

7. Wallace, interview with the author, Nov. 9, 2007.

scholars," the idea that the best journalists were produced by scholars with a substantive interest in the field, not by retired journalists, and that students should study the role of journalism in society.[8]

While Coffin may have been the only journalism dean to appear as a fictional character in a novel, Luxon was likely the only dean whose exact name was given to a character in a nationally syndicated comic strip. Milton Caniff, the cartoonist who produced the "Steve Canyon" feature from 1947 to 1988, was Luxon's student at Ohio State in 1929, and Luxon kept framed, autographed originals of Caniff's panels on his office wall. In the cartoon's strip on Oct. 26, 1952, the Canyon character twice addressed a journalist character as "Luxon."

State of the School

In addition to screening candidates for the deanship in 1953, the search committee produced a three-page report detailing the condition of the school and its many needs. The conclusions were based on information that committee members gathered from faculty members, university officials, and state newspaper leaders, but nothing in surviving documents indicates how the faculty members and newspaper representatives on the committee participated in the discussions and the drafting of the report. The picture the report painted was bleak, but it suggested opportunities for improvement.

The school occupied three offices and classrooms on the east side of the top floor of Bynum Hall, which had been converted from the university's gymnasium, and the report said not a single room was suited for its purpose. The rooms had poor lighting and ventilation and no space for writing laboratories or a reading room. The only advantage of the conditions in Bynum, according to the report, was that the building's limitations and handicaps familiarized students with the difficulties of working in typical newspaper offices. Jack Adams, who was a faculty member at the time and who later became dean, said Bynum was a "pigpen," with offices arranged around a running track in the balcony.[9]

The report said the school needed a newsroom, an advertising classroom, a reading room, an assembly room, a photographic darkroom, a typography lab, classrooms, and offices. It said the need for a building was imperative and that university officials had made a firm commitment to

8. Danielson, interview with the author, Feb. 26, 2008.
9. David Perry, "Howell Has History of Spreading Smiles," *UNC Journalist*, Nov. 9, 1974, 1.

assign Howell Hall to the School of Journalism after the School of Pharmacy moved from Howell to a new building. The report said Howell would not be available for five years, but it turned out to be seven. The committee suggested that additional space in Bynum occupied by the University Press might be assigned to the school, and they proposed the addition of space in an annex to Caldwell Hall.

The committee identified gaps in the curriculum, saying the school needed courses in journalism ethics, press law, magazine journalism, propaganda and public relations, advertising, and newspaper management. A majority of members expressed grave doubts about establishing a graduate program in journalism, however, and said graduate work for journalists should be in a relevant subject outside the school. The committee did suggest that the school might create a graduate minor in journalism for students in other academic disciplines, such as English, history, or political science.

Committee members differed in their opinions about the appropriate relationship between the school and student publications such as the *Daily Tar Heel*. Some sources had suggested that the school should assume control of the student newspaper to give students more practical experience. Committee members agreed, however, that it would not be practical to change the tradition of student control of the newspaper and that closer cooperation without control by the school would be a better alternative.[10] Such a move would have been difficult to accomplish, however, because students on the paper were fiercely independent and somewhat contemptuous of the School of Journalism. Ed Yoder, who was editor of the *Daily Tar Heel* in 1954–55, said in 2008 that he and other staff members, including Barry Farber, Rolfe Neill, and Charles Kuralt, majored in liberal arts disciplines instead of journalism and felt that professional journalism education should take place at the graduate level. They also believed that their student newspaper experience was more valuable than courses in the journalism school. Yoder said he'd had some tangles with Luxon, whom Yoder and others on the *Daily Tar Heel* suspected of trying to take over the newspaper. It was an unfair suspicion, Yoder later admitted, and Luxon strongly denied it at the time.[11]

10. "Report Concerning the State and Present Needs of the School of Journalism," W. W. Pierson to R. B. House, Aug. 12, 1953, Chancellor's Records: R. B. House Series #40019, University Archives and Records Service, University of North Carolina at Chapel Hill Library.

11. Yoder, interview with the author, Jan. 25, 2008.

Luxon's Fast Start

An area newspaper showed Luxon hard at work a few days after he assumed his new duties as dean. The story was written by Robert Madry, director of the UNC News Bureau, and was accompanied by a photograph of Luxon with Coffin and professors Phillips Russell and Walter Spearman. W. Whatley Pierson, who had chaired the search committee and was dean of the Graduate School, had taken Luxon on a campus tour to meet other deans and faculty members. Being politic, Luxon paid homage to his predecessor: "I am informed that O. J. Coffin has done a good job since he came here 27 years ago, and it is my intention to build on the solid foundation laid by him." Luxon said he did not plan any immediate changes but wanted to make a thorough study of the school to determine if any changes were needed. He said his first priority was to learn about North Carolina, and he had already asked where he could get a good road map of the state.[12]

Looking back 20 years after he became dean, Luxon recalled what he had inherited in 1953. He said the school had previously focused on training students for regional, small-town newspapers. Luxon added, "There were no books in the library because my predecessor believed the only books you needed were *Webster's Collegiate Dictionary* and the *Bible*."[13]

He wasted no time in starting to improve conditions in the school. Two months after becoming dean, he outlined his goals to his friend, Ralph Casey of the University of Minnesota, saying he wanted to add "three men of distinction" to the faculty and start a graduate program. The Journalism Foundation had given him $2,000 a year to help the school and promised to double its endowment. He said he had been well-received by the state press and other departments on campus. Saying he did not want to appear boastful, he said, "The four or five significant schools of journalism in the country, among which Minnesota is at or very near the top, are going to be joined in the not-too-distant future by the School of Journalism at the University of North Carolina."[14]

Two weeks later, Luxon told another friend, Harvey Davis, the provost at the University of Iowa, that the most intelligent action he had taken in

12. Madry, "New Dean Hard at Work," Raleigh *News and Observer*, Dec. 6, 1953, 10-IV.

13. Robert Peterson, "Luxon Fought for Expansion," *UNC Journalist*, Nov. 9, 1974, 6. Luxon later told his friend A. H. Kirchhoffer that Coffin had spent only $12 on book purchases in 1953. Luxon to Kirchhoffer, Dec. 1, 1959, Luxon Papers.

14. Luxon to Casey, Feb. 1, 1954, Luxon Papers.

many years was the decision to take the job at North Carolina. He said he had already accomplished 10 things since he had arrived in Chapel Hill:

1. Added three new courses.
2. Changed the credit hours of one course and the title of another.
3. Ordered 200 books for the school's reading room.
4. Changed the graduation requirements for journalism students.
5. Started plans for a master's program.
6. Arranged for a joint appointment of a new faculty member with the Institute for Research in the Social Sciences.
7. Arranged for James Paul from the Institute of Government to teach a course about journalism law in the school.
8. Received cooperation from everyone at the university, especially President Gordon Gray.
9. Spoken at several meetings of newspaper people.
10. Arranged with the dean of the School of Pharmacy to cooperate in a campaign to get a new building for that school so the School of Journalism could move into Howell Hall.[15]

Luxon also launched a whirlwind effort to meet leaders of the state press. He spoke to the Eastern North Carolina Press Association (ENCPA) at Greenville on Dec. 4, after driving to the meeting with editor Frank Daniels and three staff members from the *News and Observer*.[16] He later claimed that during National Newspaper Week of 1954, he spoke on nine occasions in eight cities in six days to tell people what he planned to do at the School of Journalism.[17]

Luxon met with Gray on Jan. 4, 1954, and told him that he had already met several officials on campus: Albert Coates of the Institute of Government to talk about someone (James Paul) to teach the press law course, Earl Wynn to talk about the Communication Center, and Dean Brecht of the School of Pharmacy to talk about Howell Hall. In addition to addressing the ENCPA, his activities with newspaper leaders included a Christmas party at the *Durham Morning Herald* and *Sun*, a meeting of the Mid-West North Carolina Press Association, a Freedom of Information meeting, and the NCPA newspaper institute. He said his to-do list for the school included faculty conferences, the issue of retaining Phillips Russell on the faculty through 1955, the replacement of Weimar Jones on the faculty in 1955, the stimulation of faculty research, and planning the

15. Luxon to Davis, Feb. 14, 1954, Luxon Papers.
16. Luxon to Earl English, Dec. 8, 1953, Luxon Papers.
17. Luxon to Mark Ethridge, July 25, 1963, Luxon Papers.

graduate program.[18] Luxon wrote a five-year plan for the school that said the major emphasis in most schools of journalism was training students to enter newspaper work, but at least four schools were also doing significant work in research and in training graduate students: the University of Illinois, the University of Minnesota, Stanford University, and the University of Wisconsin. The UNC program, he said, would be modeled after those four.[19]

Eight months into his term, Luxon sent a three-page progress report to North Carolina newspaper leaders, saying the school's greatest needs were books, a new building, and equipment. The UNC Graduate School had already approved a graduate minor in journalism for graduate students in other fields, and Luxon said it was the first step toward a graduate program in journalism. The school printed a brochure for distribution to newspapers in the state and created an advising system for new students. Finally, he invited ideas: "We want your criticism and we shall be happy to receive your praise if and when we merit it."[20]

Luxon launched another initiative in 1954 when he created the *Journalism Newsletter* to inform school alumni about the school and their fellow alumni. The first issue, on Dec. 1, 1954, included a list of faculty and staff members, news notes about the school, and alumni news. It also described the activities of the foundation and UNC administration in support of the school. Luxon pleaded for editors to help persuade the state legislature to appropriate money for a new building for the School of Pharmacy and for the renovation of Howell Hall. The newsletter's second issue, July 5, 1955, was delayed because of the "magnificent" response of 238 alumni to the first issue. It reported that the legislature had not appropriated money for a new building for the School of Pharmacy, which meant the School of Journalism would not move into Howell Hall as early as planned. "New facilities and new equipment for the School of Journalism must and will be found, one way or another, in the near future," Luxon stressed. "Professional education for journalism at the University of North Carolina needs and deserves better housing and adequate equipment to enable the school to prepare young men and women for careers in journalism."[21]

18. Luxon, agenda for meeting with Gordon Gray, Jan. 4, 1954, Luxon Papers.
19. Luxon, "School of Journalism Five-Year Plan, 1954–1959," April 29, 1954, Office of the Dean of the Graduate School Records #40107, University Archives, University of North Carolina at Chapel Hill Library.
20. Luxon to North Carolina Newspapermen, Aug. 7, 1954, Chancellor's Papers: House Series, and Luxon Papers.
21. "New Building Meets a Snag," *Journalism Newsletter*, July 5, 1955, 1.

Three years after he became dean, Luxon reaffirmed his satisfaction with being at UNC, but he complained that he had suffered personal financial loss. He wrote to the dean of the faculty (now known as the provost) to discuss his salary for 1957–58, asking to be given the same consideration as other deans. He claimed he had been making more than $14,000 when he left Ohio State and was offered $15,000 to stay there, while the person who took his place was making $20,000. After arriving in Chapel Hill, he had expressed disinterest in dean's positions at four other schools, with salaries that ranged from $12,500 to $18,000. He said his future was "inextricably interwoven" with the School of Journalism. He cited his accomplishments in the three years he had been dean: strengthening the faculty, increasing the number of books and tripling the number of newspaper subscriptions in the reading room, improving the curriculum, establishing a graduate program, increasing overall enrollment, starting a newsletter for alumni, attracting better students, and making significant progress toward his goal of turning the journalism school into "one of the outstanding professional schools of journalism in the United States."[22]

Curriculum Changes

The 1954–55 catalog of the School of Journalism reflected several changes Luxon had made to the curriculum, revealing a more formal approach to the study of journalism. The curriculum had already changed in 1950 when the school was created, and Luxon led the faculty to make more changes, especially in enforcing admission requirements, which Coffin had frequently waived or ignored.[23] The number of majors in the school dropped by more than 50 percent, from 98 in 1951 to 45 in 1954, reflecting the school 's tighter adherence to admission standards. The decline concerned Luxon, and he asked editors to be patient about the low supply of graduates while he tried to recruit more students to the school. In 1954, the school graduated 28 men and 15 women, and 16 of the men went directly into the armed services.[24] The number of majors remained at or near 60 until 1961, when it reached 78 (that number grew to 85 in 1963 and 100 in 1965). In 1957, Luxon thanked the director of UNC's summer school for allowing the school to offer courses in the summer of 1958—after a lapse of three years—as a test to see if there was sufficient enrollment to offer

22. Luxon to Corydon Spruill, Dec. 13, 1956, Chancellor's Papers: House Series.
23. Luxon to Gray, Aug. 28, 1954, Luxon Papers.
24. Military service was mandatory for men at that time.

summer school courses.[25] He told Morrison that low enrollments in fall and spring semesters were a concern and he had to "do some hard talking" to persuade university administrators to permit the school to offer certain courses. He reiterated what he had told the faculty earlier: summer school courses would be offered for the convenience of students and not simply to provide additional income for faculty members.[26]

Students at UNC could not declare an academic major until they were juniors. After being in the General College for their first two years, they needed at least a C average to enter the School of Journalism as juniors. Men and women were admitted to the school on an equal basis, but the university limited freshman admission to men, except for women whose families lived in Chapel Hill. Women who had completed General College requirements at other schools could be admitted to UNC and the school as junior transfer students.

The journalism credit-hour requirement was increased from 18 to 24 semester credits, including a required core of "News Writing," "News Editing," "History of Journalism," and "The Press, the Constitution and the Law." In addition to the law course, two other courses were added to a list of electives in the school: "Functions and Responsibilities of Contemporary Journalism" and "Seminar in History of American Journalism." Luxon told Kirchhofer he was being pressured to assume responsibility for two news programs on WUNC-TV, the university's new public television station, which was scheduled to go on the air on Oct. 15, 1954. Luxon seemed to think that the programs would be too heavy a burden, and the idea apparently was dropped.[27]

The 1955 catalog expanded the statement of the school's objectives, affirming the school's responsibility to prepare young people for positions on newspapers in the state. It said the school was guided by the belief that journalists had to understand the political, social, economic, and cultural forces affecting society and had to be able to interpret and report them. To that end, graduates of the school had to have a background in the humanities, social sciences, and natural sciences. Students were supposed to take from 60 to 80 percent of their courses outside the school. The number of courses in the school's curriculum had increased to 26, and changes were notable in two areas: five "nonskills" or "issues" courses and six graduate-

25. Luxon to Guy B. Phillips, Dec. 17, 1957, Joseph Morrison Papers #3787, Southern Historical Collection, University of North Carolina at Chapel Hill Library. (Summer school courses that did not meet minimum enrollment levels were cancelled.)

26. Luxon to Morrison, Dec. 19, 1957, Morrison Papers.

27. Luxon to Kirchhofer, Aug. 4, 1954, Luxon Papers.

level courses. In addition to journalism history and press law, the school offered nonskills courses in international communication, communication and opinion, and the responsibilities of journalism. The graduate curriculum included a research methods course, three seminar courses, a readings course, and a thesis course. JOUR 53 was limited to news writing, and JOUR 54 and JOUR 55 were changed to reporting courses. The radio journalism course was expanded to include television news, and Morrison's business journalism course dealt primarily with writing stories for business publications and not with the reporting of business news.

The catalog advised students in the General College who planned to major in journalism to talk to advisers in the school. Students had to be able to type with reasonable skill, accuracy, and speed, and knowledge of shorthand was said to be useful, especially for women. Journalism majors were advised to work for student publications such as the *Daily Tar Heel*, and some students had to work on the student newspaper to fulfill requirements for courses in the school. The school recommended newspaper internships in the summer and offered assistance in getting those positions. A placement service—provided by the dean, faculty members, and a placement committee—was available for students and graduates. A chapter of Kappa Tau Alpha, the national honorary fraternity for outstanding journalism students, was established in the school on May 17, 1955, and was named the Norval Neil Luxon Chapter after his retirement in 1969.

Faculty Changes

Luxon also wanted to strengthen the school by hiring faculty members with doctorates who could begin a program of research and guide graduate students. In 1954, he hired Roy E. Carter Jr., one of the first persons to receive a doctorate in mass communication research from an American university (Stanford), as a cornerstone for the graduate program. Carter dealt a blow to Luxon's plans four years later, however, when he resigned to return to the University of Minnesota, his alma mater. He told Luxon that only Minnesota's offer of a professorship and a research directorship could have lured him away from UNC.[28] Undeterred, Luxon told Chilton Bush of Stanford that his goal was to get young faculty members with doc-

28. Carter to Luxon, April 21, 1958, Chancellor's Records: William B. Aycock Series #40020, University Archives and Records Service, University of North Carolina at Chapel Hill Library.

torates, men trained by Bush, Ralph Casey of the University of Minnesota, Ralph Nafziger of the University of Wisconsin, and Charles Sandage of the University of Illinois.[29]

In a 1971 interview, Luxon explained his philosophy of the importance of faculty research, saying that research improved teaching and the practice of journalism. Not all faculty members needed to engage in research, however, as long as they kept up with the knowledge in their field. He said the most successful schools of journalism were the ones that had a majority of faculty members who had graduate degrees and conducted research, balanced by others who were primarily interested in teaching and who had considerable media experience. He also believed that every faculty member should teach at least one undergraduate course every semester, a practice that continued in the school for many years.[30]

Luxon's recruitment efforts resulted in the hiring of three men whose potential and personalities fit his plan for the school: Jack Adams and Wayne Danielson in 1958 and Jim Mullen in 1959. Adams had a doctorate from the University of Wisconsin and was an expert in international communication who was on the faculty at Michigan State University. He became a self-taught expert on media law after he arrived at the school, even though he had never taken a law course and had been given no teaching materials about the subject. Danielson, whose doctorate was from Stanford University, was one of the leading scholars in the emerging discipline of using computers in newspapers. Mullen had a doctorate from the University of Minnesota and was teaching in the respected advertising program at the University of Illinois. Luxon told all of them he wanted them to come to Chapel Hill to grow with a school that was just developing and help build a new graduate program.

Luxon was able to give the new faculty members a reduced teaching load (two courses per semester instead of three) so they would have more time to conduct the research he felt was so important. Adams said there was no resentment among other faculty members about that arrangement. Adams and his colleagues soon had respectable visibility among researchers on campus, and they used the campus Univac 1103 computer more than any other unit on campus except the computer science department, according to Adams.[31] Danielson recalled that faculty members in

29. Luxon to Bush, May 23, 1958, Luxon Papers.
30. Luxon, interview with Max McCombs, Sept. 26, 1971, Luxon Papers.
31. Adams, interview with the author, Aug. 21, 2007.

other departments were amazed that someone from the journalism school knew what a standard deviation was.[32]

Soon after Mullen was hired, he proposed changes in the advertising curriculum that met with resistance from other professors on campus who saw the changes as impinging on their academic territory. Mullen wanted to drop the school's existing newspaper advertising courses and replace them with four courses he had created to expand the school's advertising focus beyond newspapers and into advertising principles, copywriting, media planning, and advertising campaigns.[33] Dean Maurice Lee of the School of Business Administration objected to the new, broader advertising courses, saying advertising courses in the School of Journalism should be limited to newspapers. He said the proposed courses would be an unnecessary duplication, even though the business school did not offer or intend to offer courses in copywriting, media planning, or campaigns. He admitted that he and Luxon had found it distasteful to have to take sides in the issue, and he expressed admiration for what Luxon was doing in the School of Journalism.[34] Luxon countered that the advertising courses in the School of Journalism were from the perspective of the creators of advertising, while those in the School of Business Administration took the perspective of business executives who used and managed advertising. He cited four other schools of journalism that offered advertising courses in universities where business schools offered similar courses: Illinois, Minnesota, Stanford, and Wisconsin.[35]

Opposition to the advertising course revisions from another department on campus foreshadowed a deeper conflict over academic boundaries. Professor Wesley Wallace, a future chairman of the Department of Radio, Television, and Motion Pictures (RTVMP), objected to the school's broad claim to be preparing students for all media of mass communication and not just newspapers. He claimed that RTVMP should have responsibility for preparing students for careers in radio, television, and motion pictures. While Luxon had claimed that newspaper communication could not be separated from other mass media, Wallace maintained that there should be such a separation and that the School of Journalism's ad-

32. Danielson, interview with the author, Feb. 26, 2008. Standard deviation is a statistical measure of variability.

33. Luxon to Administrative Board of the Graduate School, Dec. 1, 1959, Graduate School archives, UNC–Chapel Hill.

34. Lee to William B. Aycock, Nov. 2, 1959, Graduate School archives. An advertising course was taught by Charles Henry Fernald, assistant professor of sales relations in the Department of Economics and Commerce, as early as 1922.

35. Luxon to William B. Aycock, Oct. 31, 1959, Graduate School archives.

vertising courses should be limited to print media.[36] His opposition was not enough to prevent approval of the changes on Jan. 7, 1960.

Joe Morrison achieved some degree of national fame in 1958 while he was on leave from the university and completing his master's degree at Columbia University. With time on his hands after completing his thesis, he was accepted for an appearance on the nationally telecast quiz show, "Twenty-One," on the NBC network. He and his competitor, Elfrida von Nardoff, matched answers on two successive shows. Morrison stumbled on the third week's show, however, when he failed to name three famous wives in history who had been killed by their husbands. He correctly named Catherine of Aragon by Henry VIII and Octavia by Mark Antony, but he mistakenly said Calpurnia had been killed by Julius Caesar (Pompea was the correct answer).[37] It was later revealed that the producers of "Twenty-One" and other quiz programs had rigged the shows by providing answers to selected contestants, including von Nardoff when she faced Morrison. In 1963, he sued her, the National Broadcasting Company, and Barry-Enright Productions, the show's producers, for $500,000. He had received $1,500 for his losing effort, but von Nardoff won $146,000 against him and eventually won $220,500. Morrison said the incident held him up to public scorn and contempt by his friends and the general public.[38] The suit was dismissed because the statute of limitations had expired, and Morrison received no money for damages.

Luxon told Casey in 1959 that he had more ambitious plans for the faculty, saying he wanted to add a few more "good research men." To do so, however, he said he would have to get rid of some existing faculty members. He said they probably wouldn't leave the school even if he got them new jobs elsewhere at an increase in salary, which he would not do.[39] The nature of faculty activity in one summer was reflected in a letter Luxon wrote to the editor of *Editor and Publisher* in response to a story that had reported low interest in summer newspaper jobs on the part of U.S. journalism faculty members. He recounted what his own faculty members were doing in the summer of 1964: Danielson was a consultant to a newspaper chain in Florida, Spearman took over the editorship of the *Smithfield Herald* for three weeks, Sechriest worked on the copy desk at the

36. Wallace to Administrative Board of the Graduate School, Dec. 11, 1959, Graduate School archives.

37. "UNC Prof Trying for Big TV Money," *Charlotte Observer*, April 21, 1958, 12-A.

38. "Tar Heel Is Suing Rival in Quiz Show Aftermath," Raleigh *News and Observer*, June 14, 1963, 1-A.

39. Luxon to Casey, Jan. 30, 1959, Luxon Papers.

Durham Morning Herald, Byerly spent time at the newspaper he owned in Montana, Mullen taught summer school at the University of Illinois, and Adams and Morrison worked on research projects.[40]

It wasn't all hard work in the school, however. In 1958, the junior class defeated the seniors, 34-9, in a softball game at Camp New Hope, north of Chapel Hill, that was reported in the *Daily Tar Heel*. Professor Stuart Sechriest, the home plate umpire, smoked a cigar even though he wore a protective mask, and he fired a cap gun at players and spectators, who tossed bats, threw tantrums, and set off firecrackers. The other faculty umpires, Ken Byerly (first base) and William Caldwell (third base), threatened to give a failing grade to any player who disputed their calls, and Jo Anne Smith (another faculty member) was the scorekeeper. Luxon was not present but sent his regrets. Seniors on the team included Buzz Merritt (pitcher), Leonard Sullivan, Al Elmer, John Ashford, Dick Crouch, Bill Cheshire, Jerry Shields, Glenn Keever, and Ed Butchard. On the junior side were Al Resch (pitcher), John Hubbard, Thurman Worthington, Roy Lucas, Wyndham Hewitt, Ben Taylor, Jerry Alvis, Alex Coffin, and Tommy Bolch.[41] Sechriest later said the game was a one-time event.[42]

Graduate Program

Luxon had started thinking about a graduate program even before he arrived in Chapel Hill. He wrote to W. W. Pierson, dean of the Graduate School, from his home in Columbus, Ohio, on Oct. 27, 1953, to ask how soon he could start a graduate minor in the school, tied to a graduate major in fields such as psychology or sociology. He acknowledged that it would be the first step toward a graduate major (master of arts) in journalism. He said he needed to know because he wanted to start recruiting faculty members and tell them about a graduate program. Russell was in his last year of teaching, and Luxon wanted to replace him with a young person with a doctorate to teach research courses.[43]

The graduate minor in journalism was approved with "hearty unanimity" by the administrative board of the Graduate School in 1954,[44] and

40. Luxon, "Working Teachers," letter to the editor, *Editor and Publisher*, Oct. 3, 1964, 7.

41. Ann Frye, "J-School Softball Game Has Gun-Toting Umps," *Daily Tar Heel*, April 25, 1958, 1.

42. Sechriest, interview with the author, Aug. 18, 2008.

43. Luxon to W. W. Pierson, Oct. 27, 1953, Luxon Papers.

44. Pierson to Luxon, May 25, 1954, Graduate School archives.

Luxon submitted a proposal for an M.A. major in journalism a year later. It was designed to meet the needs of several types of students: journalists who wanted to teach at the college level or who wanted to study the role of the media, recent journalism graduates who wanted to maximize their preparation for journalism careers, working journalists interested in media research, and superior students from other academic disciplines who wanted to become journalists. Luxon said the proposed program would be based on sound academic practice, high admission standards, and a high level of student performance. Students could not receive credit for courses in journalistic skills and techniques, however.[45] The first M.A. degree in journalism was awarded in 1957, and Luxon later said the graduate program marked a "break with the past" in journalism education on the campus and was an indication of its future.[46]

Students with undergraduate degrees in fields other than journalism had to complete five courses (15 credits) of undergraduate journalism work before they were admitted to unconditional graduate standing, but that requirement could be waived for students with professional journalism experience who passed competency exams. Students had to complete 30 credits at the graduate level, including six credits for their thesis. Usually, 18–21 credits were taken in journalism, and 9–12 credits were taken in a single outside department, constituting a graduate minor. Students had to have a reading knowledge of or complete a minor in a foreign language, pass written and oral exams, and write a thesis. Graduate fellowships of $1,500 were available from the university, and the school awarded one $1,500 fellowship each year.

Luxon was concerned about low enrollment in the early years of the master's program and feared it might jeopardize the school's plan to start a Ph.D. program.[47] Those fears were never realized, and in 1963, Luxon submitted a proposal to Dean Hugh Holman of the Graduate School for a program leading to the doctor of philosophy degree with a major in mass communication research.[48] Consistent with that title, the proposal mentioned other mass media more than it did newspapers, and RTVMP was not listed as one of the departments participating in the program. The participating departments were Business Administration and Economics, History, Political Science, Sociology, and Psychology.

Once again, RTVMP objected to what it feared as encroachment on

45. Luxon to Pierson, Dec. 17, 1954, Graduate School archives.
46. Luxon, "Annual Report of the Dean, 1963–64," Luxon Papers.
47. Luxon to Ralph Casey, June 16, 1959, Luxon Papers.
48. Luxon to Holman, Aug. 20, 1963, Graduate School archives.

its academic turf. Wallace, by then the chairman of RTVMP, told Luxon he was delighted to know that the School of Journalism wanted to start a doctoral program, but he strongly objected to the fact that courses in the School of Journalism's Ph.D. program would cover the fields of radio, television, and motion pictures, domains that he said were RTVMP's responsibility. He suggested that the name of the degree be changed to a Ph.D. in Journalism, but he said that he really preferred for the School of Journalism and RTVMP to establish a "truly joint activity."[49]

In response, Luxon said the school was prepared to include RTVMP courses in the Ph.D. program and take other steps to make the doctoral program appealing to students from RTVMP. He cited the specific example of Grover Cleveland Wilhoit, "an outstanding master's candidate in RTVMP," as someone who might want to earn a Ph.D. from the School of Journalism.[50] Despite what Luxon wrote to Wallace, he told Ralph Casey that RTVMP, which he described as "low status on campus, a staff without competence in research, and courses without content," had bitterly opposed his proposal.[51]

Holman appointed a subcommittee of the administrative board of the Graduate School to consider the proposal for the Ph.D., and he urged the subcommittee to consider Wallace's objections. However, he also downplayed those objections by pointing out that RTVMP "had regarded itself as working in the area of new art forms in a creative and critical-aesthetic fashion," and it had not been carrying out any kind of "analytical or detailed, scientifically based studies" of the sort that the School of Journalism was proposing.[52]

The Administrative Board unanimously approved the proposal, saying it would be a substantial addition to graduate study and research activities on campus. Holman was especially pleased that the new program included "newly developed techniques of research computation" at the Computation Center. He also liked the involvement of a broad range of departments and hoped the program would be expanded to include RTVMP courses. He praised the school for its excellent equipment and "highly qualified" faculty.[53] On Aug. 7, 1964, Wilhoit was admitted as the first student in the Ph.D. program, and he became its first graduate in 1967.[54]

49. Wallace to Luxon, Oct. 14, 1963, Graduate School archives.
50. Luxon to Wallace, Oct. 29, 1963, Graduate School archives.
51. Luxon to Casey, Nov. 2, 1963, Luxon Papers.
52. Holman to Charles Bowerman, Oct. 18, 1963, Graduate School archives.
53. Holman to William B. Aycock, Oct. 31, 1963, Graduate School archives.
54. Wayne Danielson to C. Hugh Holman, Aug. 7, 1964, Graduate School archives.

8. Accreditation and a New Home

With a cadre of research-trained faculty members on board and a new curriculum in place, Luxon turned his attention to two other important matters: accreditation and a new home for the school. He had been an early leader in the American Council on Education for Journalism, the national accrediting body, and he came to UNC with the goal of achieving accreditation for the School of Journalism. He knew it would take time to improve conditions enough to achieve accreditation, and he had to quell a rumor in 1954 that the school would be visited by an accreditation team that year. He told his friend Casey emphatically that a school could not be visited without an invitation: "I have never requested a visitation and have no intention of requesting one before 1956–57, when, I hope, I'll have three well-qualified men in the graduate and research area added to the staff and will have the school housed in a well-equipped, adequate building." He said he did not think UNC could be accredited in 1954, and he would not ask for a visit until he knew the school would pass.[2]

1. Luxon to Carl Jeffress, May 1, 1958, Chancellor's Records: Aycock Series #40020, University Archives and Records Service, University of North Carolina at Chapel Hill Library.
2. Luxon to Casey, March 13, 1954, Norval Neil Luxon Papers #4585, Southern Historical Collection, University of North Carolina at Chapel Hill Library.

Accreditation Achieved

Luxon believed the school was ready three years hence, and he asked the chancellor to invite an accrediting team to visit the school during the 1957–58 academic year.[3] Just before the visit, Luxon predicted that the only accreditation criterion that the school would fail would be physical facilities, and that deficiency would be remedied by the remodeling of Howell Hall.[4] A six-man team came to campus Feb. 19–20, 1958: Burton W. Marvin, dean of the School of Journalism at the University of Kansas and chairman of the ACEJ Accrediting Committee; John H. Colburn, managing editor of the *Richmond Times-Dispatch*; I. W. Cole, dean of the School of Journalism at Northwestern University; C.A. "Pete" McKnight, editor of the *Charlotte Observer*; Willis C. Tucker, director of the School of Journalism of the University of Tennessee; and Walter Wilcox, executive secretary of the Accrediting Committee.

Luxon's prediction proved to be true, and the site visit team recommended accreditation for the school's news-editorial sequence[5] at the end of its visit. Table 8.1 summarizes the team's findings. The school was lauded for its administrative leadership, its status within the university, strong relationships with North Carolina newspapers (including the School of Journalism Foundation), and high student morale. The team was concerned about the "shallow" requirement of only two skills courses and insufficient practical work in those courses. While Luxon had made substantial progress in creating a climate for scholarly research among the faculty, the team concluded that overall faculty research accomplishments were limited. Predictably, the team said the school's quarters in Bynum Hall were inadequate, but it was impressed by the university's promises for a new building. The Accrediting Council confirmed the decision at a meeting in New York on April 20 and notified UNC president William Friday, praising the support the school had received from him and the state press.[6]

Relaying the news to Chancellor William Aycock, Luxon said the com-

3. R. B. House to Walter Wilcox, Feb. 8, 1957, Chancellor's Records: Robert House Series #40019, University Archives and Records Service, University of North Carolina at Chapel Hill Library.

4. Luxon to William B. Aycock, Feb. 14, 1958. Aycock became chancellor on July 1, 1957.

5. A sequence was an area of specialization, and the school had only one at the time. The advertising sequence had not yet been created.

6. John Stempel to Friday, April 28, 1958, Chancellor's Records: Aycock Series.

Table 8.1 Summary of 1958 Visitors' Report for the School of Journalism by the American Council on Education for Journalism

Category	Rating	Comments
Administration	High	Excellent status within university, adequate financial and moral support, strong relationships with North Carolina newspapers and alumni, high student morale. Academic standards strengthened.
Faculty	Median	The rating would have been "median high" if the two faculty members on leave had been present and if the school were to fill the two vacancies with well-qualified teachers. A few faculty members needed to strengthen their standards. Faculty enjoys respect of others at the university.
Curriculum (news-editorial sequence)	Median high	Recommended accreditation for this sequence. Concerned about shallow requirements for skills courses (only two) and about need for more practical exercises in courses. Concerned about too much emphasis in the news photography course on film and camera operation.
Service	High	Commended faculty for involvement with state and area professional organizations. Commended the support of the North Carolina Journalism Foundation as a sign of strong relationship with state press.
Research	Median high	Said Luxon had made substantial progress in creating a climate for scholarly activity, but overall faculty accomplishments were quite limited.
Quarters and facilities	Low	Quarters were inadequate, but the team was impressed by the university's support for the new building and the plans for it.

ing weeks would be a crucial time because he was trying to recruit three new faculty members, one of whom might be his successor when he would be forced by university policy to relinquish the deanship in 1964.[7] Luxon also reported the accreditation news to the 18 directors of the School of Journalism Foundation with the superlative statement that May 1, 1953, was one of the most important dates in the school's history.

The *Daily Tar Heel* exuberantly reported the news with a two-page special section and a large headline. The section was compiled by a committee of students who were trying to form a chapter of Sigma Delta Chi, the national professional journalism fraternity: Charlie Sloan, John Ashford, Tom Bolch, Ben Taylor, Stan Fisher, Clark Jones, Paul Rule, Don Shaw, and Walt Shruntek.[8] Luxon told a reporter that the school was pleased to have achieved one of its goals, and he cited faculty research efforts that had produced several publications. He said he was especially grateful to the state press for its support.[9]

The *Tar Heel* also saw the occasion as an opportunity to profit from the event by publishing congratulatory advertisements by Julian's College Shop, a men's clothing store on Franklin Street; the *Winston-Salem Journal* and the *Twin City Sentinel*, whose ad lauded the 31 Carolina alumni on their staffs; the *Chapel Hill Weekly*, which erroneously said journalism was first taught by its founder (Louis Graves) and that the department was formed in 1926; the Bank of Chapel Hill; Graham Memorial Union, the student union on campus; and the Intimate Bookshop on Franklin Street. The newspaper's editorial reaction to the news about accreditation—"A small milestone has been passed in furthering the journalistic enterprise on the UNC campus"[10]—was significant, in light of a previous *Tar Heel* editor's strong charges in 1953 that Luxon was a poor choice for dean because he had been hired just to achieve accreditation.

New Home in Howell Hall

University officials had assured Luxon when he was hired in 1953 that the school would move into Howell Hall as soon as it became available, after the School of Pharmacy moved out of Howell into its new home in Beard Hall. Howell Hall was called the Chemistry Building when it was

7. Luxon to Aycock, April 30, 1958, Chancellor's Records: Aycock Series.
8. Ben Taylor, "Sigma Delta Chi Group Staffs Special Section," *Daily Tar Heel*, May 1, 1958, 3.
9. "J-School Wins Accreditation," *Daily Tar Heel*, May 1, 1958, 3.
10. "Journalism School," *Daily Tar Heel*, May 1, 1958, 2.

completed in 1906 for the chemistry department. The pharmacy school moved into the building in 1925, when the name was changed to honor the first dean of that school, Edward V. Howell.[11] In August 1954, prior to the accreditation visit, Luxon had emphatically told the state press that no school of journalism in a major university in the United States was as inadequately housed and as ill-equipped as UNC's, and his immediate goal was to remedy the situation. He asked newspapers to help by endorsing the School of Pharmacy's request for a $1.4 million legislative appropriation for a new building and more than $188,000 to renovate Howell. The expenditures, he said, would lift the school to near the top of the 100 schools and departments of journalism in the country.[12]

Luxon sent editors an example of an editorial from the *Asheville Citizen* headlined "The State Needs More Pharmacists." He added his own note: "It also needs, and according to your frequent calls on us, can use more young newspapermen. It can get both by providing a new building for the School of Pharmacy."[13] Many newspapers in the state answered Luxon's call and published editorials supporting the request for funding for the Pharmacy building. Holt McPherson said in an editorial that the university's request for money was important because the state needed pharmacists and because when the School of Pharmacy moved out of Howell Hall the School of Journalism would get badly needed buildings that would improve its chances for reaccreditation. He said the school was "cramped in the old gymnasium, so inadequately housed that it dares not ask again for accreditation pending better space facilities."[14] In a 1975 interview, McPherson talked about his efforts to persuade the legislature to appropriate money for the two schools: "One legislator was dragging his feet on it," he said, "but I told him that if he would arrange to get the pharmacy building included in the budget for the next year, we could get the journalism school to work and promise him a better class of newspapers. He said, 'Hell, yes, I'll vote for it.'"[15]

Although the pharmacy-journalism package got top priority in the uni-

11. Arthur S. Link, *A History of the Buildings at the University of North Carolina* (honors thesis, University of North Carolina, 1941), 167–68.

12. Luxon to North Carolina Newspapermen, Aug. 7, 1954, Chancellor's Papers: House Series. Also in Luxon Papers.

13. Luxon to North Carolina Newspapermen, Nov. 19, 1955, University Development Program Records #40136, University Archives, University of North Carolina at Chapel Hill Library.

14. "Two Buildings for One Offers Good Proposition at University," *High Point Enterprise*, Sept. 19, 1956, 4A.

15. Interview with Holt McPherson by E. P. Douglass, April 9, 1975, Southern Oral

Howell Hall, ca. 1930. Home of the School of Journalism, 1960–99. When the school moved into Howell Hall, Dean Neil Luxon said the facilities were as good as any in the country. *(North Carolina Collection, University of North Carolina at Chapel Hill Library. Reprinted with permission.)*

versity's 1956 state budget request, and voter approval of a state bond referendum guaranteed money for Howell, subsequent state action did not come as quickly as Luxon and others had hoped, and renovation work did not begin until the fall of 1959. Jack Adams recalled Luxon taking faculty members on a tour of the unfinished building: "It smelled like a chemistry lab. Everything looked as if it had a thick layer of grease. It was dark, dreary, dirty."[16] The interior was completely remodeled, including new floors and a new staircase. Ceilings were soundproofed and lowered, and air conditioning ducts were installed—without an air conditioning system. The result was "as fine a journalism plant as any in the United States,"

History Program Collection, Southern Historical Collection, University of North Carolina at Chapel Hill Library.

16. David Perry, "Howell Has History of Spreading Smiles," *UNC Journalist*, Nov. 9, 1974, 1.

according to Luxon.[17] The school had to wait until August 1960 to move to its new home, after the university had spent $225,000 for the renovation.

The 1960–61 school catalog proudly described the new home as having 22,000 square feet, two news-writing labs with typewriters, a news-editing lab with a copy desk and wire-service machines, an advertising classroom, student work space, and a reading room. It also had photographic facilities with four film-processing darkrooms and a printing darkroom with four enlargers, a contact printer, print washers, and driers for negatives and prints. Speed Graphic and Rolleiflex cameras were available to students. Luxon boasted to Casey and Ralph Nafziger that Howell Hall was better than any school he had seen. He bragged about the 75 new typewriters (costing more than $12,000), new furniture, new photographic equipment, small offices for research assistants, and a large auditorium. Each faculty office had a conference table and enough chairs for seminar classes. He said the photo lab was better than any newspaper's in the state. He also confided that he was happy with the faculty he had built, but he worried that they might be lured to other schools. One of the things that he thought would keep them was the teaching load of two courses per semester.[18]

Stuart Sechriest said in a 2007 interview that he had been bothered by a steam pipe that passed through the photographic lab in Howell Hall. From Howell, it continued to the home of UNC president William Friday and also to the Chapel of the Cross church, which purchased steam from the university to heat its building. The pipe made the photo lab very hot, and Sechriest turned off the steam one day, which prompted a complaint from Mrs. Friday about the lack of heat in the Fridays' house.[19]

The NCPA mistakenly believed it could influence the naming of the new building. In 1949, McPherson had told President Frank Porter Graham that the NCPA wanted the university to name a building to honor Josephus Daniels and to make it the home of the journalism program.[20] In 1960, as the school was getting ready to move into Howell Hall, the NCPA brashly appointed a committee to consult with Friday about renaming Howell Hall to honor Beatrice Cobb, the longtime NCPA secretary, al-

17. "Howell Hall Renovated to House Journalism School; Ready by Sept.," *Daily Tar Heel*, Dec. 12, 1959, 1.

18. Luxon to Casey, May 3, 1960, and to Naziger, July 19, 1960, Luxon Papers.

19. Sechriest, interview with the author, May 21, 2007.

20. McPherson to Graham, Frank Porter Graham Records #40007, University Archives, University of North Carolina at Chapel Hill Library. Daniels had been publisher of the Raleigh *News and Observer* and Secretary of the Navy during World War I.

though Luxon had advised McPherson that university policy made such a change impossible.[21] Aycock later told McPherson that university policy would not permit changing the name of a building.[22]

Howell Hall was formally dedicated as the home of the School of Journalism on Oct. 21, 1960, with programs in the building's auditorium, lunch at the Morehead Building, and an evening session in the Hill Hall auditorium. More than 200 people attended, including 50 alumni.[23] The list of speakers was impressive: UNC chancellor William B. Aycock; William D. Snider, associate editor of the *Greensboro Daily News;* Ashley B. Futrell, president of the NCPA; McPherson; North Carolina governor Luther Hodges; President William Friday; Gordon Gray, the former UNC president who had become special assistant to U.S. President Dwight Eisenhower; Mark Ethridge, publisher of the *Courier-Journal* and the *Times* of Louisville, Ky.; Montgomery Curtis, director of the American Press Institute; and Clifton Daniel, assistant managing editor of the *New York Times* and a graduate of the school, who was the main speaker. (Daniel was also the son-in-law of former U.S. President Harry Truman.)

The student newspaper again trumpeted the school's accomplishments. Editor Jonathan Yardley commended the school on the day of the dedication: "Recognizing that good newspapers are not made of technicians, it has moved continuously in the direction of strong foundation in the liberal arts, while continually striving to improve its own curriculum." Yardley said journalism courses were no longer filled with only journalism majors, and the school had risen to the top of national rankings. Noting that many of the guests for the dedication were graduates of the school, Yardley concluded, "If Bynum, with all its failures, could produce men and women such as these, there should be no limit to what Howell can do."[24]

Help from the Journalism Foundation

McPherson later recalled that UNC president Frank Porter Graham had tied support from the Journalism Foundation to a new home for the school, saying that if newspaper people could raise $100,000 for the foundation, Graham would see to it that the school could move into Howell Hall.[25] When Luxon came to his first foundation board meeting on Jan. 29,

21. Luxon to McPherson, July 18, 1960, Luxon Papers.
22. Aycock to McPherson, July 26, 1960, Luxon Papers.
23. *Journalism Newsletter*, January 1961, 1.
24. Yardley, "An Occasion Worth Celebrating," *Daily Tar Heel*, Oct. 21, 1960, 2.
25. McPherson, interview with E. P. Douglass, April 9, 1975.

1954, he told the board that the school had a greater need for books and equipment than for salary supplements. He said foundation funds should not be used to supplement faculty salaries because faculty compensation should come exclusively from the North Carolina General Assembly.[26] That statement contrasted with what he had previously told McPherson when he was anticipating the job offer from UNC and asked if the foundation could supplement the $10,000 salary he expected to receive.[27] The board resolved to give the school $2,000 each year; after giving $500 for books in 1954 and $676 in 1955, the foundation fulfilled its pledge in subsequent years. Annual allocations to the school generally came from investment income. Luxon and subsequent deans submitted annual requests for funds that were based on the expected interest income, and unspent funds were returned to the principal to ensure continued growth. The market value of the foundation's principal grew from just less than $12,000 in 1950 to just more than $39,000 in 1954. With the principal at nearly $38,000 in 1953, the board decided to diversify its investments beyond U.S. Treasury notes, and it authorized the executive committee to invest in the stock market.

President Gray and Chancellor House came to a special foundation board meeting in Chapel Hill on Feb. 27, 1954, when Gray suggested that all newspapers in the state should be asked to make an annual foundation contribution in the amount of 2.5 cents per subscriber. At another special meeting on June 11, in Lake Junaluska, N.C., the board formally adopted Gray's idea for raising money from newspapers, divided the state into 16 fundraising districts, and decided to solicit graduates of the school for donations. The board also ratified an agreement by which Wachovia Bank and Trust Company would manage the foundation's funds and investments.

A year later, McPherson suggested to Aycock that the foundation set up a retirement fund for the dean, both to benefit Luxon and to help lure a top person to be the next dean. Luxon reiterated his opposition to the supplement and said he would not accept one. He said he had chosen faculty members with the notion that one of them would succeed him, and he noted that there would not be a faculty vacancy when he left the dean's office and continued to teach. He said the school had more im-

26. Minutes of the School of Journalism Foundation Board of Directors, Jan. 29, 1954, Office of the Dean, School of Journalism and Mass Communication, UNC—Chapel Hill.

27. Luxon to McPherson, Aug. 11, 1953, Luxon Papers.

portant needs at the time, including graduate assistantships.[28] Luxon and McPherson may have gotten a bit too eager in their fundraising efforts, because Gray had to ask McPherson for better coordination in solicitation efforts. McPherson had apparently asked the management of the *Charlotte Observer* for contributions but did not coordinate that effort with the university's Development Council, headed by Charlie Shaffer, House's assistant. Gray again suggested that the state's newspapers should be asked to make annual contributions based on circulation,[29] and he made the same suggestion to Luxon a few days later.[30]

McPherson advised foundation directors in 1959 that some newspapers had not met their pledge of 2.5 cents per subscriber. That was unfortunate, he said, because 76 percent of the school's graduates in the last five years had taken jobs at North Carolina newspapers.[31] By 1956, income from the foundation account had enabled the school to establish four $300 scholarships to honor Louis Graves, Gerald W. Johnson, O. J. Coffin, and Quincy Sharpe Mills.[32] (Tuition at the time was $75 per semester.) While Luxon was dean, from 1953 to 1964, annual donations to the foundation ranged between $11,000 and $20,200, averaging more than $14,400. School expenditures from foundation funds during that time increased from $500 in 1953 to more than $17,600 in 1964, averaging nearly $5,000. In 1963, for example, foundation support totaled $12,700, including $6,900 for scholarships and assistantships, nearly $1,400 for a lecture series, $1,700 for school publications, and $1,200 for faculty travel.

Luxon was shocked in 1962 to learn that McPherson's will apparently included High Point College but not the UNC School of Journalism. In a three-page letter, Luxon said he had previously understood that McPherson would divide his money between the two institutions. Seeming to contradict what he had said earlier about faculty salary supplements, Luxon reminded McPherson of the personal financial loss he had suffered by leaving Ohio State and coming to UNC—more than $3,000 in one year and an estimated $73,000 over the course of eight years. He said financial considerations would force him to continue to teach after he left the deanship, pointing out that the mortgage on his house would not be paid

28. Luxon to Aycock, June 6, 1960, Chancellor's Records: Aycock Series.
29. Gray to McPherson, Feb. 6, 1954, Luxon Papers.
30. Gray to Luxon, Feb. 12, 1954, Luxon Papers.
31. McPherson to Steed Rollins, Feb. 20, 1959, Chancellor's Records: Aycock Series.
32. Mills graduated from UNC in 1907 and was a journalist in New York City before being killed in France in World War I. The money for the Mills scholarship came from a bequest by his mother, Nancy B. Mills.

off until 1965. He acknowledged that McPherson had already given more than any other individual ($7,000) to the Journalism Foundation, but he wanted him to think about establishing a McPherson Distinguished Professorship or provide more money for financial aid. He asked McPherson to consider what other North Carolina newspapermen would think if he did not leave some money to UNC's school. He also said some people might think that McPherson's failure to include the school would be seen as a repudiation of Luxon. Finally, he said that if McPherson were to create a distinguished professorship, he would be proud to be the first to hold it.[33] The school eventually received more than $185,000 from McPherson's estate, in addition to his annual contributions.

"Fewer and Better Schools of Journalism"

As he transformed UNC's School of Journalism into one of the nation's best, Luxon also became nationally known as a gadfly who wanted to eliminate journalism programs that did not measure up to his high standards. He used UNC's school as an example when he espoused those beliefs in several venues, and he often referred to his effort when he signed letters: "Yours for Fewer and Better Schools of Journalism" or "Yours for F and B SoJ." He launched his campaign in 1957 in his presidential address to the Association for Education in Journalism at Boston University, when he said the number of journalism schools should be reduced drastically. He said 40 or 50 truly professional schools would be sufficient as long as they met the following conditions:

- Their budgets were adequate;
- they had rigid requirements for the first two years of study;
- their faculty members were interested in teaching, research, and public service;
- and their parent universities had outstanding libraries and nationally recognized departments in the humanities and social sciences.

In other words, schools like his.

Luxon repeated the arguments in articles for the nation's newspaper editors, saying that more than 200 colleges and universities (too many, in his opinion) offered at least one journalism course. He proudly cited his faculty of nine, which included five Ph.D. degrees, six M.A.'s and eight

33. Luxon to McPherson, Jan. 23, 1962, Luxon Papers. As reported in Chapter 4, McPherson had told William Carmichael, UNC's comptroller, in 1948 that he was bequeathing his estate to UNC for the improvement of journalism education.

B.A.'s. All faculty members had some media experience, and many were engaged in research. He bragged that only a small number of the 29 undergraduate courses in the school dealt with journalism techniques. Luxon said, however, that too many of the more than 200 journalism programs were still operating under the philosophies of the 1920s, and their faculty members did not have academic respect on their campuses. He claimed only about 10 programs were truly excellent and highly respected, but too many had "inadequately prepared personnel offering shoddy academic fare in a physical and intellectual environment discouraging to intelligent students." He said he had carried on an extensive effort to reduce the number of schools but had met defeat. He believed schools and newspapers were better than they were in the 1920s but were not as good as they could be. While college enrollments had increased more than 40 percent in the previous decade, Luxon said, journalism enrollments had remained at the same levels. One way to pare programs, he suggested, was to eliminate journalism programs at private colleges. The number of publicly funded programs could be reduced to one per state, and some states could eliminate their programs completely.[34] Few people took Luxon's exhortations seriously, and the number of journalism programs continued to grow.

Luxon Steps Down

As required by university policy at the time, Luxon took his mandatory retirement at age 65, on June 30, 1964. The NCPA gave him a new Volkswagen Karmann Ghia automobile as a retirement present. The money to purchase the automobile came from 40 individual contributions totaling $2,870, ranging from $5 to $500 each. (One contribution was from the auto dealer, suggesting a donation or discount.) Luxon said he was embarrassed by all the attention to his departure from the dean's office, and he reminded people that he planned to be an active teacher for five more years.[35] Luxon had chosen new faculty members with the idea that one of them would succeed him as dean, and he seemed to have favored Wayne Danielson from the beginning. In 1963 he told Chilton Bush, head of the Department of Communication and Journalism at Stanford University, that he had secured Danielson's promotion to full professor at age 33. He admitted that other faculty members resented the fact that he had pro-

34. Luxon, "There Are Still Too Many J-Schools," *Bulletin of the American Society of Newspaper Editors*," March 1, 1964. Also, "Prune Journalism Schools," *Nieman Reports*, June 1963, 2.
35. Luxon to Mark Ethridge, July 31, 1964, Luxon Papers.

moted Danielson while doing nothing about promotions for five others who ranged in age from 42 to 55. That did not deter him, Luxon said, because he believed in merit raises and promotions.[36] Bush had known Danielson as a graduate student at Stanford, and he told Luxon that the University of Iowa might try to lure Danielson there as part of an effort to hire Paul Deutschmann, another well-known mass communication scholar. He advised Luxon to do what he could to keep Danielson happy at UNC.[37]

Chancellor Aycock intended to replace Luxon with someone from within the faculty.[38] Luxon told McPherson that if anyone offered to bet money that Luxon's successor would come from another state, McPherson should take the bet.[39] In December, Luxon told Wesley Clark, dean of the School of Journalism at Syracuse University, that the dean of the faculty was going to interview the seven faculty members about their preference, and he assumed the next dean would come from the faculty.[40] Jack Adams and Jim Mullen later recalled that Luxon found them sitting in an office with Danielson one day and pointedly announced that one of the three was going to be the next dean. Adams and Mullen both said they simultaneously pointed to Danielson and said, "Him!"[41]

Aycock made the selection after James Godfrey, the university's dean of the faculty, interviewed the seven faculty members. All seven said the new dean should come from the faculty, and only Danielson named someone other than himself as his preferred candidate.[42] Godfrey told Aycock on Dec. 16, 1963, that Danielson's appointment would be the wisest move for the university.[43]

Julian Scheer, a UNC journalism graduate who was a public relations executive with the National Aeronautics and Space Administration, praised the job Luxon had done and recommended to Aycock that Walter Spearman be given careful consideration as dean when Luxon stepped down. Acknowledging that Spearman did not have a Ph.D., Scheer said a doctorate in journalism was a "rather nebulous thing in both educational and

36. Luxon to Bush, May 15, 1963, Luxon Papers.

37. Bush to Luxon, May 27, 1963, Luxon Papers.

38. Aycock to Nelson Woodson, Nov. 6, 1963, Provost's Records #40039, University Archives, University of North Carolina at Chapel Hill Library.

39. Luxon to McPherson, Nov. 19, 1963, Luxon Papers.

40. Luxon to Clark, Dec. 7, 1963, Luxon Papers.

41. Adams, interview with the author, Aug. 21, 2007; Mullen, interview with the author, Aug. 22, 2007.

42. *Journalism Newsletter*, January 1964, 1.

43. Godfrey to Aycock, Dec. 16, 1963, Provost's Records.

Chuck Stone, the first Walter Spearman Distinguished Professor in the School of Journalism and Mass Communication, 1991–2005. *(School of Journalism and Mass Communication, UNC–Chapel Hill. Reprinted with permission.)*

journalistic circles." He praised Spearman for being an inspiration to many students and for having the respect of the working press. He believed that many North Carolina newspaper people would also endorse Spearman.[44] Aycock quickly told Scheer that the Board of Trustees had already approved Danielson's appointment.[45] A few days later, Luxon told Ralph Casey that Danielson was the unanimous choice of the faculty and called him "the most brilliant man in the field today."

Spearman once again dealt with the disappointment of not being chosen as dean of the school. He continued to teach, however, and he became one of the most beloved teachers in the history of the school and a popular stage actor in Chapel Hill. In 1967, he received a Tanner Award for teaching excellence, the university's highest teaching award at the time, and he directed the North Carolina Scholastic Press Institute for high school journalists and teachers for 30 years. He won the university's Thomas Jefferson Award in 1978, the year he retired. He was inducted into the North Carolina Journalism Hall of Fame in 1983, in the third group of inductees and the first faculty member so honored. Upon Spearman's death in 1987, William Friday, UNC president emeritus, lauded his teaching, theater performances, and writing: "Walter Spearman was one of those noble spirits who made Chapel Hill the much loved place it is." Chancellor Christopher Fordham said many North Carolina journalists called him their favorite teacher. Dean Richard Cole called him an institution and said he was the "Mr. Chips of Chapel Hill." It was estimated that Spear-

44. Scheer to Aycock, Jan. 10, 1964, Chancellor's Records: Aycock Series.
45. Aycock to Scheer, Jan. 13, 1964, Chancellor's Records: Aycock Series.

man taught more than 5,000 students in his 43 years on the faculty, from 1935 to 1978.[46]

He was further honored by the creation of the Walter Spearman Distinguished Professorship in the school. Chuck Stone was selected in 1991 as the first Walter Spearman Professor. Spearman's widow, Jean Spearman, later said Stone was the perfect person to fill the chair: "It was remarkable. If Walter could have selected his own candidate, he could not have found one who was closer to his own ideals and understanding than Chuck Stone, who has been a joy to us and who would have made Walter proud."[47] Stone had had a distinguished career as a journalist, including the editorship of the *Chicago Defender*, before he joined the faculty. By the time he retired in 2005, he was one of the most popular professors in the school and in the university, especially for his course in censorship.

Luxon continued to teach until he retired in 1969, and he died on Sept. 4, 1989, at age 90. Friday praised Luxon upon his death, saying he came to the university "with a sense of mission about the future of the School of Journalism, and he achieved what he set out to do."[48] Luxon's will included a $1,000 gift to the school.

46. University of North Carolina News Bureau, "Renowned Journalism Professor Walter S. Spearman Dead at 79," Feb. 24, 1987.

47. Spearman, quoted in *Carolina Innovator*, the printed program for the Richard Cole retirement dinner, April 29, 2005, 3.

48. "Luxon Dead at Age 90," *UNC Journalist*, October 1989, 4.

9. The Danielson Years

The transition in the dean's office would not be as dramatic as it was when Luxon moved into it in 1953. Wayne Danielson maintained the momentum that Luxon established, and the school achieved accreditation again, expanded the graduate program and faculty research, and explored the revolutionary idea that computers could produce newspapers. During this period, the school and the university experienced the challenge of racial integration.

At 34, Danielson was the youngest dean in the university's history when he assumed the deanship of the UNC School of Journalism on July 1, 1964. The university had initiated a new policy on administrative appointments, and deans were appointed to five-year terms that could be renewed. A native of Iowa, he had joined the UNC faculty in 1958 after earning a B.A. from the University of Iowa and an M.A. and Ph.D. from Stanford University. Danielson had written for the college newspaper at the University of Iowa and for the *San Jose Mercury-News* in California. In a story about his appointment, the *Daily Tar Heel* reported that Danielson planned no major changes in the school's undergraduate program, but said the faculty anticipated an increase in the school's graduate enrollment. The article identified him as a nationally known scholar in mass communication, especially concerning computer applications in journalism.[2] In *Editor and Publisher*, the story of his appointment identified him in the headline as a

1. Yoder, "The Stuffed Shirt Era," *Greensboro Daily News*, Jan. 21, 1964, 6-A.
2. Mickey Blackwell, "News Researcher Danielson Named Dean of J School," *Daily Tar Heel*, Jan. 11, 1964, 1.

Wayne Danielson, dean of the School of Journalism, 1964–69, became nationally known for his prediction that computers would change newspapers. *(North Carolina Collection, University of North Carolina at Chapel Hill Library. Reprinted with permission.)*

computer expert.[3] That kind of identification revealed how unusual it was at that time to think of computers and newspapers together, but Danielson would play a leading role in changing that perception.

He said later that he patterned his administrative philosophy and style after Luxon's but allowed that he was probably more democratic than Luxon. Danielson also said he wanted to be remembered for continuing Luxon's work and for strengthening the scholarly reputation of the school. Many journalism schools had underemphasized research, Danielson said, but he thought it was very important. Some people who wanted to join journalism faculties, he said, desired a break from working in journalism and thought it would be great to join a faculty somewhere and tell "war stories" of their experiences. Instead, he wanted a faculty of younger people who would be fully integrated into academic and scholarly activities on campus.[4]

Reactions to Danielson's Appointment

Danielson's elevation to the deanship prompted critical responses from several sources. In an editorial that appeared the day his appointment was

3. "Computer Expert to Become Dean at Chapel Hill," *Editor and Publisher*, Jan. 18, 1964, 62.
4. Danielson, interview with the author, Feb. 26, 2008.

reported, the *Tar Heel* expressed high regard for him as a teacher and researcher. However, the writer disagreed with Danielson's statement that no changes were needed at the undergraduate level, pointing out that a student could graduate from the school and write fewer than 40 news stories—and none of them would have to be printable—because only one of the four courses required for graduation was directly concerned with writing news. The writer said one of the other required courses, journalism history, was superfluous and should be replaced by a course more useful to aspiring journalists.[5]

Danielson's limited newspaper experience provoked a strong negative response from a prominent UNC alumnus who had not been a journalism major while a student. Edwin M. Yoder, a columnist for the *Greensboro Daily News*, attacked journalism education in general and Danielson's appointment in particular. Yoder was a 1956 graduate of UNC and former editor of the *Daily Tar Heel* whose only journalism courses had been Phillips Russell's creative writing courses. In his column, Yoder connected the death of famed newspaper critic A. J. Liebling on Dec. 28, 1963, to "the laying of apostolic hands" on Danielson as the new dean of the school. He said Liebling had guarded American journalism against false values, and Danielson, like Coffin and Luxon before him, had become the symbol of North Carolina's journalism's values. Yoder said an increasingly complex society made it imperative that the field of journalism recruit people who understood the modern world and could explain it with integrity. However, he said, journalism schools—"gaudy journalism factories"—were dispensing a "cult of technique" that hampered understanding. The journalism schools' ambitions, he said, were to convert journalism to a profession that combined the laboratory scientist's research mystique and the "stuffed-shirt responsibility of the more self-conscious bar and clergy." Journalism education suffered, he said, from "creeping academic snobbery."

That had not always been true at the UNC School of Journalism, Yoder claimed, because its aim had been to turn out good writers. Its faculty members were journalists "rather restlessly pastured in academe" who deemed the English sentence the "noblest of human artifice." He called the faculty a kind of "patriciate of journalism, secure enough in its values to be contemptuous of the parvenu's attention to fads." Coffin's departure had meant a change, Yoder warned, and the school had decided that the state press had outgrown the "homely craftsmanship" that Coffin preached and had become "big-time and Midwestern." The school had emerged from its rustic quarters and had begun to hire "research scien-

5. "Tempering Applause with Hope," *Daily Tar Heel*, Jan. 22, 1964, 2.

tists whose experience in mock-scientism is as great as their experience of workaday journalism is limited." Yoder said the school "set about with keen success to ape the Big Ten athletic conference—the *locus classicus* of the big 'J-School' and muscular football."

Yoder believed the appointment of Danielson (whom he mocked as a "doctor of journalism") had accelerated that process. Danielson was a journalist only in the "most literal academic sense" who had worked briefly as a reporter, research manager, and research consultant for a few newspapers, Yoder charged. Danielson as a journalism dean, he said, was like a law school dean who had studied in a rural courthouse but had not argued before its juries or a medical school professor of surgery who had never cut human flesh. Journalists were not like lawyers or doctors or clergymen who guarded and practiced an established body of learning, lore, or doctrine, Yoder said. The journalist "is not a vessel or a container," he contended. "He is a midwife, a transmitter, a vehicle, a lens. A law professor who never faced a jury is conceivable if undesirable; a teacher of journalists who has rarely written about a trial or a murder or a political campaign is conceivable but ridiculous."[6]

Danielson said in 2008 that he had not been bothered by the reception he received from North Carolina newspapers when he was appointed dean. The state's newspapers had had a long relationship with the university, and those ties were so strong that most newspaper people accepted him although they thought he was a strange person to run the school. Danielson recalled that the Raleigh *News and Observer* published a critical article about him, but the editor called him to say that the newspaper's warm feelings toward the school were still strong. He told Danielson that if he ever needed assistance, he would be "on the veranda" ready to help.[7]

The School and the Student Newspaper

Yoder's comments about Danielson were not simply the personal reactions of one person to one dean. In fact, more than 40 years later, Yoder said he did not recall writing the column and seemed surprised to read what he had written in 1964. He said he had probably made an unfair criticism of Danielson that was predicated upon an inaccurate understanding of journalism education at that time. He said that he, Charles Kuralt, Barry Farber, Rolfe Neill, and others on the *Daily Tar Heel* staffs of their era believed that their practical experience on the student newspaper was

6. Yoder, "The Stuffed Shirt Era," *Greensboro Daily News*, Jan. 21, 1964, 6-A.
7. Danielson, interview with the author, Feb. 26, 2008.

superior to courses in the journalism school.[8] Neill recalled that he had spent so much time writing for the *Daily Tar Heel* by the time he was a junior that he thought it would have been a waste of time to take courses in the School of Journalism.[9] Such attitudes were apparent four years earlier, when an editorial, "An Idiotic Feud," by then-editor Jonathan Yardley lamented the lack of cooperation between the *Daily Tar Heel* and the School of Journalism and said the growing feud and resultant cliques could lead to an unfortunate climax. The newspaper's goal was to put out a student newspaper that informed the student body and gave aspiring journalists some experience, he said, while the school's goal was to instruct aspiring journalists in the arts and skills of journalism. It seemed "ridiculously natural" to him that the two groups should work closely together to achieve those goals.

Yardley said newspaper staffers considered journalism majors to be "nothing but trade school students" in a university that was supposed to teach overall knowledge rather than prepare people for trades or professions. Journalism students, on the other hand, thought the student newspaper was a sloppy product that was not worthy of their cooperation. He said the school's faculty was "one of the finest groups of men on this campus, men who are dedicated not only to teaching their students about journalism but also about the various aspects of an education which cannot be found between the pages of a newspaper." He admitted that journalism students were correct in their criticism of the newspaper's sloppiness, but he said it was due to "stingy appropriations, a small staff, and poor facilities." The staff was annoyed, he said, because the critics did not seem to realize that the paper "would improve immensely by their cooperaiton [*sic*]." The student newspaper had nothing to offer the School of Journalism except an opportunity for experience, he said. It was not a laboratory newspaper, however, because its purpose was to serve students.[10]

Later that year, the occasion of the Howell Hall dedication and several speakers' pronouncements about the responsibilities of the press prompted Mary Stewart Baker, an associate editor of the *Daily Tar Heel*, to say in a signed editorial that the student newspaper had to assert its responsibility every day or it would become "a toy of the Journalism School."[11] In a letter

8. Yoder, interview with the author, Jan. 25, 2008.

9. Neill, interview with the author, Oct. 5, 2007.

10. Yardley, "An Idiotic Feud," *Daily Tar Heel*, April 5, 1960, 2. There is little doubt about the authorship of the editorial because a statement on the editorial page said all editorials were the personal opinions of the editor, unless otherwise noted.

11. Baker, "A Lesson in Responsibility," *Daily Tar Heel*, Oct. 26, 1960, 2.

to the editor two years later, a student in the school, Bill McAllister, criticized the *Daily Tar Heel* for a lack of enthusiasm and poor news coverage. He said he had heard that there had been an attempt several years earlier to allow the School of Journalism to help guide the paper, but that the idea had been turned down for fear that the assistance would lead to censorship. Following McAllister's letter, an editor's note from Wayne King acknowledged the letter as a thoughtful commentary and admitted that the paper suffered from an inadequate staff. He said the idea of the school helping to publish the paper was being considered at that time, but the marriage of the two would not necessarily be a happy one, and he would not enter into it hurriedly. He also said McAllister would be welcome to work on the staff.[12]

A few months later, King reiterated his position about the problems hampering cooperative efforts between the school and the paper. He said Yardley had earlier proposed that the school might relieve the staffing problem by assuming responsibility for the news and sports sections of the student newspaper. King admitted that the paper was usually understaffed and that affiliation with the school would help both the paper and the school. However, he said, a "marriage" between the two would be undesirable. Regardless of any stipulations to the contrary, the paper would lose some freedom on its editorial page because readers would think the school was responsible for all content. He acknowledged the foibles of college editors, saying that, as a group, they were "possibly the most unbridled lot on the national campus scene." While editors were likely to make occasional mistakes, he said, they would also, from time to time, produce good results.[13] The idea of the school playing more of a role in the *Daily Tar Heel* did not take hold, however.

Computers and Newspapers

Danielson was one of the earliest scholars to predict that computers would revolutionize newspapers, and his ideas and predictions brought publicity and a degree of notoriety to him and the school. In a 2008 interview, he recalled that he had been energized in his work by a conversation he had in the early 1960s with John W. Carr III, director of the university's Computation Center. Dropping by Danielson's office one day, Carr boasted that the university's new computer had the capacity to store the contents of a

12. McAllister, "Should Journalism Students Edit DTH?" *Daily Tar Heel*, Jan. 4, 1962, 2.

13. King, "The DTH, the J-School and a Generation of Nice Guys," *Daily Tar Heel*, April 12, 1962, 2.

typical daily newspaper. Danielson had used computers for data analysis, but he had never thought they might be used to produce news stories, so his initial reaction to Carr's comment was essentially, "So what?" However, that conversation motivated him to work with Carr and other computer experts on campus and to think of ways to produce a newspaper with a computer.

In 1963, Danielson and Bruce Briggs of the Computation Center published an article in an academic computing journal about a computerized news editing program they had developed. The program could take stories from the Associated Press teletype, alter the content based on preprogrammed instructions from an editor, and cut the stories from "the bottom up" to conform to the newspaper's policy and other news of the day. In other words, it was designed to help an editor make decisions, but it was not a complete editing system that would operate on its own. Such an independent, complete editing system was feasible, Danielson and Briggs argued, but operationalizing it would be a major undertaking.[14] Danielson, Carr, and others produced in 1964 what Danielson claimed was the first newspaper produced by a computer and a computer printer.[15]

Editor and Publisher sensationalized a prediction Danielson made at a 1964 newspaper workshop at the University of Wisconsin. Under the headline, "Computers Can Write Like Machine," the story began, "If you write like a machine, you can be replaced by a machine." Danielson told the journalists that newspapers were afflicted by "humdrum, hackneyed, formula writing—writing in which the names and ages change, but the basic prose goes on forever." Such writing had been around for a long time, he claimed, but computers made it possible to replace those writers with machines. He said much in newspaper editing was repetitious and predictable: "We gather the news from our standard sources, then cut it up and fit it into a standard mold that everyone can recognize." Danielson described experiments he had conducted at UNC that showed that much of a newspaper could be produced automatically. A certain amount of newspaper work would always be routine and repetitious, and if that work were to be done by a computer, Danielson said, it would be "good riddance." He said he feared an increase in the "routine and machinelike" content of newspapers because editors would find that it would be cheap and simple to have computers produce that content.[16]

Newspapers were already using computers in 1964, primarily to replace

14. Danielson and Briggs, "A Computer Program for Editing the News," *Communications of the Association for Computing Machinery*, August 1963, 487–90.

15. Danielson, interview with the author, Feb. 26, 2008.

16. "Computers Can Write Like Machine," *Editor and Publisher*, May 16, 1964, 70.

typesetting machines at a stage in the production of newspapers that came to be called the "back end." Danielson's predictions had more to do with the creation and editing of content, or the "front end" of the production process, which is what caused his predictions to be greeted with skepticism. At a 1990 seminar in Chapel Hill about the future of communication research, Danielson recalled—"with the satisfaction of having the last laugh"—the reaction of a newspaper editor in Dubuque, Iowa, to Danielson's prediction that computers might replace writers: "So, a professor at the University of North Carolina thinks a computer may be helpful to the editor of a newspaper. Please let this fellow know that I'm building a computer in my basement. I'm making it out of an old toaster, a broken TV, and a three-way switch. It won't be very good. But it will be good enough to replace a professor of journalism who thinks computers will have anything to do with newspapers."[17]

Racial Integration

While he was making predictions about the media business and computers, Danielson and the faculty had another issue to confront—one that was affecting the entire nation. The School of Journalism had a frontline perspective on the racial integration of the university and the turbulence of civil rights demonstrations in Chapel Hill. Lester Carson, a journalism major who graduated in 1963, was the first African-American student in the school and one of the first black undergraduate students at the university. He started college at North Carolina Central University, which was then called North Carolina College (NCC). He wanted to study journalism, but because it was not offered at NCC, he transferred to UNC in 1962. More than 40 years later, he said he had been surprised in 1962 to find that people in the School of Journalism treated him very cordially, even to the point of what seemed to be indifference on the part of white faculty members and students. He said he could not recall a single unpleasant incident in Howell Hall. He considered Walter Spearman a mentor and friend who offered a shoulder to cry on, though Carson never needed it.[18]

Walter Jackson, the third black student in the school, graduated in 1967, and he also said in 2008 that he had fond memories of the School of Journalism and Howell Hall. When he was in the school, it had fewer than

17. Danielson, "The Future of Communication Research," remarks at the School of Journalism and Mass Communication, April 28, 1990, School of Journalism and Mass Communication archives.
18. Carson, interview with the author, Feb. 26, 2008.

100 students, and they got to know one another and developed a sense of camaraderie. Howell Hall was like a little home with a "cozy, comfortable feeling," where most students and faculty members knew each other. He developed good relationships with a number of fellow students, especially Karen Parker, the only other African-American student in the school. She was a senior while he was a sophomore, and for his last two years, he was the only black student in the school.

Jackson recalled supportive professors, especially Ken Byerly, whom he described as an "all-around great guy, very personable, humorous, and knowledgeable about the field." All faculty members had excellent contacts in the field and seemed to be very caring, Jackson remembered. Race did not seem to be an issue in the school, he said, and faculty members helped him develop his talents. The larger university was different, however, because black students were still very much outside the mainstream. The university had no black athletes, and black students were discriminated against in subtle ways. He said, for example, that white students sang "Dixie" and waved Confederate flags at athletic events. The university as a whole was not a welcoming, warm, hospitable place for black students, Jackson said, but he thoroughly enjoyed the School of Journalism because of the environment it provided him. All in all, he said, his experience at the school gave him the skills and confidence he needed to compete and to follow his star.[19]

Things were different for Parker, the second black student in the school and the first black female undergraduate student at UNC–Chapel Hill. Interviewed for the school's laboratory publication in 1963 while she was a student, she said so many races were represented at the university that no one paid any attention to her. She said she felt more like an individual at Chapel Hill than she did at UNC–Greensboro, which she attended for her first two years.[20] However, a diary she wrote while she was at Chapel Hill painted a different picture and revealed many frustrations for the only undergraduate black woman on campus and in the school.[21]

Parker participated in civil rights demonstrations in Chapel Hill, which were aimed at getting the town council to pass a public-accommodations law before Christmas of 1963. On Dec. 14, 1963, Parker and two other students went to Leo's Restaurant on west Franklin Street in Chapel Hill with

19. Jackson, interview with the author, March 19, 2008.

20. Susie Lewis, "Karen Parker Sees No Race Problem Here," *UNC Journalist*, October 1963, 1.

21. Karen L. Parker Diary #5275, Southern Historical Collection, University of North Carolina at Chapel Hill Library.

the purpose of getting arrested, which happened when they refused to leave the restaurant at an employee's request.[22] A month later, she was "shocked and bitter" at news that the university planned to expel students who had participated in such demonstrations. "I had always been so proud of being at Carolina," Parker wrote in her diary. "I knew it wasn't as liberal as people liked to say it was, but this statement really hurt me. I didn't care to go to school there anymore, but they were going to have to expel me because I wasn't going to give up."[23]

Female students of that era had to obey nightly curfews in dormitories, and her arrest on Dec. 14 made Parker 15 hours late for the curfew, so she had to appear before the University Women's Honor Council on Feb. 27 on a charge of missing the curfew because of her arrest. After the hearing was postponed until March 2, Byerly testified as a character witness for her. Parker told the council that her decision to participate in the demonstration had been spontaneous and that she had had not intended to violate the curfew. The charges were dropped, and the council praised her for doing all she could to comply with the curfew regulations.[24]

Parker later applied for the editorship of the *UNC Journalist*, but she confided to her diary that she was not confident about her chances of winning it. She wanted the post because of the $300 annual stipend and the prestige, but she thought the odds were against her. She was surprised to win the editorship, the Beatrice Cobb Scholarship, and election as vice president of the Press Club, but she was worried about doing a good job because everyone would be watching her.[25] A year later, Parker wrote in her diary that she had worked hard on the *Journalist,* but felt she did not get the recognition she deserved. She was also disappointed at not being selected for Kappa Tau Alpha, the national honorary fraternity for journalism students, but she reasoned that her grades must not have been high enough. She was disappointed, too, at not receiving the award for the outstanding senior woman in journalism: "After all, the j-school has its conservatives (especially the new Sigma Delta Chi officers) and I am a Negro who has overstepped most of the j-school student body. I'm the only one with a permanent sun-tan." After having drinks with Curry Kirkpatrick and other students, she cried on his shoulder and found him to be "sur-

22. "3 More Arrested as Race Protests Continue Here," *Daily Tar Heel,* Dec. 15, 1963, 1.

23. Parker diary, Jan. 10, 1964.

24. John Greenbacker, "Women's Council Frees 2 Sit-Ins," *Daily Tar Heel,* March 4, 1964, 1.

25. Parker diary, May 9, 1964.

prisingly understanding." She said that while he had achieved recognition because he was "damned good," her own achievements would have to be more tangible to be recognized.[26]

Two weeks later, Parker learned that her grade-point average had been high enough for Kappa Tau Alpha, and she didn't understand why she wasn't selected. She said a co-editor of the *Tar Heel* had been selected, even though his grades were not as good as hers, and she believed it might have been favoritism among the journalism faculty. She said journalism majors were not as politically liberal as some other campus groups.[27] In the middle of final exams, she was disappointed about her job prospects. Byerly had recommended her and another student for a job in California, but he had arranged an interview for the other student and not for Parker. She concluded, however, that it was mere personal favoritism and not racism.[28] She wrote on June 3 that she was surprised to get a note from Danielson saying she had done a good job on the *Journalist,* because she thought no one had noticed.

She was reflective as she began to prepare for graduation: "This is a beautiful, wonderful place—despite its faults. What hurts me so much is that I cannot and will not ever become a part of it. It means so much to me. . . . I'm just lonely, little old me. Karen Parker, student number 668-670, a problem for the Dean of Women's office, a resident of second floor, East Cobb, the only Negro in the School of Journalism, an 'assimilated' Negro, a marginal person, a beatnik sympathizer, the first Negro undergraduate girl to graduate from UNC—an unknown. I don't even feel as good about my accomplishments—editor of the *Journalist,* the Beatrice Cobb scholarship, vice-president of the Press Club, Toronto Exchange—if I could just do something else!"[29]

In a 2008 interview, Parker reflected on that statement, saying that she had felt very isolated at the time—and that the feeling had not completely disappeared. "When I go back to campus now," she said, "as a member of the General Alumni Association's Board of Directors and the university's Board of Visitors, and think about 45 years ago, I get the same emotional feeling—that I do not belong there. That is not because of people or the way I am treated, but those are still my emotional memories. I sometimes feel the same anger and the same hurt, and even though I am part of cam-

26. Parker diary, May 7, 1965. Kirkpatrick later became a well-known national sportswriter.
27. Parker diary, May 17, 1965.
28. Parker diary, May 30, 1965.
29. Parker diary, March 4, 1965.

pus history, those emotions will follow me for the rest of my life." She also credited Roy Thompson of the *Winston-Salem Journal* for being a source of inspiration. She said he had a lot of charisma and that he and his wife invited her into their home and gave her advice. He had faith in Parker that she did not have herself, and he was "Saint Roy" to her and others.[30]

Accreditation and a New Dean

Racial issues were not overly distracting to Danielson and the faculty, and the school continued its quest to maintain Luxon's vision and momentum. Success in that endeavor became apparent when the school enjoyed a successful accreditation visit on March 1–2, 1965. In its recommendation that the school be reaccredited, team members said they were impressed by the physical facilities and equipment, faculty teaching loads, salaries, and faculty and student morale. The team expressed concern about the meager professional backgrounds of some faculty members, however, and recommended that professional experience be given greater weight in faculty salary increases and promotions. They also suggested that the faculty consider increasing the number of required credit hours in journalism from 24 to 30 (eight courses to 10 courses) by adding writing and reporting courses. They also recommended that the school ensure that the new doctoral program not detract from the high quality of undergraduate teaching. At the time, the annual budget of the school was $124,500, $93,850 of which was spent on salaries.[31] Luxon, who was still on the faculty, complained to Earl English about the "so-called Accreditation Visitation" and said the team had not asked a single question about research, visited the library, or checked a single student record. He blasted the "damned-fool" recommendation that the journalism course requirements be increased.[32]

As Luxon had done, Danielson benefited from support from the school's foundation. During his term, annual donations to the foundation averaged $28,000, primarily because of a significantly higher figure of $43,500 in 1967, and annual foundation support to the school averaged just over $14,000. In 1967, for example, Danielson spent $6,800 from the

30. Parker, interview with the author, Feb. 20, 2008.
31. John Stempel to William B. Aycock, May 5, 1965, Chancellor's Records: Paul Sharp Series #40021, University Archives and Records Service, University of North Carolina at Chapel Hill Library.
32. Luxon to English, March 5, 1965, Norval Neil Luxon Papers, Southern Historical Collection, University of North Carolina at Chapel Hill Library.

foundation for graduate assistantships, $5,075 for scholarships, $4,700 for school publications, and $1,500 for faculty travel.

In a 2008 interview, Danielson recalled how well the faculty members worked together. Morrison was an East Coast man who seemed to live simultaneously in Chapel Hill and his hometown of New York, according to Danielson, and was a good writing coach for students. Byerly had come out of the newspaper business and taught community journalism with a practical approach, encouraging students to be entrepreneurs and buy their own newspapers. His book about community journalism had a controversial chapter about what not to publish in small-town newspapers, Danielson recalled. Spearman was a "lovely, lively man" and a good writer, whose teaching resulted in some of the best student writing in the school. Danielson said Mullen was gruff and wise-cracking but had enormous impact and improved the image of advertising education. Adams was very thoughtful, and his work in law and ethics was widely applauded. Danielson remembered Sechriest as a "wonderful old-time North Carolina person" who tried to teach Danielson how to live in North Carolina and took him fishing. Sechriest taught in a very informal way and was a good companion.[33]

Jock Lauterer also had fond memories of the faculty members of that era. He said Morrison used to throw erasers at him to wake him up in class. Morrison had a Brooklyn accent that made him sound like Elmer Fudd, and when he called Lauterer's name, it sounded like "Watuhwuh." Spearman was wonderful, Lauterer said, "and if you didn't love Spearman, there was something wrong with your DNA." Byerly got Lauterer involved in community journalism, including his first internship, and gave him advice about launching his own newspaper. Danielson helped Lauterer get started in publishing books, including their joint effort, *Only in Chapel Hill*.[34]

Danielson took a leave of absence in the 1967–68 academic year to teach at the University of Texas at Austin and help that school develop a doctoral program. He told the school's laboratory publication that he was taking the leave so he could catch up on his reading and so his family could experience living in another part of the country.[35] Luxon, who

33. Danielson, interview with the author, Feb. 26, 2008.

34. Lauterer, interview with the author, March 24, 2008. *Only in Chapel Hill: A Photographic Essay* was published for the School of Journalism Foundation by Colonial Press of Chapel Hill in 1967.

35. Mickey Henkel, "Danielson Takes Leave; Luxon Serves as Dean," *UNC Journalist*, April 1967, 1.

served as interim dean in Danielson's absence, complained to Kirchhofer that he was busier that year as interim dean than he had been when he was dean, mostly because the school had 50 percent more students and 30 percent more faculty members.[36] In a reflective document he wrote about the school that year, he said that of the variety of sources for North Carolina newspaper personnel, the school at UNC was probably the most important. However, the school had not been able to meet all of the needs of the state's papers. For the six to eight years after the reorganization of the school in 1954, 72 percent of its students were from North Carolina, and 76 percent took their first jobs in the state. However, as enrollment grew and the school's reputation spread, the percentage of out-of-state students increased to 35 percent in 1967. While most UNC journalism students planned to stay in North Carolina, an increasing number of graduates were finding jobs outside the state, and the aim of the school was to prepare students for jobs anywhere. Luxon said the 91 percent increase in graduate enrollment from 1964 to 1967 was the most significant fact to note about the school, and five of the 21 graduate students were working on their doctorates.[37]

Danielson's interest in Texas was not based solely on the appeal of living in a different part of the country for a year. The lure of the University of Texas and its multifaceted College of Communication was too tempting, and Danielson's year there turned out to be the beginning of the end of his deanship at UNC. In 2008, he recalled that one reason he was attracted to the University of Texas in 1969 was the fact that Dewitt Reddick, the college's dean, had combined departments of radio, television and film, advertising, journalism, and speech communication into one college. Danielson found the union of those faculties interesting because it broadened the concept of communication and developed new knowledge.[38] He returned to Chapel Hill for the 1968–69 academic year, but he decided to resign and return to Texas to become dean of its school. He informed UNC chancellor Lyle Sitterson of his decision on Jan. 23, 1969.[39] The faculty had heard the news earlier, however, because Morrison told Provost Charles Morrow on Jan. 21 that Danielson had told him and others of his intent

36. Luxon to Kirchhofer, Dec. 29, 1967, Luxon Papers.
37. Luxon, "A Six-Year Look to the Future, Based upon the Experience of the 1958–1967 Decade," Luxon Papers.
38. Danielson, interview with the author, Feb. 26, 2008.
39. Danielson to J. Carlyle Sitterson, Jan. 23, 1969, Provost's Records #40039, University Archives, University of North Carolina at Chapel Hill Library.

that day. Morrison told Morrow that he wanted to be considered as a candidate for the deanship, but that wish did not get any consideration.[40]

Writing to a former student, Luxon expressed disappointment at Danielson's resignation, calling him "a brilliant, ambitious young man" who felt he would have more opportunities at Texas. Luxon said he would probably not be solicited for advice about a new dean, but if he were asked, he would strongly recommend Jack Adams. He said the school was in a critical spot because it had money to hire a full professor but could not find one, and it had three vacancies to fill—the full-professor vacancy, the one to be created by Luxon's upcoming retirement, and the dean's position.[41]

Luxon complained to McPherson that he had not been consulted by university administrators for his opinion about Danielson's possible reappointment, which had been cancelled because of his resignation. Luxon was deeply disappointed by Danielson's decision but didn't blame him, speculating that Texas would pay Danielson more than what the UNC chancellor was receiving. He said people in the school were hoping the chancellor would not insist on a search committee and said several faculty members would consider leaving the school if the wrong man were appointed. Vermont Royster of the *Wall Street Journal* had been suggested as a dean, but Luxon said Royster was not interested in an administrative position and instead wanted a teaching position with classes on only two days a week.[42] At a faculty meeting on March 7, Danielson said he had received a number of telegrams from former students who were advocating the choice of Wayne King, a school alumnus, to be the next dean. A week later, however, Danielson called a special faculty meeting to announce that the university's Board of Trustees had approved the appointment of Jack Adams to be the next dean. Adams told his colleagues there would be very little change in the philosophy or programs of the school.[43] Chancellor Sitterson made Adams' appointment official on the same day.[44]

40. Morrison to Morrow, Jan. 21, 1969, Provost's Records.
41. Luxon to Laura Shackelford, Feb. 1, 1969, Luxon Papers.
42. Luxon to McPherson, Jan. 31, 1969, Luxon Papers.
43. Faculty meeting minutes, School of Journalism, March 7 and 14, 1969.
44. Sitterson to Adams, March 14, 1969, Provost's Records.

"I am proud of the ways in which
the students and faculty responded
to a situation which, elsewhere, led
to disaster, and which, in our School
of Journalism, and at UNC, did
not."—*Jack Adams*[1]

10. The Adams Years

John B. "Jack" Adams succeeded Wayne Danielson on July 1, 1969, and
perpetuated the vision and momentum created by Luxon and continued by Danielson. In Adams' 10 years as dean, the school experienced
unprecedented growth, dealt with students' spelling and grammar problems, and began to adopt computers and other new technologies. Those
developments happened while the school responded to charges of racism
and dealt with campus turbulence associated with demonstrations against
the Vietnam War.

Adams was 49 years old and had served in the Army Air Forces in Europe in World War II. He required just two years to earn his undergraduate degree at the University of California in 1953, was elected to Phi Beta
Kappa, and completed his master's (1954) and doctorate (1957) degrees at
the University of Wisconsin. While a graduate student, he was a reporter
and editor at the *Wisconsin State Journal* in Madison. He taught one year
at Michigan State University before coming to Chapel Hill in 1958 to fulfill
Luxon's desire for a professor with a background in international communication. Adams had previously corresponded with Luxon about teaching
opportunities at UNC, but none was appropriate at the time. When Luxon

---

1. Adams, "Report from the School of Journalism to the Directors of the N.C. Press
Association and Directors of the School of Journalism Foundation," May 28, 1970,
Provost's Records #40039, University Archives, University of North Carolina at Cha-
pel Hill Library.

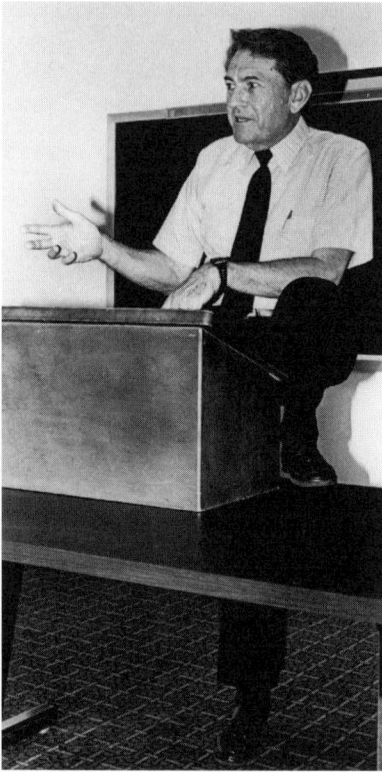

Jack Adams, dean of the School of Journalism, 1969–79, in his familiar classroom stance. *(Lori Thomas, School of Journalism and Mass Communication, UNC–Chapel Hill. Reprinted with permission.)*

later wrote to Adams about the possibility of an appointment as an associate professor, Adams informed Gordon Sabine, his dean at Michigan State, who encouraged him to consider the UNC position because Michigan State would not be able to offer a salary increase that year.[2]

At a faculty meeting in the Club Room of the Carolina Inn on July 15, Adams revealed his priorities by proposing four ways to strengthen the school's ties with the NCPA. One was a "Seminar for Practicing Newsmen," a semester-long course that had already been approved by the university's extension division to start in spring 1970. Ken Byerly would direct the program and would thus have a reduced teaching load for one semester. Adams also encouraged faculty members to increase their use of North Carolina journalists as resources in their courses. In addition, Adams suggested a workshop for high school journalism teachers as part of the North Carolina Scholastic Press Institute for high school journalists that Walter Spearman had directed for several years. Finally, Adams wanted to explore the idea of conducting roving workshops for newspaper employees in the state.[3]

Adams had gained administrative experience in his Army Air Forces days, and he had learned that he could be more effective if he "stayed below the radar." That is how he said he operated as a dean, trying to find out which people on campus could do things for the school and quietly working with them. Administrative procedures were more informal then, he recalled, saying he often conducted business with the chancellor dur-

2. Adams, interview with the author, April 1, 2008.
3. Faculty meeting minutes, School of Journalism, July 15, 1969.

ing chance encounters while walking across the campus.[4] He had been relieved that no one wrote newspaper editorials about him when he became dean, and he thought he had been correctly perceived as a "copy editor gone wrong and a researcher by necessity and a good-old boy." In the classroom, Adams impressed students with his knowledge of media law and his ability to tell interesting stories about relevant legal cases, and most students never knew that he had not taken a media law course himself.[5] Students were also amused by Adams' way of standing in the classroom—hiking his left foot high on the table and standing on his right leg for an entire class period. Some students said that made him look like a stork or a crane, and Adams stood that way so many times that the table in his classroom eventually bore wear marks from his left shoe.

During Adams' tenure, the school had a reputation on campus as a welcoming place for students. Rick Gray, a journalism major and associate editor of the *Daily Tar Heel*, wrote a column praising Adams and three members of his staff: Mildred Stout, the school's business manager; Susan Thomas, the financial manager; and Betsy Rigsbee, the secretary. Gray said the 200 or so journalism majors were lucky to have a place where the faculty members and staff knew their names and cared about them. Gray admitted that the school did have a few bad courses and a few professors who were not ideal, but he concluded that majoring in journalism had been a good experience on balance.[6]

Jan Johnson Yopp, who received her undergraduate degree from the school in 1970, remembered in 2008 what it was like to be a student back then. The school had about 100 students and 10 faculty members, all white men. She took courses from all of them except Jim Mullen, who taught advertising. Ken Byerly taught her news writing class, and because of his laugh, students called him "Ho-Ho" Byerly. The news writing class was in Howell 106, and students typed stories on yellow copy paper and cut and pasted the stories together. The *AP Stylebook* was very small, and students had to memorize the entire book. She took editing and news photography from Stuart Sechriest, feature writing and history from Joe Morrison, media law from Adams, and international communication from Michael Bishop. Students used large box cameras in the photography course, and she took photos of student protests on campus for a class assignment. She worked for the News Bureau as part of Spearman's reporting course and got several stories published. Spearman smoked cigarettes in class, she re-

4. Adams, interview with the author, Aug. 21, 2007.
5. Adams, interview with the author, Aug. 21, 2007.
6. Gray, "J-School: A Good Place to Be," *Daily Tar Heel*, March 24, 1971, 6.

called, and students waited in keen anticipation for the ash to drop off the end of the cigarette he held in the corner of his mouth.[7]

Yopp joined the faculty in 1977 after working six years at the *Raleigh Times*. She had found that she had not been happy with editing other journalists' copy and heard about a faculty vacancy from Jack Adams and Stuart Sechriest.[8] She left the school for a few years to work in public relations for Wachovia Bank in Winston-Salem. When she returned to full-time teaching, she headed the news-editorial sequence and taught public relations courses. Yopp also was associate dean and senior associate dean of the school until she became dean of the university's Summer School in 2008.

Vietnam and Racism

Adams and the faculty had to deal with campus unrest associated with the Vietnam War and answer charges of racism. UNC students, angered by the expansion of the Vietnam War into Cambodia and the killings of students by National Guardsmen at Kent State University, went on strike one week before the end of the spring semester in 1970. The university faculty voted to give students two options in light of the strike: They could receive regular course grades on the basis of work completed in the first 14 weeks of the 15-week semester, or they could take grades of Incomplete. Individual faculty members in the school made their own decisions after consulting with students, and Adams told members of the school's foundation board and the NCPA that he did not receive a single complaint from students. He said he was proud of how students and faculty had responded to the situation.[9]

In a 2007 interview, Adams recalled thinking at the time that his function as dean was "keeping the lid on and not being terribly innovative." He said it was important then that students not be distracted from their education. Journalism students of that era were particularly concerned about press coverage of student demonstrations. Gray told Adams he had gone to the Duke University campus as a reporter to cover a demonstration and had been sprayed with Mace (a pepper-based spray designed to subdue rioters) along with the demonstrators. Obviously distressed as he sat in Adams' office, Gray asked if he could be an objective reporter when he had just been sprayed with Mace. Adams replied, "This will be a good op-

7. Yopp, interview with the author, April 15, 2008.
8. Yopp, interview with the author, April 15, 2008.
9. Adams, "Report from the School of Journalism," Provost's Records.

portunity to find out if you could." Gray wrote the story and gave no hint that he had been as angry as he had ever been in his life.[10]

Journalism students stayed in the forefront of racial integration efforts on campus. In 1969, Cureton Johnson, a journalism major, was instrumental in creating *Black Ink,* a newspaper for African-American students on campus. In 1972, Richard Epps, also a journalism major, became the first black student to be elected UNC student body president. Ernie Pitt, who received his bachelor's degree from the school in 1974, said he had no awareness of racial problems on campus while he was a student. In 2008, he sat in the office of the *Winston-Salem Chronicle,* a newspaper he founded for the city's black community, and recalled the school with admiration. He said the School of Journalism had meant everything to him and had prepared him for his life's work. He loved the newspaper business, he said, because of what he learned in the school. The faculty members and the environment were nurturing and caring and taught him a way of life.[11]

In 1978, however, the school had to deal with charges of racism. The charges began with an editorial in *Black Ink* claiming that racism had been a problem in the School of Journalism for several years and had stemmed from three causes: the absence of black faculty members, the lack of courses about the black press, and the racist treatment of black students by some white instructors. The writer said black students in the school had been "scorned at, frowned upon, criticized and stomped into the ground." In response to remarks criticizing black journalism students because of their low level of participation in campus publications, including *Black Ink,* the writer said those students were not lazy or unconcerned about their future profession. Instead, they were frustrated with the school, which the writer called one of the "chief bastions of bigotry on campus."

The writer mocked school administrators who claimed that the school had no black faculty members because there were no qualified black journalism instructors available. The editorial charged that white teachers scheduled discussions about the black press for the last day of classes in the semester so that they could say they did not have time to talk about the black press that semester. The writer also claimed there was bigotry in many writing courses, and black students were angered at the "boldness and audacity" of white professors who said black students shouldn't write stories about blacks. Black students who defied that warning almost always got a lower grade on the assignment, the writer said. The editorial

10. Adams, interview with the author, Aug. 21, 2007.
11. Pitt, interview with the author, April 28, 2008.

closed with a strong indictment of the school: "Someone once asked this writer (the great, happy journalism major that I supposedly am) whether the UNC School of Journalism is nationally ranked. Yes, it is nationally ranked. It ranks number one in bigotry, number one in hypocrisy and number 93 in academic excellency [*sic*]."[12] Allen Johnson III and Lonza Hardy Jr. were co-editors of the paper at the time, but the editorial was unsigned. In 2008, neither could recall who wrote the editorial.[13]

A month later, Hardy wrote a signed column with specifics about the charges. He said there had been "numerous cries" from black students that the school was racist because it had neither black teachers nor courses about the black press. He had interviewed four black students in the school about their opinions. Edna Brown, a junior in the news-editorial sequence, said she "got no fun" from any of her journalism courses, adding that the school saw her not just as a student but as "another one of those little black students." She felt distant from the faculty, who seemed to be more interested in the "successful student, the one who works on the *Daily Tar Heel* or the one whose father works with the Greensboro paper." Gwendolyn Wallace, a senior in the broadcast journalism sequence, admitted that she had not talked to any of her journalism professors and realized that was her problem. She, too, felt distant from her professors but doubted if they would have understood her problems. Black students could relate better to black instructors, she said.

Linda Covington, another senior in the broadcast sequence, said she had been attracted to the school because it was the only accredited one in the state. She lamented the lack of black instructors and black-press courses in the school and said the faculty didn't recognize that there was a problem. She also thought that too few black students had voiced their opinions about the problem. Finally, Lillie Love, a junior in the broadcast sequence, said she liked her professors: "They've seemed very concerned and interested about me as a student. I haven't come to any racism or prejudice that is overt." She said that if she hadn't taken AFAM 65, a course in the African-American Studies Department about the black press, she would be ignorant of the black press.[14]

A month later, a student wrote to *Black Ink* to complain that students in the School of Journalism could not get credit for the AFAM 65 course be-

12. "J-School Racist?" Unsigned editorial, *Black Ink*, Jan. 27, 1978, 4.
13. Johnson, interview with the author, April 28, 2008, and Hardy, e-mail message to the author, April 17, 2008.
14. Hardy, "J-School Depressing, Frustrating," *Black Ink*, Feb. 23, 1978, 8.

cause it was not cross-listed in the catalog as a journalism course.[15] (Cross-listing means a course is listed in two or more academic departments and is considered as being a course in each.) Another reader wrote to report that a search for a photojournalism teacher in the school had not produced a single black candidate. The writer quoted Sam Fulwood, a black student on the search committee, as saying that the committee had sent a vacancy announcement to *Still Here*, a newsletter aimed at African-Americans in higher education. Fulwood said search committee members were not allowed to ask faculty job candidates if they were black, but he said he was confident he could have discerned that by looking at materials they submitted. The letter writer complained that the search committee had not done enough to find black photojournalists, who had to find their own jobs because the school would not do it for them.[16]

Responding to the charges of racism, several faculty members in the school met with black students who had formed an organization called Journalism Organization for Black Students (JOBS) to voice their concerns. JOBS students used the pages of *Black Ink* to make their concerns known, saying "irregularities" in the School of Journalism needed to be corrected. The first problem they cited in their letter was the need for black faculty members, saying that the school had not made a concerted effort to hire black teachers. The students said they did not accept the claim that there were no blacks who were qualified to teach journalism. Turning to the second concern—the lack of a course about the black press—the letter said, "It becomes quite irritating to witness year after year a complete negligence of the contributions of the black press to American journalism." The students wanted a complete course and not just discussions about the black press in other courses. The third concern was the need for more announcements and news about job opportunities, scholarships, and conferences of interest to minority students. The fourth concern focused on student-teacher relationships, and the writers said teachers often did not give them appropriate advice on matters that concerned them. They also said some instructors showed bias toward *Daily Tar Heel* staffers or students who had important parents.[17]

Adams and the faculty succeeded in hiring a black faculty member late

15. Clarence High, "No Credit for 'Black Press,'" letter to the editor, *Black Ink*, March 13, 1978, 4.

16. Teresa Burns, "Black Faculty in J-School," letter to the editor, *Black Ink*, March 13, 1978, 4.

17. Journalism Organization for Black Students, "J-School Can Find Black Instructor if It Looks," letter to the editor, *Black Ink*, Aug. 18, 1978, 5.

in 1978. Harry Amana had worked at a black newspaper, the *Philadelphia Tribune*, for three years and was teaching journalism at Temple University in Philadelphia. In a 2008 interview, Amana recalled seeing an announcement about a position with the Southeastern Black Press Institute (SEBPI), a Rockefeller Foundation–funded program at UNC that was directed by Sonja Haynes Stone in the Department of African-American Studies (AFAM). Amana applied for the position and submitted a critical column he had written about the black press. He recalled traveling to his job interview by train from Philadelphia and experiencing a dismal taxi ride—"a long, dark passage"—from the Amtrak station in Raleigh to Chapel Hill. When he arrived at the Carolina Inn on campus, it looked to him like an "antebellum Southern mansion," especially when he saw a black waiter in a servant's uniform. His first reaction, he recalled, was to ask himself why he had come to Chapel Hill in the first place, and he said to himself, "I am never going to come back here again." During an interview with a large search committee the next day, he learned that the position called for fundraising, which he did not want to do. After the meeting, Professor Donald Shaw of the School of Journalism approached him and asked if he might be interested in a faculty position in the school, which led to discussions with Adams and other faculty members.[18]

Adams arranged with AFAM and SEBPI for Amana to be hired as a faculty member in the school and a research associate in SEBPI. In addition, his AFAM course on the black press would be crosslisted as a journalism course, allowing journalism students to get journalism credit for it. A *Black Ink* story about Amana's appointment said the leaders of JOBS, Terri Burns and Edna Brown, reported that they had a useful meeting with Adams and other faculty members and that the school had made a concerted effort to find a black instructor. In the story, Amana explained that many black journalists were reluctant to consider teaching positions because they could make more money elsewhere.[19] Allen Johnson later recalled what it meant for black students in the school to see an African-American face in front of a classroom: "This is not meant to disparage any of our white instructors, but it did something for us to see that black face [Amana's] in the school. It was nice to see the J-school move in that direction and be more diverse."[20] In 1979, *Black Ink* printed material from the school's catalog and other sources in a comprehensive profile of the school. With the racism controversy apparently forgotten (or perhaps be-

18. Amana, interview with the author, Nov. 20, 2007.
19. Carol Lewis, "Harry Amana Arrives at J-School," *Black Ink*, Feb. 5, 1979, 1.
20. Johnson, interview with the author, April 28, 2008.

Harry Amana became the school's first African-American faculty member in 1979. *(School of Journalism and Mass Communication, UNC–Chapel Hill. Reprinted with permission.)*

cause of new editors at *Black Ink*), the article did not say anything about black faculty members or courses about the black press.[21]

Amana later recalled that teaching at UNC was not much different from what he had already experienced. The high school and college (Temple University) he had attended were almost entirely white, and he had not had any black teachers. When he enlisted in the Army and traveled by train to Ft. Jackson, S.C., he was refused service in a restaurant in Raleigh. Columbia, S.C., was even worse because soldiers there were segregated. He said he had been in a lot of situations where he had been the first or the only minority person, and it never crossed his mind that he was in an unusual situation at UNC. "It was the way the world was for me at that time," he said. As long as he was around good people who were committed to change, he was fine. He said he had met many people like that in Chapel Hill, especially Richard Cole and others in the School of Journalism. Black faculty members in other departments, like Carolyn Stroman and Genna Rae McNeil, were also strong advocates for change and black pride, he said. While the racial composition of UNC classes was similar to that at

21. "J-School Among Best in the State, the U.S.," *Black Ink*, Sept. 24, 1979, 6.

Temple, he did find one difference: UNC students were more polite, less confrontational, and less challenging of authority. He started teaching at UNC on a three-year contract and stayed for 28 years, including a stint as head of the Sonja Haynes Stone Center for Black Culture and History when plans were finalized for its new building.[22]

Enrollment and Faculty Growth

Early in Adams' tenure as dean, the school had to deal with increasing enrollment, leading him to tell the provost in 1971 that the number of majors had doubled since 1966 and quadrupled since 1959, but the faculty had only grown from seven to 11. Some students could not enroll in journalism courses because most journalism courses needed to have a small number of students to meet accreditation standards and to fit physically into the school's small classrooms. In addition, 45 percent of the students in journalism courses in the fall 1971 semester were nonmajors. Adams considered the presence of nonmajors in school courses to be positive because it indicated the high opinion other students had of the school. He lamented the dim prospects for hiring additional faculty, limited physical facilities with little hope for expansion, and insufficient secretarial support. In addition, the number of jobs available to graduating students was insufficient for the number of graduates. The faculty had hoped to raise the minimum grade-point average for admission to the school from 1.5 to 2.0, but the provost had vetoed that proposal as well as a limit on the number of transfers from the General College. Adams said another option, capping the number of junior-class transfers from other universities, was being considered.[23] The faculty had initiated a policy of restricting some courses to journalism majors to ensure that those students could enroll in the courses they needed.

The number of majors increased 79 percent in 10 years, from 164 in 1969 (135 undergraduate and 29 graduate) to 294 in 1979 (257 undergraduate and 37 graduate). Over the same time period, the number of degrees awarded increased 97 percent, from 62 in 1969 (48 undergraduate and 14 graduate) to 122 in 1979 (113 undergraduate and 9 graduate). The proportion of women students in the school increased from 48 percent to 65 percent, largely due to the university's decision to admit women as first-year students on the same basis as men beginning in 1965.[24] The enrollment in-

22. Amana, interview with the author, Nov. 20, 2007.
23. Adams to J. C. Morrow, Nov. 22, 1971, Provost's Records.
24. Pamela Dean, "Women on the Hill: A History of Women at the University of

crease in the school was fueled in part by what was called the "Watergate" effect or the "Woodward and Bernstein" effect. Some said the famous exploits of *Washington Post* reporters Robert Woodward and Carl Bernstein, who had helped uncover the Watergate scandal of the early 1970s, had boosted journalism school enrollments around the country, but enrollments had been increasing before the scandal broke.

In response to the growing number of majors, Adams sought ways to increase the number of classrooms and offices in Howell Hall. In 1973, when the school was given additional staff positions, Adams reduced the physical space of the dean's office to create new offices, and he reduced the size of the student lounge (room 204) to create a seminar room. In 1978, he inquired about the possibility of reducing the size of the building's auditorium to create additional classrooms and offices.[25] Provost Charles Morrow forwarded the request to the university's space committee, which turned it down because the university needed the 225-seat auditorium for large-enrollment classes.[26] By 1979, the school had to limit each graduating student to two guests at the school's commencement ceremony in the Howell Hall auditorium.[27]

The faculty grew in numbers and became much more diverse while Adams was dean. At the start of his term in 1969, the faculty consisted of nine white men: Adams, Walter Spearman, Joe Morrison, Stuart Sechriest, Neil Luxon, Ken Byerly, Jim Mullen, Donald Shaw, and Max McCombs. The faculty was much more diverse by 1979. Four white women—Margaret Blanchard in 1974, Carol Reuss in 1976, and Jane Brown and Jan Johnson in 1977—had joined the faculty, as had Amana, the first African-American, in 1979. Serving on the faculty with them in 1979 were 10 white men: Adams, Mullen, Shaw, Richard Cole, Tom Bowers, Jim Shumaker, Bill Chamberlin, Bob Stevenson, Rich Beckman, and Raleigh Mann.[28] In a 2007 interview, Adams recalled that faculty recruitment was easy in his time. When he was ready to hire someone, he called the dean or director of that person's school to ask about him or her. That good-old-boy network, Adams said, resulted in some "cotton-picking good people."[29]

North Carolina" (Chapel Hill: Division of Student Affairs, University of North Carolina at Chapel Hill, 1987). An electronic version of this booklet is available online at http://www.lib.unc.edu/ncc/ref/unc/womenonthehill.pdf (accessed Jan. 11, 2008).

25. Adams to J. C. Morrow, May 10, 1978, Provost's Records.

26. Claiborne Jones to Morrow, July 28, 1978, Provost's Records.

27. Faculty meeting minutes, School of Journalism, March 19, 1979.

28. The author remembers his first faculty meeting, in 1971, when 12 white men gathered around a conference table in the dean's office.

29. Adams, interview with the author, Aug. 21, 2007.

Spelling and Grammar Exam

Faculty members became concerned in the 1970s about students' weak writing skills, and they discussed ways to remedy the problem, believing that no other school or department on campus was doing anything about it. The faculty decided to experiment with the Purdue Placement Test in English and considered ways to incorporate such a test into the curriculum. When faculty members realized that the test was too long and too elementary, Cole and Bowers designed a shorter exam limited to spelling and grammar questions based on students' spelling and writing errors collected from faculty members. Upon a recommendation of a student-faculty committee, the faculty made the test part of the news writing course in the fall 1974 semester. A student on the committee wanted the passing score to be 80 percent, but the faculty settled on 70 percent. Students who did not attain that score received a grade of Incomplete in the course, and they had one year to pass the test and receive the course grade they had otherwise earned. If they did not pass the exam, they could not receive a grade higher than D for the course. In response to a proposal that the school offer a remedial course in spelling and grammar, Adams told the faculty that Professor Doris Betts of the English Department had volunteered to work with journalism students who needed help.[30]

In 1975, the faculty changed the requirement and made a score of 70 percent a requirement for graduation from the school instead of the completion of the news writing course. The requirement has remained a part of the school's curriculum, and no student has graduated since then without passing the exam. In a 2007 interview, Adams said he was still amazed that the university allowed the school to impose such a graduation requirement.[31]

When the new test was given for the first time, in the fall 1975 semester, 68 students took it, and 25 (37 percent) passed. Only 69 percent had passed it by the end of the semester. Professor Vermont Royster mentioned the exam and the results in his *Wall Street Journal* column, which was cited in a nationally syndicated column by James J. Kilpatrick. NBC News sent a reporter and crew to the school to film a report about the test, and it aired on NBC's national television news show on Feb. 1, 1975. Other schools of journalism followed the school's example, and some used the UNC test. The faculty soon realized students would need extra instruction to learn

30. Faculty meeting minutes, School of Journalism, Sept. 19, 1973.
31. Adams, interview with the author, Aug. 21, 2007.

Jim Shumaker administers the spelling and grammar exam in Howell 203 while being filmed by a crew from NBC News in January of 1975. *(School of Journalism and Mass Communication, UNC–Chapel Hill. Reprinted with permission.)*

the material to pass the test, and the school created a series of remedial sessions that came to be known as "Grammar Slammer."

Curriculum and Technology Changes

The school had traditionally focused on preparing students for careers in print journalism, but changing student interests in the 1970s led the school to create additional specializations in the undergraduate curriculum called "sequences." When the advertising sequence was created in 1971, the school began calling the existing newspaper-oriented specialization the "news-editorial" sequence. In 1974, Adams told the faculty that William Melson, chairman of the Department of Radio, Television, and Motion Pictures (RTVMP), wanted to strengthen that department by creating a broadcast journalism sequence that combined courses from RTVMP and the School of Journalism. Adams warned the faculty, however, to guard against a merger of the school and RTVMP, saying the school should remain newspaper-oriented.[32] That broadcast journalism sequence became

32. Faculty meeting minutes, School of Journalism, Oct. 21, 1974.

official in 1975, but it changed significantly 20 years later, when the school assumed sole responsibility for it.

The faculty modified the requirements for courses outside the school in 1977. Students had to complete at least one course each in economics, state and local government, U.S. government and politics, recent U.S. history, sociology, and psychology. They were also required to complete an outside concentration of at least nine credits in one academic subject outside the school.[33] Journalism 53, "News Writing," was increased from three credits to four.

Technology was altering the school as well. In 1973, Adams purchased three electric typewriters for the news editing classroom. Some newspapers were using electric typewriters to operate typesetting machines, and Adams thought it was important for students to have opportunities to practice on them. Four years later, he used $12,000 from the foundation to buy three CompuEdit video display terminals, a traffic box, a printer, and a spare-parts kit for the news editing lab. The terminals had a punched-paper tape input capability, and students could edit stories by keyboard.[34] The addition of that computer-editing system came only 15 years after Danielson had predicted—in the face of great skepticism—that computers would someday become commonplace in newspaper newsrooms. By 1975, faculty members and students could access the university's mainframe computer via a terminal in Howell Hall.

As Luxon and Danielson had done before him, Adams benefited from the largess of donors to the school's foundation. While Adams was dean, from 1969 to 1979, annual contributions to the foundation hovered around $30,000 until 1975, when they jumped to $45,000, and they averaged approximately $34,000. Expenditures of foundation funds by the school during that period increased from just under $20,000 to slightly more than $50,000, averaging almost $30,000. Adams spent a total of $27,245 in foundation funds in 1975, including $17,500 for scholarships and assistantships, $2,000 for school publications, $3,100 for educational materials, and $3,000 for faculty travel.

Schoolwide Accreditation

The school had two successful accreditation visits while Adams was dean, including a precedent-setting accreditation for the entire school. On Oct.

33. Debbie Barnes, "J School Approves Requirement Changes," *UNC Journalist*, December 1977, 6.

34. Laura Jeffress, "J-school Foundation Buys Video Display Terminals to Update News Editing Labs," *UNC Journalist*, February 1977, 1.

25–26, 1971, a team visited the school and recommended reaccreditation. Data in the report showed that the school's annual budget was $214,250, of which $146,250 was spent on salaries; enrollment was shown as 173 undergraduates and 19 graduate students. The report lauded the school for strong administrative support from the university, mutual respect between the dean and the faculty, excellent media relationships, unusually effective encouragement of faculty research, excellent student record keeping, excellent facilities, high faculty morale, unshakable student morale, and strict adherence to stated degree requirements. The team also said the faculty needed to devote more thought to photojournalism in the curriculum and publishing outlets for students.[35]

Adams was a member of the Accrediting Council of the American Council on Education for Journalism, and he was chair of the council's Accrediting Committee in 1977. At the time, accreditation was bestowed on a sequence-by-sequence basis, meaning a school could have one sequence accredited and another not accredited. At a meeting when the Accrediting Council discussed a new idea of granting accreditation on a schoolwide basis instead of for individual sequences, Adams volunteered the UNC program to be a test case for such a process. The visit occurred on March 16–17, 1978. Data from the report showed an annual budget of $395,000, including $250,000 for salaries and an enrollment of 244 undergraduates and 23 graduate students. The team report commended the school for having strong administrative support from the university, a faculty that accorded the highest respect to the dean, highly supportive newspapers, high student opinion of advising and faculty access, high student and faculty morale, and high-quality master's degree students. The team also expressed concern about low levels of professional experience on the faculty and unevenness in promotion policies for faculty members with professional backgrounds. The major negative aspect of the team's review was what it called the "rather poorly conceived" broadcast journalism program. All broadcast journalism courses were taught in RTVMP, and students who spoke to members of the visit team were "harshly critical" of those courses. The team said the school should either make broadcast journalism a first-class program or drop it. If it was to be offered, it belonged in the School of Journalism.

The team recommended accreditation for the undergraduate news-editorial and advertising sequences, as well as the M.A. news-editorial program. Under the new policy, that meant the entire school was accred-

35. Milton Gross to J. Carlyle Sitterson, April 26, 1972, Chancellor's Records: Nelson Ferebee Taylor Series #40023, University Archives, University of North Carolina at Chapel Hill Library.

ited, and for one year, the UNC School of Journalism could boast that it was the only accredited journalism school in the country. The report said the experiment in schoolwide accreditation was greatly aided by the "extremely high quality and effective leadership" of the school.[36] Holt McPherson wrote to Chancellor Ferebee Taylor to praise the report, saying he would share the news with the NCPA in July. He especially wanted to report what the team said about the School of Journalism Foundation, and McPherson reminded Taylor that he had headed the foundation since its beginning in 1947. He said he had visited many accredited schools but did not think he had ever seen a finer report than the one about UNC.[37]

Adams Steps Down

Adams was reappointed to a second five-year term as dean in 1974, and McPherson had hoped that Chancellor Taylor could persuade Adams to continue in the deanship after 1979, saying Adams had handled it "more effectively than any other dean yet."[38] Near the end of his second term, on May 25, 1978, Adams told Provost Charles Morrow that he did not want to serve another term and wanted to be replaced at the earliest possible time, preferably before July 1, 1979. Morrow concluded that Adams was serious, but he told Taylor it would not be practical to find a replacement so soon.[39] Adams made his decision official in a letter to Taylor on June 1, saying he wanted to return to full-time teaching and research.[40] He broke the news to the faculty on June 19, saying the main reason for the timing of his departure was that Mildred Stout would be retiring as the school's business manager in August 1979, and Adams thought the new dean should have a chance to work with her before she left.[41]

Taylor appointed a search committee chaired by Gordon Cleveland of the Department of Political Science.[42] The committee included four fac-

36. Milton Gross to N. Ferebee Taylor, May 3, 1978, Chancellor's Records: Taylor Series.

37. McPherson to Taylor, June 2, 1978, Chancellor's Records: Taylor Series.

38. McPherson to Taylor, June 2, 1978, Chancellor's Records: Taylor Series.

39. Morrow to Taylor, May 26, 1978, Chancellor's Records: Taylor Series.

40. Adams to Taylor, June 1, 1978, Chancellor's Records: Taylor Series.

41. Faculty meeting minutes, School of Journalism, June 19, 1978.

42. Search committees were not used when Danielson (1964) and Adams (1969) were selected; the chancellor and provost made the decisions after consulting with members of the school's faculty. By 1979, the university's commitment to affirmative action in hiring mandated the use of formal procedures, including search committees, in the hiring of faculty members and deans.

ulty members from the school: Reuss, Shaw, Shumaker, and Stevenson. Two other UNC faculty members were also on the committee: Robert Headen of the School of Business Administration and Elizabeth Czech of RTVMP. Two students were selected: Deborah Jane Moose, an undergraduate, and Robert Friedman, a graduate student. The NCPA was represented by its president, James H. Parker of the *Sampson Independent*. Taylor asked the committee to give him no fewer than two and no more than three names in alphabetical order.[43]

In a letter to the provost, Mullen said his discussions with his faculty colleagues had led him to conclude there was unanimous agreement that the next dean should come from the present faculty.[44] Nevertheless, after interviewing two internal candidates (Cole and Bowers), the search committee expanded the search beyond the faculty.[45] Four months later, its deliberations concluded, the committee submitted three names (in alphabetical order) to the chancellor: Bowers, Cole, and Keith Sanders of the School of Journalism of the University of Missouri.[46] Three weeks later, Taylor told Cole he had been selected to succeed Adams on July 1, 1979.[47]

43. Taylor to members of the search committee, Aug. 24, 1978, Chancellor's Records: Taylor Series.

44. Mullen to Morrow, July 24, 1978, Chancellor's Records: Taylor Series.

45. Cleveland to Taylor, Oct. 6, 1978, Chancellor's Records: Taylor Series.

46. Cleveland to Taylor, Feb. 26, 1979, Chancellor's Records: Taylor Series.

47. Taylor to Cole, March 21, 1979, Chancellor's Records: Taylor Series.

11. Richard Cole—New Programs and a New Name

Richard Cole, a 37-year-old Texas native who had joined the faculty of the School of Journalism in 1971, became its fifth dean on July 1, 1979. He had received his bachelor's and master's degrees from the University of Texas and his Ph.D. from the University of Minnesota. Cole had worked at newspapers in Mexico City and London and taught one year at West Virginia University before coming to UNC. By the time he left the dean's office 26 years later in 2005, the school had changed in ways that made it almost unrecognizable in comparison to when he started. Cole's vision, unwavering dedication, and legendary fundraising accomplishments transformed the school's curriculum and programs, increased the size of the faculty and staff, moved the school to a new and much larger home, and gave it international prominence.

Changes in Curriculum and Focus

Cole became dean 70 years after the first journalism course was taught at the university. During that time, the curriculum had evolved from a limited focus on newspapers to encompass other forms of mass commu-

1. Cole, interview with the author, March 25, 2008.

Richard Cole, dean of the School of Journalism and Mass Communication, 1979–2005, transformed the school by raising millions of dollars in private contributions and moving it to Carroll Hall in 1999. *(e.noonan IMAGES [www.eileennoonan. com]. Reprinted with permission.)*

nication. Early journalism courses in the Department of English and later the Department of Journalism and the School of Journalism concentrated on newspapers and reflected the extant job opportunities for graduates and the backgrounds of the faculty members, all of whom had newspaper experience. Most of the early journalism courses had a practical approach; students learned skills they would need if they were to work at a newspaper. When the department was created in 1924, two of its six courses were not skills courses—a course about public opinion and one about comparative newspaper editorial policies and the role of the newspaperman and the public. In 1937, Phillips Russell taught the first journalism history course, which was related to journalism but did not teach a journalism skill. In 1953, James Paul of the Institute of Government taught the school's first press law course, and Neil Luxon taught the first course about the social responsibilities of the media. The newspaper-oriented courses formed what later became known as the school's news-editorial sequence. The first graduate-level courses appeared in 1955.

Expansion into advertising began in 1941, when J. Roy Parker taught the first newspaper advertising course, and an advertising copywriting course was added in 1950. The advertising curriculum changed significantly after Jim Mullen arrived in 1959, and it became a separate sequence in 1971, when Tom Bowers joined the faculty to teach in the advertising sequence. The addition of John Sweeney in 1981 came in response to a growing number of advertising students. Sweeney, who had worked at a Chicago advertising agency, eventually expanded the school's curriculum into sports marketing and communication.

Public relations instruction had begun in 1926, when Robert Madry taught two courses in educational publicity while he was head of the uni-

Richard Cole (left) prepares to assume the deanship of the School of Journalism from Jack Adams in 1979. Mildred Stout, the school's business manager, looks on. *(School of Journalism and Mass Communication, UNC–Chapel Hill. Reprinted with permission.)*

versity's news bureau. Students in the 1960s who expressed interest in public relations work were told to work for newspapers first. Ken Sanford, who earned his B.A. from the school in 1954 and was in the second class of M.A. students in 1958, recalled Dean Luxon's reaction when Sanford told him he wanted to work in public relations. "That's fine," Luxon said, "but promise me you will work for a newspaper for five years before you do." Sanford worked for the *Winston-Salem Journal* for five years and then had a distinguished career in public relations and was inducted into the North Carolina Public Relations Hall of Fame.[2]

Public relations instruction began in earnest when Carol Reuss joined the faculty in 1976 after working for business magazines and getting her Ph.D. at the University of Iowa. In 2007, she remembered coming to UNC for her job interview, when she landed at the small Raleigh-Durham airport and took narrow Highway 54 to Chapel Hill. Because there were so few women on the faculty, she ate many lunches with male colleagues and made friends that way. Reuss said the female secretaries in the school sometimes brought punch and cookies for students during final exam

2. Sanford, interview with the author, Oct. 5, 2007.

week and expected female faculty members to do the same—until Reuss told them otherwise.[3]

Reuss knew the school had been newspaper-oriented, so she did not push a public relations program. The faculty anticipated negative reactions from newspaper people when the first public relations course was created in 1980, so they called the first course "Business and Organizational Communication," but later changed it to "Principles of Public Relations." The faculty added other public relations courses, and in 1982 public relations became an optional specialization of the news-editorial sequence. The faculty believed that public relations professionals should have news-editorial skills and needed to know how the news media operated. Public relations was made a separate sequence in 1991 and eventually became the largest sequence in the school. Dulcie Straughan, who had worked in public relations in Virginia before receiving her Ph.D. from the school, joined the faculty in 1987 and became head of the public relations sequence when Reuss retired. Straughan also became associate dean and senior associate dean of the school.

Stuart Sechriest joined the faculty in 1946 and taught news editing, and he created the first news photography course. When Rich Beckman came to the school in January 1978 after Sechriest's retirement and entered his Howell Hall office for the first time, he found two Speed Graphic cameras, two viewfinder cameras, and a 35mm Nikon-F camera still in its shipping container. Students in the early photography courses had to buy their own equipment or use cameras owned by the school or borrowed from Canon, the camera manufacturer. Technological requirements for the early color-photography courses were especially challenging. Processing color transparency film required a precise water temperature, and Beckman bought aquarium thermometers at a pet store to monitor the temperature. The photography program was darkroom-based while it was in Howell Hall, but it had become almost completely digital by the time it moved to Carroll Hall in 1999. Beckman was involved with digital photography from its early days, and eventually the school got its first Macintosh computer for processing images. From there, Beckman recalled, the school's adoption of new technologies was a "windstorm down the digital path."[4] He and his colleagues expanded the number of photojournalism courses to include color and advanced photojournalism, and they added courses in graphic design and publication design. Visual communication became a separate sequence in 1991, and the school added a multimedia Web and CD-ROM

3. Reuss, interview with the author, Aug. 2, 2007.
4. Beckman, interview with the author, June 2, 2008.

production option to that sequence in 1998. Students who completed the courses in that option learned to integrate text, photographs, video, audio, and animation into CD-ROMs and Web sites.[5] By the time Beckman retired in 2008, the school's multimedia program was considered the best in the world.

The broadcast journalism sequence also changed significantly—after the school's name was changed. As the school broadened its focus into career fields beyond newspapers, Cole thought a new name was appropriate. A faculty committee recommended in 1990 that the school change its name to the School of Journalism and Mass Communication (JOMC) to reflect the diversity and direction of the program, and the faculty approved the recommendation with only two dissenting votes.[6] Cole explained to alumni that the school was not trying to expand into new territory or to attract students from other majors. By 1990, he said, 70 percent of the school's undergraduates were in sequences other than news-editorial. He was also careful to explain that he was proposing "communication" without an "s" because it was a more encompassing term than "communications."[7] Faculty members in the Department of Radio, Television, and Motion Pictures (RTVMP), who thought the new name would be confusing and detrimental to their department, opposed the change.[8] Cole and the journalism faculty prevailed, however, and the change became effective Nov. 1, 1990.[9] The titles of the school's graduate degrees were changed to Master of Arts in Mass Communication and Doctor of Philosophy in Mass Communication.

Evolution of Broadcast Journalism

The school's other sequence, broadcast journalism, was launched in 1975. That sequence changed significantly because of two developments in the 1990s: the dissolution of RTVMP and the school's move to Carroll Hall. The first courses in radio journalism had been added to the Department of Journalism curriculum in 1943, and television news courses were added

5. Boris Hartl, "School Expands its Media Vision," *UNC Journalist*, Fall 1998, 10–11.

6. Faculty meeting minutes, School of Journalism, Jan. 10, 1990.

7. Cole, "Why the School of Journalism Wants to Become the School of Journalism and Mass Communication," *JAFA News*, Summer 1990, 6–7.

8. Gorham Kindem to Richard Cole, Feb. 16, 1988, Chancellor's Records: Paul Hardin Series #40025, University Archives, University of North Carolina at Chapel Hill Library.

9. Paul Hardin to C. D. Spangler, Oct. 26, 1990, Chancellor's Records: Hardin Series.

in 1955, but RTVMP eventually assumed responsibility for all broadcast journalism courses. In 1975, a cooperative effort with RTVMP allowed students in the School of Journalism to take the RTVMP courses in broadcast journalism, and the school created a broadcast journalism sequence that combined journalism and RTVMP courses. However, even as early as 1963, Dean Neil Luxon had expressed misgivings about RTVMP,[10] and an accrediting site-visit team had reached the same conclusion in 1978.

By 1992, concerns about the situation in RTVMP had spread to higher administrators within the university. Provost Richard McCormick wrote to Stephen Birdsall, dean of the College of Arts and Sciences, about proposals that Birdsall and others were considering for the future of the "often troubled" RTVMP department. He told Birdsall that Cole and the JOMC faculty had a vested interest in the future of RTVMP because of the broadcast journalism sequence, and he told Birdsall to keep him (McCormick) informed of all plans because of their impact on JOMC.[11] An external review committee appointed by Birdsall in 1993 concluded that RTVMP students were poorly served by a faculty that was "too fragmented and lacked vision." The committee based its recommendations on the assumption that there were two legitimate intellectual traditions for studying the mass media: a pragmatic or industry-based approach (which it said was already well-represented in JOMC) and a critical, liberal arts approach (which it said should continue in the College of Arts and Sciences). Consequently, the committee recommended that RTVMP be "disestablished" and that JOMC be given sole responsibility for teaching broadcast journalism. It also recommended that most RTVMP faculty members be transferred to the Department of Speech Communication, which would be renamed the Department of Communication Studies.[12]

The recommendation drew scores of protests from RTVMP alumni opposed to the recommendations and the change in the department's mission. E. Reese Felts Jr., a member of the RTVMP class of 1952, said he had included a large gift to RTVMP in his will, but he said he would "disestablish" that bequest if the department were abolished.[13] One protest came from the president of the Motion Picture Association of America, almost certainly at the request of a UNC alumnus in the motion picture indus-

10. Luxon to Ralph Casey, Nov. 2, 1963, Norval Neil Luxon Papers #4585, Southern Historical Collection, University of North Carolina at Chapel Hill Library.
11. McCormick to Birdsall, Nov. 23, 1992, Chancellor's Records: Hardin Series.
12. "Report of the External Review Committee of the Department of Radio, Television and Motion Pictures," March 10, 1993, Chancellor's Records: Hardin Series.
13. Felts to Paul Hardin, April 12, 1993, Chancellor's Records: Hardin Series.

try. Jack Valenti's letter said UNC was a great American university, and "beneath its canopy ought to be as fine a school of the mystery and magic of film as is possible to assemble."[14] The protests were to no avail, however, and Hardin announced on July 19, 1993, that he had adopted the external committee's recommendation to eliminate RTVMP. Felts followed through on his threat and became a major benefactor of the School of Journalism and Mass Communication, even designating funds to provide coffee in the school's mailroom, a practice that continues to the present.

As a result of the elimination of RTVMP, JOMC assumed responsibility for broadcast journalism and video production courses. Two professors transferred from RTVMP to the school: Richard Elam in 1993 and Richard Simpson in 1994. Professor John Bittner had transferred from RTVMP at his own request in 1991 and headed the broadcast sequence until his death in 2002, and Professor Anne Johnston transferred to the school in 1993 after winning a sex discrimination claim against RTVMP.[15]

The additional faculty members and the school's move to Carroll Hall in 1999 made it possible for the school to expand its broadcast journalism sequence, which had been renamed "electronic communication" in 1994. Bittner and Simpson created a core of broadcast courses in writing, reporting, and production. Additional space in Carroll Hall made it possible to build a television studio and production facilities, and students started producing a weekly newscast, "Carolina Week," on Feb. 2, 2000, under the leadership of Simpson and Professor Charlie Tuggle. The school's broadcasting efforts expanded in 2004 to two 30-minute television news programs a week and a news magazine show on radio. The broadcast journalism program quickly established a reputation for excellence and has won scores of national awards.

As the school met the needs of an expanding student population with new sequences and expanded course offerings, dramatic changes occurred in the percentages of students in the undergraduate sequences between 1980 and 2005. Figure 11.1 shows that the news-editorial sequence—the largest sequence in 1980, with 64 percent of the students—became smaller percentagewise when students had more choices. By 1985, advertising had surpassed news-editorial in size, and advertising and public relations combined included more than 50 percent of the students in the school. Public relations continued to grow, and it became the largest sequence in 2005 as advertising leveled off to about one-fourth of the students. The advertis-

14. Valenti to Paul Hardin, May 4, 1993, Chancellor's Records: Hardin Series.

15. Christine Tatum, "Professor Finds New Home at School," *UNC Journalist*, May 1993, 3.

Figure 11.1 Percentages of Students in Undergraduate Sequences, School of Journalism and Mass Communication, 1980–2005

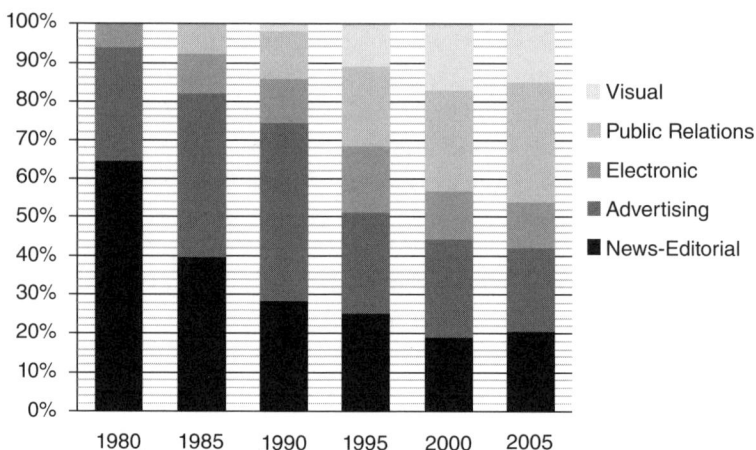

ing and public relations sequences tended to attract more female students than the other sequences, and the percentage of women in the school has remained at about 75 percent.

The changes in the school's undergraduate and graduate curriculum during Cole's term as dean are reflected in the number of courses that were offered. In 1980, the school offered 42 courses, including 13 for undergraduates, 18 for advanced undergraduates and graduate students, and 11 strictly for graduate students. In 2005, the total had increased more than 150 percent to 106 courses, including 17 for undergraduates, 58 for advanced undergraduates and graduate students, and 31 strictly for graduate students.

Graduate Program

The school awarded its first master's degree in 1957 and its first doctorate in 1967. The graduate program remained small relative to the undergraduate program and did not surpass 30 students until 1978. Graduate enrollment then grew steadily until it surpassed 100 in 1995. That was also the year the Park Foundation of Ithaca, N.Y., pledged $5.5 million for the first five years of the Roy H. Park Fellowship program to give financial support to Ph.D. and M.A. students, beginning in 1997.[16] Roy Hampton Park was

16. Jennifer Palcher, "$5.5 Million Grant is Largest School has ever Seen," *UNC Journalist*, Fall 1996, 13.

Roy Hampton Park was a North Carolina native who built Park Communications into a media empire that included newspapers, radio and television stations, and outdoor billboards in 24 states. Through the Park Foundation created at his death in 1993 and the subsequently created Triad Foundation, the Park family is a major benefactor of the School of Journalism and Mass Communication. *(School of Journalism and Mass Communication, UNC–Chapel Hill. Reprinted with permission.)*

a graduate of N.C. State University who, by the time he died in 1993, had amassed ownership of seven television stations, 21 radio stations, and 144 newspapers in 24 states. Combined with an outdoor advertising company, the Park media empire reached 25 percent of the American public. His son said in 2008 that his father had always been interested in education, and his family wanted to continue his legacy with the Park Foundation.[17]

The first Park Fellows in the master's program received a $10,000 stipend plus tuition, fees, and health insurance for each of two years and $4,000 for travel. The first Park Ph.D. students received a $17,500 stipend plus tuition, fees, and insurance for each of three years and $6,000 for expenses. (The fellowship amounts have increased since the program was launched.) The Park program increased the number of graduate students in the school and made UNC the best-funded program in the country, attracting outstanding students to the school. Graduate students from the school have consistently ranked first in the number of scholarly research papers presented at national and regional meetings of journalism education associations.

In 2003, Triad Foundation, headed by Roy H. Park, split off from the

17. Roy H. Park , interview with the author, July 14, 2008.

Roy H. Park of the Triad Foundation continued his father's exceptional support of the School of Journalism and Mass Communication. *(Jon Reis/ jonreis.com. Reprinted with permission.)*

Park Foundation, but it continued to make regular contributions to UNC's Park Fellows program. (The Triad Foundation's support for the graduate program is the equivalent of income from a $20 million endowment, based on an assumed 5 percent annual yield.) As of August 2008, the Park and Triad Foundations had given and pledged to the school more than $20 million, in addition to $1 million for the Park Library in Carroll Hall.

Cole scored another coup in 1995 when he secured funding ($216,000 for the first year) for the Freedom Forum Ph.D. program from the Freedom Forum, a foundation that had been affiliated with the Gannett Company. The program was designed to help veteran news professionals prepare for college teaching by giving them enough financial support to allow them to be full-time students and complete the school's regular Ph.D. program in 24–27 months, compared to the usual 36 months or more. Freedom Forum Fellows received an annual stipend of up to $50,000 each, plus tuition, fees, and money for research.[18] The first four Freedom Forum Fellows, in 1995, were Joseph Campbell, 42, a staff writer for the *Hartford*

18. "New Freedom Forum Program Brings Journalists from the Newsroom into the Classroom," *UNC Journalist*, Summer 1995, 5.

(Conn.) *Courant*; Frank Fee Jr., 52, copy desk chief at the *Democrat and Chronicle* in Rochester, N.Y.; Tamela Hultman, 48, executive editor of Africa News Service; and Alice Bonner, 46, former reporter and editor at the *Washington Post*. In a letter of congratulations to Campbell, Everette Dennis, executive director of the Freedom Forum, explained why the Freedom Forum had partnered with the school: "North Carolina has long been the premiere school in the field where first-class scholarship lives alongside first-class professional practice."[19] The program ended in 2002, however, when the Freedom Forum eliminated most of its educational funding to build its $450 million Newseum in Washington, D.C.

Adopting Technology

The school had to keep pace with rapidly changing technologies in communication during Cole's tenure. In addition to funds from private donors, Cole used money from UNC's student technology fee, which was collected from all students at the university and allocated to individual schools and departments. (In some years, the school's allocation has exceeded $300,000.) Cole and the faculty ensured that the school's com-

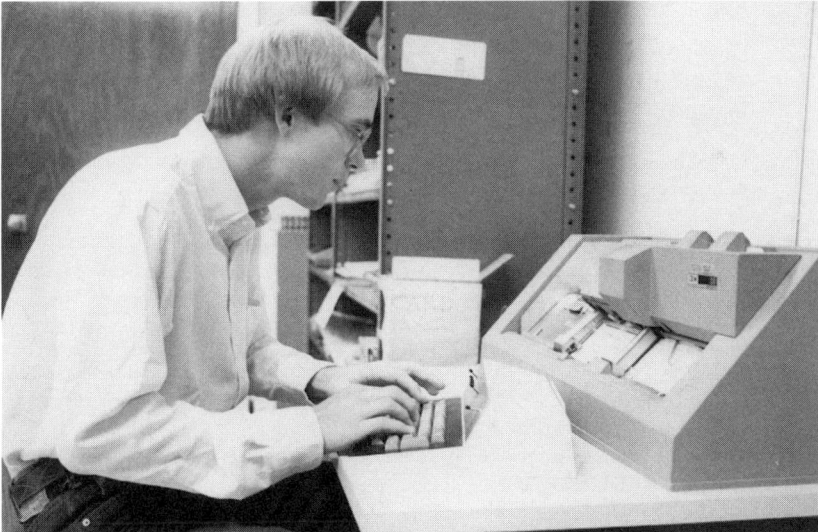

Ph.D. student Walker Smith prepares IBM data cards in Howell Hall, ca. 1985. *(School of Journalism and Mass Communication, UNC–Chapel Hill. Reprinted with permission.)*

19. Dennis to Campbell, April 14, 1995, Provost's Records #40039, University Archives, University of North Carolina at Chapel Hill Library.

Table 11.1 Timetable of Selected Technology Adoptions in
the School of Journalism and Mass Communication

1973 Electric typewriters purchased for the news-editing classroom.

1975 Computer terminals for access to university mainframe computer installed in Howell Hall.

1977 Three CompuEdit video display terminals purchased for use in news-editing courses.

1981 R. J. Reynolds Industries Center for Editing and Graphics created with 17 video display terminals and a phototypesetter.

Professor Phil Meyer teaches "Precision Journalism" for the first time. Some students write SPSS programs, enter them onto punched cards with an IBM keypunch machine in the graduate student lounge, and take them to Phillips Hall for batch processing. Typing classrooms on the first floor of Howell Hall are rewired to accommodate electric typewriters.

1982 The school's first three personal computers (Commodore 8032s) arrive and are used as terminals to send data and programs to Phillips Hall or the Triangle Universities Computing Center.

1986 Howell 201 is converted to a Macintosh lab, and Howell 107 becomes the Knight Advertising Center, with networked IBM PCs.

1987 Howell 106 is converted to an IBM computer lab in 1987, and Macintosh MacIIs are installed in Howell 06 for graphics and editing courses. DOS versions of SPSS and SAS are installed on PCs for data analysis.

1990 In 1990, Phil Meyer and Judy Woods of the School of Information and Library Science teach an information-gathering course.

1992 Ranjeev Singh is hired as the school's first computer systems administrator, when the school had four computer labs and no computers connected to the Internet.

1993 Librarian Barbara Semonche, who had helped Meyer teach database journalism courses, becomes one of the first people in the school to have an e-mail address.

1994 The school puts its first home page on the World Wide Web. Archived versions of early sites are available at http://web.archive.org/web/*/http://sunsite.unc.edu/jomc/.

1995   Some teachers begin teaching students how to create material for the
        Web, and Paul Jones, a computer expert at UNC, is hired to teach
        "Cyberpublishing and Cybercasting." The school's first e-mail distribution
        lists (listservs) go online, the *UNC Journalist* makes its first online
        appearance, and Professor Rich Beckman begins teaching students about
        digital scanning and printing. Professor Debashis Aikat, a "media futurist,"
        is hired to create and teach a course called "Electronic Information Sources,"
        in which students learn to find information on the Internet and create their
        own Web pages. Professor Bob Stevenson uses a program called Eventware
        to allow students in his class to communicate by computer with students
        and journalists in Chile, Germany, Iceland, Lebanon, and Kuwait.

1996   Ryan Thornburg, a student in the school, founds *The Fifth Estate* as
        UNC–Chapel Hill's first student-run online magazine. Frank Biocca teaches
        "Multimedia Design and Electronic Publishing."

1997   A group of faculty members receives a $100,000 grant for a project called
        "Enabling Students to Put Video and Audio Content on the World Wide
        Web." Debashis Aikat teaches the first online course for credit, "Introduction
        to Internet Issues and Concepts."

1999   The school moves to Carroll Hall and greatly expands the number of
        computer classrooms.

2003   The school introduces a distance education graduate-level certificate
        program in "Technology and Communication."

munication technology was as up to date as possible. Table 11.1, compiled
from a variety of sources, including a 1995 article in the *UNC Journalist*,[20]
summarizes some of the major steps in the adoption of new technologies
in the school. In addition to those uses of technology, all faculty and staff
members regularly received upgraded office computers.

Special Programs

The school also added many activities outside of classroom instruction as
Cole introduced a variety of special programs to enhance the school and its
service to media professionals. One of the first was the Journalism Alumni
and Friends Association (JAFA), which was formed on Jan. 26, 1980, with
Reed Sarratt as the first president.[21] Sarratt, a 1937 graduate of the Depart-

20. Richard Cole, "A National Pacesetter Instead of Roadkill," *UNC Journalist,*
Summer 1995, 2.
21. An earlier attempt to organize the school's alumni occurred on Nov. 9, 1968,

ment of Journalism, was executive director of the Southern Newspaper Publishers Association. JAFA's activities had been launched with a Homecoming Weekend reception for alumni on Nov. 10, 1979, prior to a football game against Clemson University.

The North Carolina Journalism Hall of Fame was created to honor individuals who had made outstanding and career-long contributions to journalism. Honorees had to have been born in North Carolina, educated in the state, or distinctively identified with North Carolina. The first banquet for honorees was on April 12, 1981, and Halls of Fame for advertising and public relations were added in 1988. The school's Board of Visitors was created in 1988–89 by Cole and Gene Roberts of the *Philadelphia Inquirer*. The board is a means for involving a variety of alumni and other media professionals more closely in the school. Its name was changed to the Board of Advisers in 2008.

The Program on Southern Politics, the Media and Public Life (later called the Program on Public Life) was launched on March 1, 1997, as part of the Center for the Study of the American South. It was designed to bring together politicians, journalists, policy-makers, and others. The program's director, Ferrel Guillory, joined the faculty after having been a political writer for the Raleigh *News and Observer* for more than 20 years. The school began a continuing education program of workshops and other instruction for media professionals in 1998. The first workshop was about newspaper design, followed by programs that year on North Carolina media law, trends in photojournalism, the North Carolina General Assembly, and integrated marketing communication. Other topics have included an annual multimedia boot camp, business journalism, natural disasters, and energy issues. Professor Tom Linden, a physician, created a master's program in medical journalism in 2000, and Professor John Sweeney created a sports communication program in 2001 with a $1 million gift from an anonymous donor. Lecturer Jock Lauterer started the Carolina Community Media Project when he joined the faculty in 2001. In addition to a course on community journalism, the project has featured an annual "Newspaper Academy" in the school and summertime "Johnny Appleseed" visits by Lauterer to community newspapers throughout the state.

The Carolina Business News Initiative started by Professor Chris Roush in 2003 has included regular courses in the school, summer internships, and workshops for journalists. Professor Deb Aikat taught the school's

---

when approximately 25 people met to discuss the formation of an alumni association. That attempt was reported in the minutes of a faculty meeting on Nov. 22, 1968, but it was not mentioned again.

first online course for credit, "Introduction to Internet Issues and Concepts," in 1997. It had 15 students from New Jersey, Florida, Kentucky, and North Carolina. By 2008, other courses were offered online, including "News Writing," "Professional Issues and Ethics," and "Public Records Research." The graduate faculty added a certificate program of four courses in Technology and Communication in 2003, and by 2008 more than 41 students had completed the program.

International Activities

One of Cole's teaching and research interests had been international communication, and he and other faculty members expanded the school's international presence in significant ways. Several faculty members traveled to many countries to teach, do research, and offer guidance to journalism educators and professionals. Those efforts led to several exchange programs and other cooperative efforts that benefited students from UNC and the other countries. Early international activities included Rich Beckman's summer multimedia courses in Chile and South Africa and Robert Stevenson's participation in the University of Dayton's summer program in London. Stevenson became the driving force behind many international activities, and an article in the *UNC Journalist* called him the school's link to the world's media. His reputation as a scholar and a personal host in Chapel Hill attracted many international students to the school's graduate program. Several students temporarily lived in his home until they could find a place to live, and he hosted many dinners and other events for international students.[22] After Stevenson's death in 2006, a bequest from his estate and contributions from alumni and friends created a large fund to enhance the school's support of graduate students.

In 1994, the school received a $227,000 grant from the International Media Fund for a cooperative program with the School of Journalism at Ural State University in Yekaterinburg, Russia, 900 miles east of Moscow. Ural State had one of the most prestigious journalism schools in Russia and a reputation for training aggressive journalists. Its dean and several faculty members visited UNC, and UNC faculty members went to Ural State to visit with students, faculty members, and university officials. Professor Richard Elam taught broadcast journalism there for an entire semester in spring 1995 and helped Ural State establish a computer classroom. The school also participated in a university linkage program with Moscow State University of International Relations (MGIMO).

22. Robin Harp, "The School's Traveling Man," *UNC Journalist*, December 1989, 3.

A grant in 1995 from the John D. and Catherine T. MacArthur Foundation brought three professors from the University of Havana and two Cuban journalists to the United States. Cole taught a course about Mexican and Cuban media several times and escorted students and others to those countries until U.S. government travel restrictions made the Cuban visits impractical. When Cole retired in 2005, a visa restriction prevented Dr. Gladys Fernandez of the University of Havana from coming to his retirement celebration, but she sent a message expressing the "great honor and gratitude" that Cuban professors, journalists, and students felt for Cole and his contributions to Cuban journalism.[23] Starting in 1995, the school was part of a university effort, funded by the U.S. Agency for International Development, to rebuild the University of Asmara in Eritrea. Faculty members visited Eritrea or taught there, and several Eritrean students studied at the school. Professor Cathy Packer taught at the University of Tirana in Albania in spring 1993.[24] Professor Xinshu Zhao has guided efforts by several faculty members to enhance joint programs with Chinese universities and created opportunities for students from the school to participate in media coverage of the 2008 Olympics in Beijing.

Many international students have come to the school for degree and nondegree programs. A report prepared for the 2003 accreditation visit showed that between 1995 and 2001, the school hosted more than 50 students from 24 countries, including seven each from Korea and Taiwan, and four each from Eritrea and Germany. During the same period, more than 35 visiting international scholars came from 23 countries, including five from Korea and four from Germany. They included academics who wanted to spend a semester or year at UNC doing research, journalists and faculty members who were selected for professional-development programs, and senior scholars.

Several exchange programs and other international projects were established during the same period, including one with the Pontifical Catholic University in Santiago, Chile. An exchange program with the Instituto Tecnológico y Estudios Superiores de Monterrey (also known as Monterrey Tech), in Mexico City, brought three students to the UNC program. A special Ph.D. program was developed by the school and approved by the UNC Graduate School for Monterrey Tech faculty members. It combined in-residence study with video conference courses and visits by UNC faculty members to Mexico. Several Korean students earned doctorates in

23. Fernandez, quoted in *Carolina Innovator*, the printed program for the Richard Cole retirement dinner, April 29, 2005, 1.

24. Julie Corbin, "Mission Abroad," *UNC Journalist*, Winter 1995, 12–15.

the school, and the school has established several formal relationships with Korean and Chinese universities.

Impact of Growth

The growing reputation of the school, additions to the curriculum, and school activities led to tremendous expansion in student enrollment and the size of the faculty and staff. Journalism–mass communication programs throughout the nation saw large increases in enrollment between 1975 and 2000, and North Carolina was no exception. Cole encouraged growth and was able to persuade university officials that increased enrollment and activities deserved to be matched by increases in the number of faculty and staff members, and he had a steady string of successful pleas for additional faculty and staff positions.

The school occasionally met resistance to enrollment growth, however, and the faculty had to raise admission standards for students coming from the General College (freshmen and sophomores). In 1981, the faculty raised the minimum grade-point average for admission from 1.75 (with 2.0 equal to a C and 4.0 equal to an A) to 2.0. In two responses to Cole's requests for additional funding and faculty positions for the school, Provost Samuel Williamson suggested that the school should tighten its admission standards even more to reduce the number of majors.[25] The faculty responded by raising the GPA required for admission from 2.0 to 2.2 in 1987, to 2.4 in 1990, and to 2.7 in 2002.

Table 11.2 shows that from 1980 to 2005, the number of majors in the school increased almost 200 percent, from 294 to 876. The enrollment peak was 989 in 2002, when the school had 882 undergraduates and 107 graduate students. A surge in enrollment from 1999 (842) to 2002 coincided with the school's first years in Carroll Hall, when the new facilities probably attracted more students. Enrollment in the graduate program increased from 37 in 1980 to a peak of 108 (a 192 percent increase) in 2000, before it dropped to 90 in 2005. Much of that growth can be attributed to the creation of the Park Fellowship program. For several years, the school had one of the largest academic programs on campus, counting premajors (freshmen and sophomores) through graduate students.

The size of the faculty and staff had to grow to keep up with expanding enrollment and new programs. The number of faculty members increased 221 percent, from 14 in 1980 to 45 in 2005. In 1980, the school had approximately five staff members to support faculty members and school

25. Williamson to Cole, July 31, 1986, and March 21, 1988, Provost's Records.

Table 11.2 Enrollment and Faculty Size, School of Journalism
and Mass Communication, 1979–2005

	1980	1985	1990	1995	2000	2005
Majors	294	464	565	586	912	876
Undergraduate	257	416	502	486	804	786
Graduate	37	48	63	100	108	90
Faculty	14	19	25	32	28	45

Source: Office of the University Registrar, UNC–Chapel Hill.

programs, including a business manager, a financial secretary, typists, and a part-time librarian. (Before it became the School of Journalism in 1950, the Department of Journalism did not have a secretary, and a faculty member was designated as the departmental secretary.) By 2005, the staff had increased to more than 20 full-time and several part-time employees and student assistants, including three staff members in development and alumni affairs, three to support the school's computers and computer networks, and three for executive and distance education. When Cole became dean, he created the first associate dean position; by 2005, the school had a senior associate dean and two associate deans.

Increasing minority presence among students and faculty was another goal for Cole and the school. One of the first African-American undergraduate students at UNC—Lester Carson—was a journalism major who entered the university as a junior transfer student in 1962. Karen Parker, the first female black undergraduate student at the university, was also a journalism major who enrolled in the school in 1963. Minority representation in the school grew slowly after that, reaching six students (5 percent of the school's 115 undergraduates) in 1968 and 30 students (9 percent of the school's 338 students) by 1980. In 2005, 140 (16 percent) of the school's 876 students were minorities.

Harry Amana, the first minority faculty member, had been hired in 1979; the second, Regina Sherard, was hired in 1983. Faculty diversity increased further with the hirings of Xinshu Zhao in 1990, Chuck Stone in 1991, Lucila Vargas in 1994, Debashis Aikat in 1995, Sri Kalyanaraman in 2002, and Napoleon Byars in 2005. The school created a number of programs designed to increase minority presence, including scholarships, recruitment efforts, and new courses. The school hosted a conference on "Minorities in Journalism" in 1981, participated in the Minority Professional-in-Residence program of the American Society of Newspaper Editors,[26] and joined the National Consortium for the Advancement of Minorities in Journalism in 1982. In 1985, the school was selected as a site for a Dow Jones Newspaper Fund minority training seminar, and in 1990, the school supported the formation of a new student organization in the school called Association of Minorities in Media, which was succeeded by the Carolina Association of Black Journalists.

26. Cole to J. C. Morrow, Nov. 11, 1980, Chancellor's Records: Christopher C. Fordham Series #40024, University Archives, University of North Carolina at Chapel Hill Library.

12. A New Home in Carroll Hall

The growth in the number of students, faculty members, and staff, and the expansions in curriculum and special programs, created a space shortage in Howell Hall in the 1980s. Cole turned his attention to finding a new home for the school and used his prodigious fundraising abilities to pay for it. The result was a school that was vastly different from what it had been when he assumed the deanship in 1979.

Grim Conditions in Howell Hall

One measure of the crowded conditions in Howell Hall was the overall square footage per student, which dropped from 299 in 1959–60 to 31 in 1989–90. In addition to being overcrowded, Howell had deteriorated physically as well. Within days of becoming dean, Cole wrote to the vice chancellor for business and finance to detail a long list of problems in Howell, including the lack of security for windows, peeling paint, shabby furniture, flooding faculty offices, sagging floors, broken classroom seats, termites in the basement, and a hot, decrepit auditorium. Cole said conditions were so bad in the auditorium that students had asked to have the school's annual awards convocation moved to the Carolina Union building. He also said the poor conditions were embarrassing when important visitors came to the school, and he asked what options he might have for improving the conditions.[1]

As the school continued to expand, the only computer terminals that students could use outside of classrooms were in the already overcrowded reading room. Howell Hall had only two sets of restrooms, and students wanting to use them formed long lines between classes. The auditorium had become too small for the school's commencement ceremonies and for all the students in the school to meet at one time, and disabled students had to be carried by hand to get to classrooms on the second floor. However, the cramped conditions may have had one benefit. Jock Lauterer, who was a student in the school in the early 1960s and who returned to teach in the early 1980s and again in 2001, said the limited number of restrooms in Howell increased the opportunities for faculty members to interact in the building. He recalled an instance when Jim Shumaker and Chuck Stone met on the stairs one day and began a conversation. They became so involved in their discussion that they forgot their original destinations.[2]

To meet the growing demand for more offices in Howell, Cole divided existing offices and converted dusty storage rooms to make additional offices. He walled off the ends of the hallway on the main level to create a small office at each end. One of the most unusual spaces was a storage room on the basement level under the main stairway that was converted to an office for Professor Anne Johnston, who could barely hear when students rushed up and down on the stairs above her between classes. Cole enlarged the reading room by taking over a faculty office and making a doorway between it and the reading room. The school could not add classrooms to Howell Hall, so teachers and students had to go to many buildings on campus (more than 10 in some semesters) for classes. The school had gotten so large by 1989 that it had to hold two commencement ceremonies in Hill Hall: one for graduates of the news-editorial sequence and the M.A. and Ph.D. students, and another ceremony for graduates of the advertising sequence.

An example of Cole's efforts to create more space in Howell Hall can be seen in a 1989 memo he wrote to Provost Dennis O'Connor after escorting him through the building to see how spaces could be divided to make more rooms. O'Connor vetoed the idea of dividing Howell 203, a classroom that seated 60 students, because the university needed classrooms of

1. Cole to John Temple, July 9, 1979, Provost's Records #40039, University Archives, University of North Carolina at Chapel Hill Library.
2. Lauterer, interview with the author, March 24, 2008.

that size. After the tour, Cole asked O'Connor for $38,200 to make several renovations: reduce the size of the graduate student lounge (room 206) to make an office for a senior faculty member, divide a faculty office (004) into two faculty offices, create an office from the only remaining storeroom (009), and renovate room 109 to make an office for the placement service.[3]

An accrediting team that visited the school in 1991 concluded that it had taken "considerable ingenuity" to accommodate the "enormous" growth in students and faculty in a physical space that had remained static. The result, however, was tiny faculty offices, some without windows, and some that had previously been closets or stairwells. Faculty members told the team they felt depressed about their work space, in contrast to their positive feelings about the rest of the school.[4] In 1992, the school was given space in Carr Building for offices for Professors Bob Stevenson and Frank Biocca and for Ph.D. students, but the space was less than desirable. In 1995, the school obtained space for four faculty offices on the second floor of the Porthole Building on Porthole Alley near Franklin Street, and professors Stevenson, Biocca, Donald Shaw, and Xinshu Zhao used them until the move to Carroll Hall in 1999.

Finding a New Building

While he was dealing with space problems and conditions in Howell Hall, Cole set about the task of getting an addition to Howell or a new building. In 1983, he asked Chancellor Christopher Fordham for permission to raise money for a new building, saying the school had outgrown Howell and was "jammed into it like sardines." He worked with the university's facilities planning office to develop plans for a four-story building connected to Howell and extending west from the front of the building toward Alumni Building. It would contain about 25,000 square feet and cost $5 million. Cole identified R. J. Reynolds Industries as his top prospect for funding the building.[5]

Fordham discussed the proposal with his administrative council on

3. Cole to O'Connor, June 16, 1989, Provost's Records.
4. Accrediting Council on Education in Journalism and Mass Communications, "Report of On-site Evaluation of the School of Journalism and Mass Communication at the University of North Carolina at Chapel Hill," Feb. 19, 1991.
5. Cole to Fordham, Aug. 29, 1983, Chancellor's Records: Christopher C. Fordham Series #40024, University Archives, University of North Carolina at Chapel Hill Library.

March 20, 1984, and he accepted the council's recommendation to deny the request because of the proposed building's intrusion into campus green space, its appearance and expense, and the fact that other construction projects had higher priorities. The council did acknowledge the school's need for larger and better facilities and suggested that the needs of the school and the Department of Radio, Television, and Motion Pictures (RTVMP) might be met by a new mass communication building. Provost Charles Morrow asked Cole to think about how the school might occupy several floors in such a new building.[6]

Cole met with a new provost, Sam Williamson, and the vice-chancellor for business and finance, Farris Womack, on May 10, 1985, to talk about the need for more space in Howell Hall. Cole later recalled Williamson striding across a grassy area as he stepped off possible dimensions of additions to the building.[7] Cole wrote a note summarizing the meeting and gave a copy to Williamson, and it survives in the provost's office archives. Cole and Williamson suggested an addition on the east side of Howell, between it and the Coker Arboretum. The three of them agreed on a 40,000-square-foot building on four levels, described as a "twin" to Howell and sited on the location of Howell's auditorium, which would be demolished. Womack estimated the addition would cost $4 million, and renovations to the existing structure would cost $750,000. He said the first step would be a preliminary drawing to show the relationship of the proposed addition to the existing building, neighboring Davie Hall, and the Arboretum. Cole immediately called Gordon Rutherford, head of facilities planning, to tell him that Womack had said the spatial drawing was a "front-burner" project and should be done immediately.[8] A few months later, Rutherford gave Cole a site plan for such an addition to Howell, but he said he could not support the idea because of its impact on the Arboretum, and he anticipated strong negative reactions from the university's Buildings and Grounds Committee and the Board of Trustees. He raised the possibility of a 36,000-square-foot building to the north of Howell, between it and the Morehead Building.[9]

Neither plan—building to the east of Howell, or to the north of it—was seriously considered, and in 1988, the university dropped the idea of building an addition to Howell and began discussing a new mass commu-

6. Morrow to Cole, March 21, 1984, Provost's Records.

7. Cole, interview with the author, March 25, 2008.

8. Cole, "Results of a Meeting with Farris Womack and Sam Williamson and Richard Cole," May 10, 1985, Provost's Records.

9. Rutherford to Cole, June 11, 1985, Provost's Records.

nication building on Columbia Street in the space occupied by Abernethy Hall, Swain Hall, and the Scuttlebutt snack bar. It would cost $36 million and include two five-story wings—one for the School of Journalism and one for RTVMP—connected by a 500-seat auditorium and main entrance. In 1988, leaders of student media organizations wrote the provost to express their support for such a building.[10]

The possibility of the mass communication building remained bright until Cole was startled in 1989 to read a news report that Chancellor Paul Hardin wanted to speed up plans for a new building for the School of Business Administration, a plan that would scuttle the mass communication building idea. Cole told O'Connor that he thought he had assurances from both O'Connor and Hardin that the mass communication building had been given the university's highest priority for new construction.[11] After discussing the matter with O'Connor, Cole wrote a memo for his files and sent a copy to the provost. It said O'Connor had told him the priorities had not changed but that Hardin "got caught out on a limb with a reporter." Frank Kenan, a major university benefactor, wanted to give $5 million to the business school, tied to an increase in graduate tuition for that school, but UNC system president C. D. Spangler vetoed the tuition aspect. Kenan was anxious to donate the money and also wanted the business school to have a new building, as did Spangler.

Cole changed his strategy and started his own campaign to obtain state funding for a new building. He informed the provost that he had asked two members of the North Carolina General Assembly (representatives Anne Barnes and Joe Hackney) to press for planning money for a mass communication building. He also told the provost he wanted to talk about the possibility of the school moving to Carroll Hall if the business school got its new building.[12] Carroll, which was named for Dudley Dewitt Carroll, founder of the School of Commerce, had been completed in 1953, with an addition completed in 1972. At the same time, Rolfe Neill, chairman and publisher of the *Charlotte Observer*, wrote to legislators to push for $1 million in planning money for the mass communication building. He said the School of Journalism was one of the best in the country and that its current facilities were "grossly" inadequate.[13] Meeting a few days later, the North Carolina General Assembly did not include money for

10. Leaders of campus media organizations to Dennis O'Connor, Sept. 20, 1988, Provost's Records.

11. Cole to O'Connor, Feb. 28, 1989, Provost's Records.

12. Cole to O'Connor, July 12, 1989, Provost's Records.

13. Neill to Rep. Howard C. Barnhill, July 12, 1989, Provost's Records.

the proposed mass communication building in its approved list of capital requests from the university, but it did include $7.5 million as a first step toward a new building for the School of Business Administration. In a newspaper story about the legislative action, Cole was quoted as still being hopeful of getting $1 million in planning money for a mass communication building.[14] That was not to be, however, and Cole had to announce at the first faculty meeting in the fall semester that the legislature did not allocate the planning money. He said that he and Professor Rich Beckman would start working on a photographic slide presentation to make the case for a new building and would try to show it to legislators around the state.[15]

The prospects for a new mass communication building then became even dimmer. Cole told the faculty in early October that he had met with O'Connor and representatives of the College of Arts and Sciences and the university's planning office. RTVMP and the school had been asked to reduce their space requests in the planned building by one-third. He also said RTVMP faculty members were having second thoughts about the idea of sharing a mass communication building and were thinking instead of asking for an addition to Swain Hall, their existing building. The provost was also concerned about whether the proposed building would fit in the physical space occupied by Swain, Abernethy, and the Scuttlebutt snack shop.[16] RTVMP ceased to exist after 1993, and that made the issue of a mass communication building moot.

Cole was able to give the faculty good news in November 1989: O'Connor and Hardin had assured him the school could occupy all or part of Carroll Hall after the business school moved out, scheduled for 1993 or 1994. (The move into Carroll did not occur until July 1999.) On Nov. 10, 1989, the faculty unanimously passed a resolution saying that a new building would be the best solution for the school's space needs but that they were also enthusiastic about the possibility of moving into Carroll Hall, as long as the school could have the entire building and that appropriate renovation money would be provided.[17] Hardin responded to the resolu-

14. Mark Schultz, "Journalism School Running out of Room Fast," *Chapel Hill Herald*, July 18, 1989, 1.

15. Faculty meeting minutes, School of Journalism, Aug. 28, 1989.

16. Faculty meeting minutes, School of Journalism, Oct. 9, 1989.

17. Unanimous resolution of the faculty of the School of Journalism, Nov. 10, 1989, Provost's Records and faculty meeting minutes.

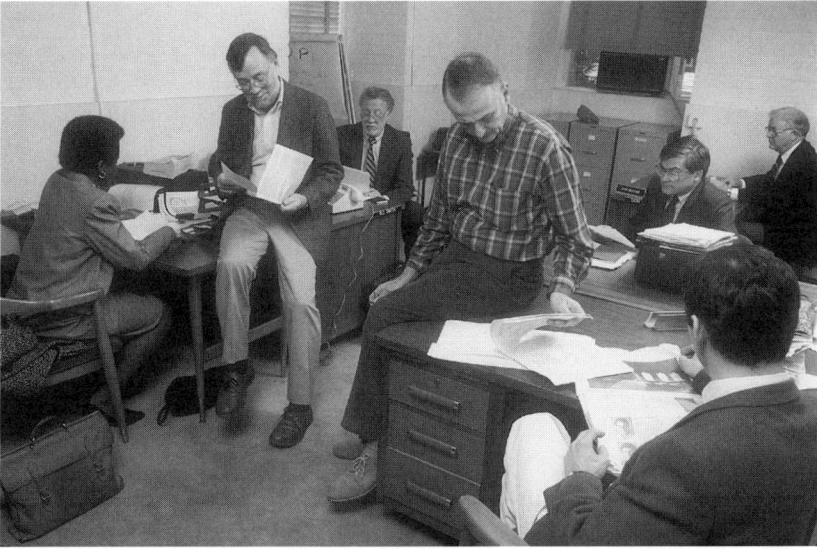

Dean Richard Cole used this photograph of part-time faculty members who shared an office in 1990 to illustrate space problems in Howell Hall. *(School of Journalism and Mass Communication, UNC–Chapel Hill. Reprinted with permission.)*

tion with a handwritten reply to Cole, saying he had received his memo and noted his request.[18]

O'Connor came to a faculty meeting early in 1990 to discuss the issue of a building. He said the school could move to Carroll Hall after the business school moved out, and the target date was 1993 at the earliest. He was optimistic about funding renovations, saying money could come from the university's Bicentennial Campaign or the legislature. The school would be given as much space in Carroll as it needed, he said, but it would have to document its needs.[19]

By June 1990, Cole had started a letter-writing campaign to the school's alumni to get them to write to state legislators about the school's need for a new building or for renovation funds for Carroll Hall.[20] He extended the campaign with stories in school publications. A story in *JAFA News,* the school's publication for alumni and friends, showed pictures of a crowded classroom, the crowded school library, a photo lab, and an office that was

18. Hardin to Cole, Nov. 28, 1989, Provost's Records.
19. Faculty meeting minutes, School of Journalism, Jan. 10, 1990.
20. Michelle Rosen, "J-School Outgrows Howell Hall," *Chapel Hill Newspaper*, June 19, 1990, A2.

used by 10 part-time faculty members (seven were in the picture). The article said the school had had about 50 majors and eight faculty members when it moved into Howell Hall; by 1989, it had 25 faculty members and more than 900 majors (first-year students through graduate students).[21] In July, Cole reminded O'Connor that both he and Hardin had assured him that the school could have Carroll Hall after the business school moved out. Cole said he had not been promised the entire building, however, and he suggested that the *Daily Tar Heel*, which needed more space, might be moved to Carroll Hall, too.[22]

The following May, an extensive article in the *UNC Journalist* reiterated the message about Howell Hall and the need for Carroll Hall, describing how Professor Cathy Packer sat in her windowless third-floor office dreaming about having windows. It cited other problems, including lack of space to give students computer access, only two sets of restrooms, the inadequate auditorium, and very limited access for handicapped students. JOMC courses were being taught in 11 buildings on campus that semester, and some faculty members did not teach a single class in Howell. The library had only 30 seats, plaster was falling off many walls, and some offices flooded after heavy rains. Cole said a new building was not very likely, so the school had its sights on Carroll Hall.[23] The faculty and staff got their initial look at Carroll Hall at the first faculty meeting in 1992. After assembling in the faculty lounge in Carroll (which later became the Freedom Forum Conference Center), they toured the building.

In 1993, Cole had to review the history of his building campaign for yet another provost—Richard McCormick. (At that point, Cole had worked on the issue of a new building with five provosts, three chancellors, at least two vice-chancellors for business and finance, and several other administrators.) In the spring semester of 1993, the school held classes in 15 classrooms outside of Howell Hall. Cole reminded McCormick that the school had been promised Carroll Hall, but not necessarily all of it.[24] Cole reiterated the school's needs again in 1994, citing the 1991 accrediting report that criticized the school's lack of space. He said five new faculty members would be joining the school and that the transfer of broadcast journalism to the school created the need for studios and special classrooms. He also said four staff members were sharing two offices.[25]

21. Amy Wearmouth, "Out of Space, Out of Time," *JAFA News*, Winter 1990, 1.
22. Cole to O'Connor, July 10, 1990, Provost's Records.
23. Jim Greenhill, "The Space Crisis," *UNC Journalist*, May 1991, C1.
24. Cole to McCormick, May 21, 1993, Provost's Records.
25. Cole to McCormick, Jan. 31, 1994, Provost's Records.

Cole arranged for McCormick to tour Carroll Hall, and he stationed faculty and staff members throughout the building to show how the school needed all the offices and the classrooms. McCormick thanked Cole for the "impressive and informative" tour and said Carroll Hall would be "a wonderful new home" for the school.[26] Cole had still not gotten assurance that the school could have all of Carroll Hall, however, and he sent McCormick a detailed memo and large notebooks showing how the school needed considerable space for its expanding graduate program.[27] A few weeks later Cole responded to a report that the College of Arts and Sciences had also requested space in Carroll Hall, and he reminded McCormick that he had already given him the notebooks with justification for giving all of Carroll to the school. He pointed out that the Arts and Sciences memorandum included inaccurate data about the size of the JOMC faculty. He said the space was also needed for special activities such as the Halls of Fame and the placement service.[28]

Cole eventually convinced Hardin and McCormick that the school deserved all of the space in Carroll Hall, and he intensified his efforts to raise private money to supplement the state's appropriation for the renovation. The cost of renovations and new equipment and furnishings eventually totaled approximately $12 million, and Cole raised approximately $7 million from private donors. Contributors were given opportunities for rooms and other facilities to be named after them.[29] The largest single gift was $1.1 million from the Park Foundation for the Park Library. Other large contributions came from the A. J. Fletcher Foundation and WRAL-TV ($250,000), the Gannett Foundation ($225,000), McClatchy Newspapers ($200,000), and the *Charlotte Observer* ($200,000). The smallest gift was $5.[30]

Cole and the faculty and staff spent two years working with an architectural firm, Pearce Brinkley Cease and Lee of Raleigh, to plan the renovations to Carroll. In October 1997, Cole announced the timetable for the move from Howell to Carroll. Removal of asbestos was to begin in December, and the contractors would begin renovation in February 1998. The move would take place in the summer of 1999.[31] The "Last Big Blowout

26. McCormick to Cole, April 12, 1994, Provost's Records.

27. Cole to McCormick, May 9, 1994, Provost's Records.

28. Cole to McCormick, Aug. 1, 1994, Provost's Records.

29. Cole, "Working for a World-Class Home: Carroll Hall," *UNC Journalist*, Fall 1996, 2.

30. Asta Ytre, "Moving on Up," *UNC Journalist*, Fall 1999, 12–14.

31. Faculty meeting minutes, School of Journalism and Mass Communication, Oct. 24, 1997.

Carroll Hall, home of the School of Journalism and Mass Communication since 1999. *(School of Journalism and Mass Communication, UNC–Chapel Hill. Reprinted with permission.)*

in Howell Hall," on April 23–24, 1999, featured an open house, presentations about the school, a banquet, and tours of Carroll. One highlight was the viewing of Professor Richard Simpson's video tribute to Howell, titled "Hell No, I Won't Go!" The faculty and staff did go, however, as they packed boxes of books and other materials from their offices and walked out of Howell on Friday, July 16, 1999. They went to work in Carroll on Monday, July 19, to wait for the moving company to bring the boxes that had been picked up in Howell over the weekend. The move went smoothly, and the Carroll Hall dedication weekend was held March 31–April 2, 2000. Interim Chancellor William McCoy joined Cole in cutting the ribbon on the front steps on March 31.

The 53,000 square feet in Carroll tripled the school's space and brought all faculty members, staff members, and JOMC classes under one roof for the first time in 12 years. The Park Library included a computer lab and multimedia lab, laptop computer connections, public access terminals, and several computers dedicated to database access. The Charles Kuralt Learning Center, which was completed a few months later, housed furniture, books, and other items from the famed broadcaster's New York City office and displayed his Emmy Awards and three Peabody Awards. The Halls of Fame room included space for photographs of members of the North Carolina Journalism, Advertising, and Public Relations Halls of

Fame. The Freedom Forum Conference Center, supported with a gift from the Freedom Forum, was outfitted as a spacious meeting room equipped with a projector and screen, ample seating, and Internet, PowerPoint, and video capabilities. Students had access to seven computer laboratories in the building, and the electronic communication sequence had a television studio, control room, and 13 electronic editing suites. The visual communication sequence had a communication laboratory, digital darkroom, and many other upgrades. Facilities for graduate students included more than 15 offices, seminar rooms, a research center, and a lounge. The Career Services suite included three rooms for recruiters to interview students.

A Fundraising Giant

The new equipment and technological advances, growing enrollments, expanded faculty and staff, new programs, and the renovation of Carroll Hall required enormous infusions of money, and Cole's extraordinary fundraising made it possible. He realized that state money would not be enough for the school to grow and prosper, so he approached fundraising in new ways and created an infrastructure in the school for building relationships with alumni and other donors. He recalled in 2008 that he had no qualms about sitting in someone's office and asking for $1 million or $10 million. He was not asking for the money for himself but for the good of the school, the university, the students, and the field of mass communication. He was turned down at times, but the effort was worth it.[32]

Cole's approach to raising money brought in millions of dollars and fundamentally changed the school. Instead of waiting for donors to make gifts on their own initiative, Cole actively sought funding from corporations and individuals to create new programs, honor individuals with professorships, and help fund the renovation of Carroll Hall. He also took a significant step in 1987 when he arranged with the university's development office to hire Barbara Habel as a half-time development director for the school. In 1989, Paul Gardner became the school's first full-time development director. Starting in 1993, when the university development office stopped supporting development officers in individual schools, Cole paid the salaries and expenses of the school's development office and staff with foundation funds, justifying it on the basis that those activities brought in more contributions.

Contributions came to the school by two routes. Many individual donors, corporations, and foundations made contributions to the School of

32. Cole, interview with the author, March 25, 2008.

Figure 12.1 Gifts to the School of Journalism and Mass Communication and Its Foundation, 2000–2004 (in millions)

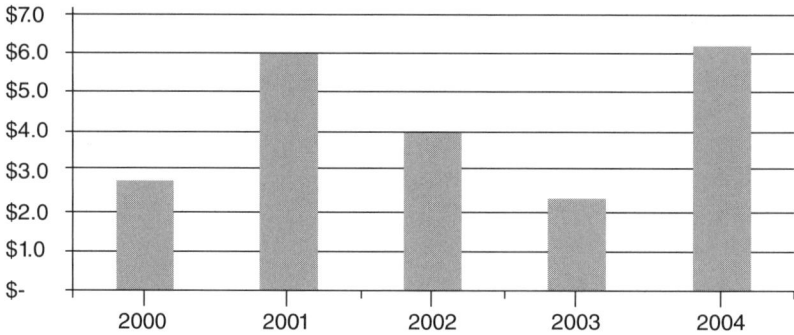

Journalism and Mass Communication Foundation that had been created at the end of 1949. The foundation invested the funds in accordance with the expertise of foundation board members and outside investment management firms. Alternatively, gifts went to separate school accounts that were maintained and managed by the university. In 2007, the foundation board determined that the university's investment fund managers could produce higher yields than private companies, and it placed the school's foundation funds under the university's management.

Figure 12.1 shows the total dollars raised per year from 2000 to 2004 from both routes. The five-year total was $21.4 million, and the yearly average was $4.3 million. The 2001 total included gifts for the Kerr and Parker professorships, the 2002 total included a major gift for the sports communication professorship, and the 2004 total included a $3 million gift for the Cole professorship.

Gifts to the school have supported students, faculty members, and programs. Some funds are endowed, and the dean uses the annual income for restricted purposes. Some are expendable and designated for restricted or unrestricted purposes. Private dollars, regardless of their source, have made the difference between the school being good and the school being great by supplementing money the school received from the state. Gifts from alumni, friends, corporations, and foundations have made the school the envy of other academic units on campus and journalism–mass communication programs at other universities across the country. The additional support has proven to be especially helpful in years of budget cuts mandated by the General Assembly or the governor's office. In 1990, for example, the school faced a loss of $29,000 in its operating budget and had to use foundation funds for supplies.[33] Similar budget cuts took place in 1999 ($50,000) and 2002 ($240,000).

An example of how outside funding affected the school in a typical year can be seen in the self-study report for the 2003 accreditation visit that explained state and private support for the school in the 2001–2002 academic year. The school's total expenditures were approximately $5.8 million, with 75 percent coming from state appropriations and special university sources, and the rest from private gifts. The largest portion of state money ($3.5 million) paid faculty and staff salaries, and other major categories of state funds expenditures were communication (telephones and postage), printing and binding school publications, educational and office supplies, repairs and maintenance, and travel. The school received nearly $335,000 from the education and technology (E and T) fee paid by all UNC–Chapel Hill students and apportioned back to academic units by the provost. The E and T funds that the school has received each year have made it possible to upgrade computers and other equipment on a regular basis. Gifts that year provided more than $95,000 in scholarships and aid to students, not counting an additional $1.8 million from the Park family for graduate support. Other private money provided nearly $60,000 for library materials and the librarian's travel, $50,000 for faculty travel, $25,000 for educational materials, $19,000 for the *Carolina Communicator*, $15,000 for the Board of Visitors, $10,000 for equipment maintenance, and $9,000 for the Journalism Alumni and Friends Association.

Fundraising efforts have sometimes been incorporated into the university's larger campaigns. The UNC–Chapel Hill Bicentennial Campaign in the early 1990s, for example, set the school's goal at $3.8 million. Thanks to Cole and the generosity of donors, gifts exceeded the goal by 50 percent, totaling nearly $5.7 million.[34] The school's goal for the Carolina First campaign, which ran from July 1, 1999, to Dec. 31, 2007, was $30 million, and it raised $45.5 million, or 52 percent above the goal.

Cole also directed fundraising efforts to raise money for endowed professorships and other enhancements for the school. Interest earnings from professorship endowments have been used to reward existing faculty members and recruit new ones by supplementing state salaries and providing money for research and travel. In 1984, the John S. and James L. Knight Foundation gave the school $900,000, including $600,000 to create a James L. Knight Professorship and $300,000 to create the Knight Ad-

33. Kenny Monteith, "School Suffers After State Budget Cuts," *UNC Journalist*, November 1990, 7.

34. "Bicentennial Campaign Closes with a Bang," *UNC Journalist*, Fall 1995, 8.

vertising Center, a classroom in Howell Hall with computers and audio-visual equipment. Subsequent contributions from the Knight Foundation and a prudent investment strategy enabled Cole to create two additional James L. Knight professorships.

Soon after Walter Spearman died in February 1987, Cole raised money to create an endowed professorship named in Spearman's honor. He raised $333,000 that was matched with $167,000 from the Board of Governors Distinguished Professors Endowment Trust Fund to create a $500,000 professorship endowment.[35] Cole secured funding in 1994 for the Glaxo Wellcome Distinguished Professorship in Medical Journalism from Glaxo Pharmaceuticals and an anonymous donor. Other distinguished professorships resulting from Cole's efforts included the Horace Carter Distinguished Professorship, the Walter Hussman Distinguished Professorship, the John Thomas Kerr Jr. Distinguished Professorship, the Knight Chair in Journalism, the James Howard and Hallie McLean Parker Distinguished Professorship, and the Distinguished Professorship in Sports Communication. In 2004, an anonymous donor contributed $3 million to create the Richard Cole Distinguished Professorship. When Cole announced that he would step down from the deanship in 2005, the school started the Richard Cole Fund for Innovation, and more than 200 donors contributed in excess of $137,000. The innovation award was prompted by a sign—"Innovate or Die"—that Cole kept on his office desk. The sign was a gift from Ed Vick, a 1966 graduate of the school and chairman and CEO of Young and Rubicam Worldwide advertising agency. In addition, Cole raised funds to create term professorships that were awarded to faculty members for two- or three-year terms: the Julian W. Scheer Term Professorship and the James H. Shumaker Term Professorship. Named professorships in the school provided by outside sources included three Kenan Professorships and an Alumni Distinguished Professorship. The number of named professorships in the school grew from none in 1979 to 11 in 2005.

David Brinkley, the distinguished broadcast journalist, donated money to create the David Brinkley Teaching-Excellence Award that is given each year to a faculty member in the school. In 1990, the William Randolph Hearst Foundation gave $200,000 to endow a program for visiting media professionals to come to the school for several days at a time to talk to students and faculty members.[36] The same year, Cole's efforts resulted in the

35. Cole to Ray Dawson, April 11, 1990, Provost's Records.
36. Cole to O'Connor, July 10, 1990, Provost's Records.

creation of a mini-sabbatical program in the school by *USA Today*, which selected staff members from the newspaper to live in Chapel Hill, attend classes, and pursue other enrichment activities. The school provided an office, and *USA Today* rented an apartment in Chapel Hill for the staff members.[37] Fewer than half a dozen staff members participated, however, and the program ended a few years later when *USA Today* stopped funding it as part of cost-cutting measures.[38]

The Rainbow Institute, one of the school's efforts to increase racial diversity, was created with an initial $46,500 grant from the Freedom Forum in 1991. The three-week program was held for four years and brought high school students of many ethnic backgrounds to Chapel Hill to improve their journalism knowledge and skills.[39] Three years earlier, the Freedom Forum funded the first Freedom Forum Seminar for Advertising Teachers, which paid for a dozen advertising teachers from around the United States and from other countries to come to Chapel Hill for a week-long exploration of ways to improve their teaching. Both it and the Rainbow Institute were eventually cancelled because of the Freedom Forum's changes in funding priorities. With support from the Ethics and Excellence in Journalism Foundation, the Rainbow Institute was reincarnated in 2007 as the Chuck Stone Program for Diversity in Education and Media. It continued in 2008 with a grant from the Gannett Foundation.

Accreditation and Other Accolades

The school received many accolades during Cole's deanship, including glowing accreditation reports and other acknowledgements of quality. The 1985 accreditation report said the school had an excellent program and overall was "one of the best in the country." It praised the strong administration, good instruction, quality of students, and private and professional support. The report warned, however, that if the school continued to grow, it would need additional faculty members, more space, and added financial support.[40] In 1991, the report said the school deserved its reputation as being "one of the best in the country" and praised the quality of instruction, faculty, students, and support from the university and

37. Cole to O'Connor, July 25, 1990, Provost's Records.
38. Cole to William Little, Dec. 16, 1991, Provost's Records.
39. Felix Gutierrez to Cole, Nov. 27, 1991, Provost's Records.
40. Joseph Shoquist to Christopher Fordham, May 17, 1985, Chancellor's Records, Fordham Series.

professionals. It also expressed concerns about the master's program and the advertising curriculum, but the overriding problem was space.[41] The 1997 accreditation report recognized the school as "arguably the best all-around program in the country."[42] The same year, UNC's Graduate School also conducted its first comprehensive evaluation of the school's graduate program. An external team of evaluators concluded that the program was "unquestionably one of the finest in the country." The team praised the faculty, curriculum, students, and administration.

In 1989, Al Neuharth, the former chairman of Gannett Newspapers and founder of *USA Today*, said in his autobiography that the school was the best in the country.[43] A paper presented at the 1994 convention of the Association for Education in Journalism and Mass Communication (AEJMC) concluded that the school was second in the nation of the 33 Ph.D.-granting programs in mass communication, based on research presentations by graduate students at AEJMC conventions over the previous six years.

By the time of the 2003 accreditation visit, adjectives used to describe the school had progressed from "deserving of its reputation as one of the best" (1985 and 1991) to "arguably the best all around" (1997) to "recognized as perhaps the best program" (2003). The report said many experts believed it was the best-balanced journalism–mass communication school because it placed appropriate emphasis on both scholarly productivity and professional excellence. Moreover, the report said, "The school combines the best in undergraduate and graduate education and is clearly focused on its mission of excellence." The report's list of strengths filled a page and praised the school's administration, faculty, professional approach, "school-wide culture of extraordinary commitment," exceptional private support, faculty scholarship, high-quality staff, superb international projects, proactive outreach, and commendable diversity. On the other hand, it said a failure to increase faculty size had caused problems with large class sizes and difficulties for students who couldn't get classes they needed. The report said the school needed to match new faculty hires with sequence needs, especially in electronic communication, and needed

41. Accrediting Council on Education in Journalism and Mass Communications, "Report of On-site Evaluation of UNC-CH School of Journalism and Mass Communication," Feb. 19, 1991.

42. Robert H. Giles to Michael Hooker, May 14, 1997, Chancellor's Records: Michael Hooker Series #40026, University Archives, University of North Carolina at Chapel Hill Library.

43. Al Neuharth, *Confessions of an S.O.B.* (New York: Doubleday, 1989), 263.

to increase faculty racial diversity to match that of the student body.[44] The school's expenditures that year were $5.6 million, primarily for salaries.

Cole Steps Down

Cole announced in July 2003 that he would step down from the deanship in June 2005. His term was to have ended on June 30, 2004, but Provost Robert Shelton persuaded him to stay an extra year. Shelton said the school faced the challenge of recruiting for a number of faculty positions that were to be vacated in 2003–2004, and adding the dean's position to that list would be unwise. Under Cole's direction, Shelton said, the school had become the best of its kind in the nation. "On all fronts, he's really led the school to new heights," Shelton said.[45]

The school faced the daunting challenge of finding a successor to a dean who had been in office for 26 years and who had utterly transformed the school. For a majority of the faculty, Cole was the only dean they had ever had, and finding his successor would prove to be more difficult than most imagined.

44. Accrediting Council on Education in Journalism and Mass Communications, "Report of On-Site Evaluation of the UNC-Chapel Hill School of Journalism and Mass Communication," Feb. 19, 2003.

45. Elliott Dube, "J-School Dean to Step Down After 24 Years," *Daily Tar Heel*, July 24, 2003, http://media.www.dailytarheel.com/media/storage/paper885/news/2003/07/24/University/JSchool.Dean.To.Step.Down.After.24.Years-1354420.shtml (accessed March 23, 2008).

"Jean Folkerts has demonstrated a
broad depth of knowledge about the
rapidly changing field of journalism
and mass communications, especially
the role that electronic media will
continue to play in informing key
audiences."—*Chancellor James
Moeser*[1]

13. An Interim and a New Dean

A search committee chaired by Professor Tom James, dean of the UNC–
Chapel Hill School of Education, set about finding a successor to Cole.
The committee worked throughout the 2004–2005 academic year to narrow the list of applicants to four finalists: Terry Hynes, dean of the College
of Journalism and Communications at the University of Florida; Frank
Denton, former editor of the *Wisconsin State Journal* in Madison; Gerald Baldasty, chairman of the Department of Communication at the University of Washington; and Joel Brinkley, an alumnus of the school who
had won a Pulitzer Prize for international reporting in 1980 and who had
worked for the *New York Times* since 1983. Hynes withdrew her candidacy
soon after her campus interview, and the committee added two finalists.
Alison Alexander was head of the Department of Telecommunications at
the University of Georgia, and Jeremy Cohen was associate vice provost
for undergraduate education at Pennsylvania State University, where he
had also been associate dean for undergraduate education and interim
dean in the College of Communications. After receiving the search committee's recommendations, Chancellor James Moeser and Provost Robert
Shelton negotiated with Baldasty about his possible appointment as dean.
The negotiations were not successful, and Tom Bowers was asked to serve

1. Folkerts Named Journalism Dean," *Daily Tar Heel*, Feb. 24, 2006, http://media.
www.dailytarheel.com/media/storage/paper885/news/2006/02/24/University/Folk-
erts.Named.Journalism.Dean-1637456.shtml (accessed March 23, 2008).

as interim dean in 2005–2006.[2] Bowers, the school's senior associate dean, had already announced that he would retire from the faculty on June 30, 2006.

An Interim Dean

Bowers had received his bachelor's, master's, and doctoral degrees from Indiana University. He was known to faculty members for his gentlemanly demeanor, knowledge of the school and university at large, and counsel to students.[3] Bowers had joined the faculty the same year as Cole to teach advertising courses but had taught news-editorial classes as well. He and Cole were finalists for the dean's position in 1979; when Cole was selected as dean, he named Bowers as the school's first associate dean.

As associate dean and later senior associate dean, Bowers' initial duties focused on scholarships as he and Cole shaped the new position. Eventually Bowers' teaching load was reduced to give him more time for administration, and he assumed responsibilities for curriculum, course scheduling, and student advising. In the latter capacity, he often counseled JOMC students with academic and personal problems. "Thanks to him, a lot of students are graduates whose lives are better," Cole said.[4] Faculty members and staff often heard Bowers say that as senior associate dean he had the best job, because he felt that in that role he could make a difference in students' lives; but Bowers was always modest about his accomplishments.

Bowers had also carved out a reputation for teaching excellence. "So much of his career revolved around excellence in teaching," Cole said, "and he embodied that excellence in his teaching."[5] Bowers created a pedagogy course, the school's first, to teach graduate students how to be effective instructors, and he received the university's John L. Sanders Award for Distinguished Undergraduate Teaching and Service in 1997. He also oversaw the School's course evaluation system that allowed students to comment on each section of each course and its respective faculty

2. Katherine Hollander, "New Search Starts for Journalism Dean," *Daily Tar Heel*, June 16, 2005, http://media.www.dailytarheel.com/media/storage/paper885/news/2005/06/16/University/New-Search.Starts.For.Journalism.Dean-1365345.shtml (accessed March 23, 2008).

3. Because the subject of this section is the author of this book, the section was written by Jan Yopp.

4. Cole, interview with Jan Yopp, July 22, 2008.

5. Cole, interview with Jan Yopp, July 22, 2008.

Tom Bowers, interim dean of the School of Journalism and Mass Communication, 2005–2006, and faculty member, 1971–2006. (*e.noonan IMAGES [www.eileennoonan. com]. Reprinted with permission.*)

member each semester. Even after his retirement, he continued to share his knowledge about teaching through a blog on the JOMC Web site.

Bowers also brought to the dean's office longtime associations with and knowledge about other parts of the UNC–Chapel Hill campus. He had served on the university's Committee on Student Conduct for more than two decades, been a member of the university's Buildings and Grounds Committee for nine years, and sat on the administrative boards of the General College and the College of Arts and Sciences. He represented the school on a campus committee that drafted the revised undergraduate curriculum that went into effect in fall 2006. He also had a national reputation for his association activities, including a year as president of the Association for Education in Journalism and Mass Communication, the national group for journalism educators, and service on the Academic Committee of the American Advertising Federation. For several years, he codirected the Freedom Forum Seminar for Advertising Teachers, a summer program for new advertising faculty members conducted at the school in the summer.

Bowers felt that it wasn't the role of an interim dean to make sweeping changes during an interim year, but he wanted the incoming dean to have a foundation for understanding the school.[6] That led him to create a "vision initiative" program in which faculty and staff examined the school's situation and envisioned what it could become in a fast-changing media environment. He formed seven heterogeneous working groups, each composed of faculty members from different sequences, because he wanted them to think beyond the boundaries of their sequences. The school's Board of Visitors participated in one weekend session that was part of the program. The groups met throughout the 2005–2006 academic year, and the entire faculty and staff participated in a retreat in January 2006. They discussed common philosophies, differences, and goals, and their efforts were useful to the incoming dean, who launched a curriculum revision effort a year later.

As an administrator in the school who worked alongside Cole, Bowers had witnessed the school's transformation from manual typewriters to computers and the enormous growth in numbers of students, faculty members, and course sections. As interim dean, he ensured that the school's equipment was up to date, upgrading the video wall in the Carroll Hall lobby and preparing the initial proposal for funds to convert the electronic journalism classrooms and studio to high-definition television. One of his most memorable experiences was calling comedian Bill Cosby to ask for a donation to the Chuck Stone Citizen of the World Award, created when the popular professor retired. Cosby did not send money; instead, he did a one-man show in Memorial Hall in June 2006, raising more than $25,000 toward the endowment.

Bowers also maintained the school's presence in international activities. He and Associate Dean Ruth Walden spent six days in China in November 2005 to visit Fudan University in Shanghai and to help celebrate the fiftieth anniversary of the School of Journalism of Renmin University in Beijing. Both visits resulted in special arrangements between the School of Journalism and Mass Communication and the Chinese universities. Bowers also committed the school to the U.S. State Department's Edward R. Murrow Program for international journalists, in which more than a dozen Arab journalists came to Chapel Hill in 2006. The reporters and writers spent seven days on campus, attending classes specifically set up for them in the school and visiting area media outlets.

---

6. Bowers, interview with Jan Yopp, July 11, 2008.

Jean Folkerts, dean of the School of Journalism and Mass Communication, 2006–present. *(School of Journalism and Mass Communication, UNC–Chapel Hill. Reprinted with permission. Photo by Steve Exum.)*

Jean Folkerts

While Bowers served his year as interim dean, a new search committee, chaired by Dean Bernadette Gray-Little of the College of Arts and Sciences, who subsequently was named provost later that year, launched a new search in August 2005. By January 2006, the committee had narrowed the field to three candidates: Laurence Alexander, former chairman of the journalism department at the University of Florida; Jean Folkerts, former director of the School of Media and Public Affairs at George Washington University; and Charles Self, former journalism dean at the University of Oklahoma. After the finalists visited the campus and school, the chancellor and provost selected Folkerts, who assumed the deanship on July 1, 2006.[7]

7. "Folkerts Named Journalism Dean," *Daily Tar Heel*, Feb. 24, 2006, http://media. www.dailytarheel.com/media/storage/paper885/news/2006/02/24/University/Folkerts.Named.Journalism.Dean-1637456.shtml (accessed March 23, 2008).

Folkerts had received her bachelor's and master's degrees from Kansas State University and her Ph.D. from the University of Kansas. At George Washington University, she was also professor of honors, associate vice president for special academic initiatives, and interim dean of the Columbian College of Arts and Sciences. She had previously taught at the University of Texas at Austin and Mount Vernon College. She had worked as a daily newspaper reporter, a public relations professional, a magazine editor and writer, and an assistant press secretary to a former governor of Kansas. She was the Freedom Forum Teacher of the Year for excellence in teaching media history in 2001 and was editor of *Journalism and Mass Communication Quarterly*, the leading academic research journal in the field, from 1992 to 2001.

A New Curriculum

When Folkerts interviewed for the deanship, she spoke about changes in the news media and said the school's curriculum needed to adapt to those changes. One of her first initiatives as dean was to lead the faculty in a significant revision of the undergraduate and professional master's degree curricula. The undergraduate curriculum had had been organized in five sequences—specialties that reflected an older media landscape of distinct differences in skills needed for careers in print journalism, broadcast journalism, advertising, public relations, and visual communication. Students completed requirements for one sequence, and they had little flexibility to take courses or learn skills in other sequences. Sparked by new developments in the digital creation, storage, and display of information, differences among the media were blurring. Multimedia techniques—combining text, audio, still photographs, and video—increasingly became part of the traditional media. Print and broadcast media added Web sites to deliver information. Those developments meant that graduates of the school needed skills in a variety of media to present information in news and promotional messages, and the restrictions of the old curriculum had become outdated in the media landscape of the 21st century.

After meetings and discussions that ranged over several months, the faculty approved fundamental changes in the undergraduate curriculum on March 7, 2008, with new requirements to become effective for students entering the school in 2009. The new curriculum is intended to help students understand the media's roles and their social, economic, and political impacts. Other aims are to enable students to understand how information is collected, written, targeted, packaged, and delivered across various media platforms. The curriculum maintains its traditional journalism–mass communication core of three required courses for all undergraduates in the school: "Introduction to Mass Communication Law," "News Writing," and "Professional Issues and Ethics." The number of JOMC credits required for graduation was raised from 28 to 34 (an increase equivalent to two courses).

The major changes are in the sequence structure beyond the JOMC core. The former news-editorial, electronic communication, and multimedia sequences were merged into a journalism sequence. Its objectives are to help students learn to write, report, and edit for multiple media formats and to produce news content that is accurate, credible, insightful, useful, and pursued within an ethical framework. Students in the journalism sequence complete two core courses. "Reporting" includes many aspects of the course that had that same title throughout the history of the school. The second journalism core course is a significant addition: "Audio-Video Information Gathering," in which students will learn to use audio and video concepts and tools to document information. Beyond the journalism core, students will choose a specialization from editing and graphic design, electronic communication, multimedia, photojournalism, or reporting.

The new school curriculum also combines the former advertising and public relations sequences into a sequence called advertising/public relations. Its objectives are to teach students about product branding, strategic and critical planning, and managing relationships with targeted audiences and publics, and to enable them to communicate accurately, credibly, and ethically in various media. The core courses required for all students in the sequence are "Principles of Advertising and Public Relations" (which combined two principles courses) and "Advertising and Public Relations Research." Beyond the core, students complete a four-course core in either advertising or public relations and a four-course specialization covering issues in advertising or public relations.

The new JOMC curriculum also added the concept of "immersions," which require students to take two courses within groupings or combinations of two or more courses in specific areas: conceptualizing the audience; mass communication theory; history, law, and regulation; online communication; diversity; political communication; communication, business, and entrepreneurship; sports communication; and honors.

A revised curriculum of the professional M.A. program, designed for students wishing to pursue media careers, was approved on April 11, 2008, to become effective in 2009. Students will complete a JOMC core of four courses: "Research Methods," "Mass Communication Law," "Reporting and Writing News," and a new course, "Multimedia Storytelling," which represents the most significant change at the graduate level. Beyond the core, students will complete a specialization in one of seven areas: electronic communication, design and editing, print journalism, visual communication, mass communication concepts and theory, medical and science journalism, or strategic communications. They must also complete two graduate courses from outside the school and write a thesis.

Hand in hand with the curriculum revisions, Folkerts succeeded in getting the school selected for the Carnegie-Knight Initiative on the Future of Journalism Education. The school will be one of a dozen schools in the country participating in the program to adapt journalism education to changes in the news industry. UNC's effort will focus particularly on North Carolina's growing Latino population, and student work documenting the Latino population will be made available to news media in the state.

Within the first two years of her tenure, Folkerts accomplished other goals, particularly fundraising and faculty diversity. She finalized arrangements for the school's Horace Carter Distinguished Professorship and the Walter Hussman Distinguished Scholar program. Total gifts to the foundation and the school were $3.7 million in 2005, $3.8 million in 2006, and $4.9 million in 2007. As with most fundraising successes, those efforts required extensive preliminary work and nurturing, which Cole had initiated. Folkerts was also successful in obtaining initial state funding to convert the school's video operations to high-definition video, and she improved the school's external communication with a new Web site and additional staff members to create Web content. The faculty became more diverse with the hiring of Paul Cuadros in 2007 and Queenie Byars in 2008. Finally, the school's national reputation in electronic communication was recognized when it was named in May 2008 as one of five schools to have a student-run digital news bureau for ABC Television.

14. Retrospective

One hundred years after Edward Kidder Graham met his first class of journalism students at the University of North Carolina, the School of Journalism and Mass Communication has become what many knowledgeable people believe is one of the best programs of its kind in the United States, with a worldwide reputation for excellence. From a handful of students in Graham's first class, the school has grown to more than 900 students and become one of the largest academic units on campus. The size of the faculty has grown from one—Graham, who was only a part-time journalism teacher in the English department—to nearly 50, and the school is supported by more than 20 staff members. Graham could not have imagined that the journalism program would move from a single classroom to occupy other buildings and eventually one of the largest buildings on campus. He could not have foreseen how the state's newspaper editors and publishers would create a foundation that would grow to have assets of nearly $20 million, providing more than $400,000 a year to enrich the School of Journalism and Mass Communication and more than $250,000 annually in financial assistance and awards to students. He could not have imagined that the school would have an annual operating budget of more than $5 million, and he could not have conceived the technological equipment and facilities that students would use to create journalism content for the digital media.

1. Friday, interview with the author, June 16, 2008.

In describing how the school has evolved, this account has focused on individual leaders and builders of journalism education at UNC–Chapel Hill because those individuals had the vision, tenacity, and leadership to create and shape the program. Other people and factors have also contributed to making the school what it is, including students, faculty, staff, alumni, university leaders, and intangibles such as the quality of life in Chapel Hill and North Carolina. In the final analysis, however, the program's leaders and one alumnus provided the vision and marshaled the resources to make the School of Journalism and Mass Communication one of the best in the world.

The relative longevity and stability of leadership has been important to the story of the school. Two men in particular played dominant roles because they were at the helm for a combined 53 of its 100 years as a program and of its 85 years as an academic unit: Oscar Coffin for 27 years and Richard Cole for 26 years. It's risky to attempt comparisons between Coffin and Cole because each provided the kind of leadership that his era demanded. At a time when print journalism was dominant and the mission of the Department of Journalism was to provide journalists for the state's newspapers, Coffin's program achieved that mission and won the gratitude and admiration of scores of North Carolina newspaper people. Near the end of his tenure, the academic environment was changing, the news media were changing, and employers wanted graduates produced by a program with more of an academic focus.

Cole, too, provided the leadership and vision that his times demanded—but his times, and the media landscape within them, were dramatically different. The number of media options had increased, and the digital revolution created a demand for graduates with a wide repertoire of technological skills and knowledge. The times also demanded that the school be more inclusive, devote more attention to teaching, lead graduate education and research, and provide more services to the media. Students also needed to think globally, and Cole brought the world to the school and took the school to the world. Coffin disdained the term "journalism," preferring "newspaperman" (and rarely acknowledged newspaperwomen). For Cole, the term "journalism" was too narrow, and he pushed for a name change to the School of Journalism and Mass Communication and made it as inclusive as possible.

Early Teachers in the English Department, 1909–24

The early journalism teachers in the English department—Graham, James Royster, Richard Thornton, and Clarence Hibbard—had little or no newspaper experience, but they played important roles in creating the basis for the department and school that were to follow. They were guided by journalism programs at other universities, with UNC's encouragement.

Graham's vision for the journalism program and his leadership—as brief as it was—were crucial to the development of the program and its success. He played an important role with his vision that the university had an obligation to serve the citizens of North Carolina and its newspapers. Graham believed that by working together, the newspapers and the university could improve the lives of North Carolina residents. With his encouragement, journalism teachers who followed him reached out to the state's newspapers. The journalism program's graduates worked for those newspapers and made the university important to those newspapers, fostering the belief in the importance of providing financial support for the journalism program at Carolina—a level of support that would later become the envy of its peers.

Without Graham, journalism at Carolina might not have achieved the prestige it gained through his support—and certainly not as quickly. One is left to speculate how the journalism program might have developed differently if Graham had not died so young. It is interesting to note that in the 100 years of journalism at Carolina, three university presidents had newspaper experience and printer's ink in their veins. Edward Graham and Frank Graham had been *Tar Heel* editors, and Gordon Gray owned a major North Carolina newspaper company while he was president. That perspective almost certainly influenced the decisions they made about the department and school, including Edward Graham's creation of the Newspaper Institute, Frank Graham's decision to seek accreditation, and Gray's selection of Luxon as Coffin's successor.

The early teachers also made journalism important to the university by supporting students in the University Press Association—who helped to publicize the university—and by incorporating functions of the university's News Bureau into their instruction. University officials' early recognition of the importance of journalism instruction became a crucial factor in the university's support of the program and its leaders in later years.

Louis Graves, the last journalism teacher in the English department, had significant newspaper experience but no teaching background. In his dual role as journalism professor and head of the News Bureau, Graves provided practical training for students and strengthened the relationship between the state's newspapers and the university. William C. Friday, who was president of the Consolidated University of North Carolina from 1956 to 1986 and who knew Graves well, said he was a pioneering influence on journalism in Chapel Hill. "He was a character, he knew he was a character, and he enjoyed being a character," Friday recalled. "He created an atmosphere that made you respect journalism because you knew it had a place."[2] Graves' experience also demonstrated that it was not practical or desirable for one person to be responsible for running the News Bureau and teaching journalism courses.

Gerald Johnson was not chairman of the department long enough to make a significant impact, but his later fame as a journalist indirectly reflected prestige on the Department of Journalism. The fact that the first chairman of the Department of Journalism had a newspaper background demonstrated to the state's newspapers that the university was serious in its aim to create a credible, sustainable journalism program closely allied with newspapers.

Oscar Coffin, 1926–53

"Skipper" Coffin, the epitome of a crusty, disheveled newspaperman, built on Johnson's program, created the curriculum, and strengthened ties with the state's newspapers. He headed the program for 27 years and left an enduring legacy, transforming it from a one-person department with seven courses to a school with eight faculty members and 20 courses. He was attuned to the needs of North Carolina newspapers and made UNC's journalism program a force in the state by meeting those needs. The Department of Journalism provided newspapermen and newspaperwomen to scores of newspapers in North Carolina and beyond. He knew all the students, they all knew him, and he helped them get jobs, either by introducing them to editors on his front porch or by driving them to visit the newspapers. The manner in which so many North Carolina newspapers hailed his legacy and contributed money to the School of Journalism Foundation after 1950 shows the esteem that former students and editors held for Coffin and the program he created. Friday was emphatic when he described Coffin's legacy. Coffin was tough, Friday said, but he turned out "a whole generation of people who could run newspapers. I can see him right now, gruff and tough as he was, but I always enjoyed him." Friday also affirmed that the school would not be where it is today had it not been for the program that Coffin built.[3]

Coffin's task was not easy. In addition to having only himself and later a small faculty, he was forced to work with meager financial resources, especially during the Depression. When former students returned from

2. Friday, interview with the author, June 16, 2008.
3. Friday, interview with the author, June 16, 2008.

military service to Chapel Hill after World War II, he and his small staff had to deal with a growing student body that strained their time and resources. Coffin stressed a practical approach to teaching the craft of journalism and had little interest in scholarly activities. He did not like the administrative responsibilities of his position, and he had no use for national journalism education or accrediting organizations. Those attitudes kept the school out of the mainstream of journalism education at the national level. He disdained research and academic rigor in courses, and the school's reputation suffered in the eyes of other academics on campus as a result. Despite that, he had the support of UNC administrators, who recognized his importance and knew the value of his connections to newspaper people in North Carolina.

Coffin made wise hiring decisions and recruited faculty members— Walter Spearman, Phillips Russell, Joe Morrison, and Stuart Sechriest— who remained with the school for years, even after he was gone. They added to the aura of the department and provided stability. They, too, were loved by students who remained loyal to them and the department. According to Friday, Spearman was a powerful force on the campus and a strong proponent of academic freedom. Spearman was colorful, Friday added, "and when you contrasted him with Skipper Coffin, you wondered how they ever got together, but you were delighted that they did." Friday said Russell was one of the reasons the school flourished because he taught students what real writing meant. "Russell loved Chapel Hill with a passion," Friday added, "and he felt a great moral duty to teach young people about the meaning of life, and he was good at it." Morrison, on the other hand, was a contrast to Coffin, Spearman, and Russell and was not in the public eye as much. Behind the scenes, Friday said, Morrison "built the core of the whole enterprise in the school and was a steady rock." Morrison had very high standards, Friday added, and he was the kind of faculty member the school needed to keep moving forward at a high level of quality. In Friday's words, "Morrison represented in one person the transition from a professional approach to a more academic approach."[4]

Coffin was the face and soul of the Department of Journalism for many years. Ultimately, he built the foundations that made it possible for his successors to build the school's reputation at a national and international level. As Friday said, without Coffin, the journalism school would not have had as much support among the state's newspapers and journalists, which in turn would have made it more difficult for his successors to raise money and create the programs they envisioned.

4. Friday, interview with the author, June 16, 2008.

Neil Luxon, 1953–64

Norval Neil Luxon was an actor on the national stage of journalism education, was active in accreditation work, and knew how excellent (accredited) journalism programs were administered. He had been an assistant to the president of Ohio State University, understood how large universities operated, and believed in the importance of state-supported universities. He had a sense of what a dean should be and do, and he acted accordingly. He came to UNC with the goal of making it one of the best journalism schools in the country, and he succeeded. He got the school accredited within five years and created the graduate program, which eventually became one of the top programs in the world. Luxon saw the value of the School of Journalism Foundation and encouraged it to support the school and to grow, and the personal and professional support that Holt McPherson gave him cannot be discounted.

When Luxon became dean in 1953, the journalism faculty consisted of six men (Coffin, Spearman, Russell, Morrison, Sechriest, and Luxon). While all had newspaper experience, only Luxon had a doctorate. He hired strong faculty members who helped build the school, enhanced the graduate program, and made the school respected on campus. He was proud of the fact that by 1964 his faculty included five men with doctorates, six with master's degrees, and eight with bachelor's degrees. Two of his hires (Jack Adams and Jim Mullen) remained in the school for many years and provided stability and leadership in new areas of the curriculum. Two who did not stay (Roy Carter and Wayne Danielson) made the school stronger while they were on the faculty and added to the school's prestige.

Enrollment in the school increased 63 percent during Luxon's deanship, and the school moved into new quarters that were among the best in the nation at the time. Donors to the School of Journalism Foundation gave the school more than $60,000, and the market value of its principal increased from zero to $230,000. One indication of how much the school had improved came when its students won first place among 47 accredited programs in the 1964 William Randolph Hearst Foundation journalism awards program, considered by some to be the Pulitzer Prizes of collegiate journalism.

Friday said Luxon changed the whole demeanor of the school. It became more of an academic program, Friday said, but it did not lose its ties to the profession. He recalled that Luxon was "a very aggressive person who pushed hard in the right places," and Friday remembered how President Gordon Gray talked in glowing terms about Luxon. He said Luxon brought the school out of the Coffin years and began the movement that made the school the No. 1 program in the country.[5]

By the time he left the deanship in 1964, Luxon had transformed the school's faculty, curriculum, enrollment, and facilities and put it on the national stage. Even without Luxon, the school likely would have become accredited and added a graduate program (at least an M.A. program), but those things would not have happened so quickly. The school would not have been acknowledged as one of the best in the country by 1965, which would have made it more difficult for those who followed him to achieve what they did, and it probably would not have achieved its present status by now. As Coffin had done, Luxon enabled the deans who succeeded him.

Wayne Danielson, 1964–69

Wayne Danielson was dean for only four years (he was on leave for one year of his five-year term), but he continued the momentum and programs that Luxon had started. Danielson encouraged faculty research and enhanced the research reputation of the school on campus and nationally through his own scholarly work. During his term as dean, enrollment in the school grew 80 percent, and the value of the foundation's assets grew more than 25 percent. In 1964, the faculty consisted of Spearman, Morrison, Sechriest, Luxon, Byerly, Adams, Danielson, Mullen, and Ethridge. By 1969, Donald Shaw and Max McCombs had been hired, bringing the faculty to 11. McCombs resigned a few years later to go to Syracuse University, but Shaw remained on the faculty for the rest of his career. Those hires were important, because the team of McCombs and Shaw and their pioneering work on the agenda-setting function of the press would forever be associated with UNC–Chapel Hill.

Jack Adams, 1969–79

As Danielson had done, Jack Adams maintained the school's momentum and growth, led efforts to increase racial diversity on the faculty, pushed for the adoption of new communication technologies, and strengthened ties with the state's newspapers. He, too, was a leader in national accreditation activities, and the school became the first program in the nation to achieve schoolwide accreditation while he was dean. The school expanded from its limited focus on newspaper journalism to include broadcast jour-

5. Friday, interview with the author, June 16, 2008.

nalism, advertising, public relations, and visual communication. Adams and the faculty provided stability at a time when the campus was in turmoil over the Vietnam war.

Friday observed that Adams came along at the right time. "Schools, like universities, go through cycles," Friday stated, "and after an aggressive leader like Luxon, the school needed someone who could consolidate the gains and set new goals, and Adams was that leader. He represented the best of Oscar Coffin's mind while being committed to Luxon's academic excellence." Adams had a personality that was necessary at that moment in the school's history, Friday said. "Adams knew how to hold the fort together and knew how to move it forward. It was a happy circumstance that he was here and that he could be the leader the way he was." Friday said it took someone with a lot of grace and an enormous amount of patience to assemble a faculty as bright and talented as the journalism school's, and Jack Adams had those qualities.[6]

While Adams was dean, the number of journalism majors increased 80 percent, and the proportion of women students increased from 48 percent to 65 percent. At the start of his term in 1969, the faculty consisted of nine white men. By 1979, four white women and the first African-American faculty member had joined 10 white men on the faculty. Many remained on the faculty and provided future leadership in administration and research. Their long service on the faculty provided the stability that created a welcoming environment and gave the school a reputation as a supportive place to work and thrive. Without Adams, the school's progress and reputation would not have grown. He, too, enabled his successors to succeed.

Richard Cole, 1979–2005

Richard Cole transformed the school in countless ways, and his impact was probably the greatest of all its leaders. He saw the size of the school increase dramatically, moved it to Carroll Hall, led its expansion into new curriculum areas and programs, and put it on the world stage. From 1979 to 2005, the number of majors in the school increased almost 200 percent, and enrollment in the graduate program increased 192 percent. For several years, the school had one of the largest programs on campus, counting premajors (first-year and sophomore students), undergraduate majors, and graduate students. While Cole was dean, the school hired 46 faculty members, and many of them became important teachers, scholars,

6. William Friday, interview with the author, June 16, 2008.

and leaders in the school. The number of faculty members grew from 14 in 1980 to 45 in 2005, and the support staff grew from five in 1980 to more than 20 in 2005. When Cole became dean, the school had one minority faculty member, and it had seven by 2005. The percentage of minority students grew to 16 percent, and the percentage of female faculty members grew to 34 percent.

Without Richard Cole, today's School of Journalism and Mass Communication would be vastly different. In his 26 years as dean, he transformed the school in many ways and made it one of the premier programs in the country. It became recognized throughout the world for its excellence and its balance between academics and preparation of students for careers in the media. He inspired and led the school to engage in activities far beyond the nation's borders. In many ways, the changes in the school were symbolized by the new facilities Cole secured for the school in Carroll Hall in 1999, which made it almost unrecognizable compared to what it had been in 1979. As an accreditation team said in 2003, the school had become perhaps the best in the country.

In Friday's assessment, Cole led the school into the 21st century and was sensitive to ongoing developments in news, journalism, television, radio, and information technology. "He was way ahead in his thinking," Friday said, "and he built on the foundation that the others had created, and he got a lot of administrative support. He set in motion what is now the finest school in the country." Accreditation people had said that to Friday, but he could see it himself. Friday said Cole had the personality, grace, and style to move the school forward. He also internationalized the school—thinking globally but never losing sight of where it came from. Friday said he used to talk with famed television journalist Charles Kuralt about journalism and the school, and Kuralt told him that the gathering of such competence was bound to produce an excellent school.[7]

Holt McPherson

Holt McPherson deserves inclusion in this accounting of individuals who have made a significant difference in the history of the school and contributed to making it what it is today. He was associated with the school for more than 50 years—beginning as a student in 1924 and continuing to his death in 1979—and actively supported four deans: Coffin, Luxon, Danielson, and Adams. He singlehandedly pushed the university to seek accreditation for the Department of Journalism, and even though that ef-

7. Friday, interview with the author, June 16, 2008.

fort failed, it marked the beginning of major changes in the focus and quality of the school. McPherson was a prodigious fundraiser for many causes in High Point, and Joe Brown, a 1946 graduate of the school who worked for McPherson for many years, said he never took "no" for an answer when he asked for money.[8] McPherson marshaled the state press and university leaders to improve the school. He was the driving force behind the School of Journalism Foundation, through which donors have given the school enormous resources to achieve and maintain its status, and he was largely responsible for bringing Neil Luxon in as dean. Without McPherson, Luxon might not have become dean, the foundation might not have been created, and the school might not be what it is today.

Faculty, Staff, and Students

As important as those individuals were to the story of the School of Journalism and Mass Communication, they could not have achieved what they did without others. The school has had a tradition of excellence and an aura or reputation that is hard to define—the result of many factors that interact synergistically. Plentiful resources and outstanding facilities have made many things possible in the school, especially attracting excellent students and faculty members. In turn, the quality of the faculty and students has enhanced the reputation of the school, and that has improved the school's image and attracted more resources to it.

One of the factors contributing to the school's reputation for excellence has been the presence of superb teachers and scholars on the faculty. The faculty has had remarkable longevity—as measured by the number of years each faculty member has served. Six were on the faculty for 30 or more years, including Walter Spearman (44); Tom Bowers (35); Stuart Sechriest (31); and "Skipper" Coffin, Joe Morrison, and Rich Beckman (30 each). Three members of the faculty in 2008 had the same level of longevity: Donald Shaw (42), Richard Cole (37), and Jane Brown (31). Eleven other former faculty members stayed 20 to 29 years, and five current faculty members already have between 21 and 27 years of service. More than half (56 percent) of the faculty members who have left the school since 1924 have done so because of retirement or death, 26 percent to go to another school, and 18 percent for other reasons. Only two left because they were denied tenure. The school has also avoided internal factions

8. Brown, interview with the author, April 28, 2008.

or conflicts, which are common at other schools. Faculty members could not have achieved all that they did without the support of dedicated staff members. The enormous contributions of the staff are especially vital, considering how they have toiled without the financial compensation they deserved because of inadequate funding from the state.

Judicious (and, to some extent, fortunate) hiring decisions have created a climate in the school in which outstanding teaching has been expected and rewarded. UNC–Chapel Hill gives only a few campuswide distinguished teaching-excellence awards each year. The consistently high level of teaching excellence in the school has been evident in the fact that its faculty members have been recognized for outstanding teaching disproportionately to their numbers at the university. Over the years, several faculty members have won campuswide distinguished teaching awards, including Debashis Aikat, Rich Beckman, John Bittner, Tom Bowers, Richard Cole, Jim Shumaker, Chuck Stone, Dulcie Straughan, and John Sweeney. In addition, several Ph.D. students have won campuswide teaching awards, including Terry Bailey, Brian Carroll, Lois Boynton, Glen Feighery, Beth Koehler, Richard Landsberg, and Karl Schmid.

The school has also provided exemplary support to research by faculty members and students. Joe Morrison was considered to be one of the preeminent historians of his era. Wayne Danielson was one of the first scholars in the country to see the potential for computers to be used in producing newspapers and for research and data analysis. Max McCombs and Donald Shaw began their pioneering, extensive agenda-setting research with a study of Chapel Hill voters in 1968. Forty years later, Shaw recalled the genesis of their interest in agenda-setting. He said McCombs had observed people in a bar talking about the previous day's news, and the two professors started speculating about the relationship between media content and voters' issue knowledge. They combined McCombs' strength in survey research and Shaw's strength in content analysis for their first study.[9] Shaw has also been recognized for his scholarly publications in media history. Phil Meyer has received international acclaim for his scholarly efforts in precision journalism and economic issues of the media and newspaper survival. Jane Brown has been a leading scholar in the study of media effects on adolescents. Bob Stevenson was internationally known for his research on the world's media systems, and Margaret Blanchard wrote important books on freedom of expression. Other faculty members

9. Shaw, interview with the author, Oct. 19, 2007.

are beginning to make names for themselves in scholarship, and the extensive research record of graduate students has made the school a leader in graduate education.

The school's reputation, including that of its teachers and scholars, has attracted outstanding students who have contributed as much to the school's quality and character as they have gained. Some of the graduates of the school's undergraduate and graduate programs probably would have succeeded and excelled without their education at UNC, but the school was fortunate to have attracted such remarkable students. The presence of excellent students has stimulated greater effort on the part of faculty members, which in turn has added even more to the school's standing.

Alumni and Friends

The school's students have been appreciative of the education and financial support they have received at the school, and they have become loyal and generous alumni. As individuals and corporate executives, they have made financial contributions that have added to the school's resources and programs. They have also contributed as visiting professionals, class speakers, mentors, and employers of the school's graduates. Since 1909, the university and the state have supported journalism education at UNC–Chapel to the extent they could, but financial support from alumni and friends of the school has made the difference in what the school has achieved.

The school's image has also benefited from the prestige of UNC–Chapel Hill, especially as the university's reputation has attracted students and faculty members. Because the School of Journalism and Mass Communication is so highly regarded, the university has recognized its contributions to the university and state and has generously supported the school. The appeal of Chapel Hill and of the state of North Carolina have also been important intangible factors in recruiting and retaining faculty and staff members. The region is recognized as an attractive place to live with an agreeable climate, top-notch schools and medical facilities, and plentiful natural attractions, such as mountains and beaches.

Impact on North Carolina

The school has also had an impact on the university and state. Rolfe Neill, who was editor of the *Daily Tar Heel* in 1953 and who eventually became one of the state's most influential journalists at the *Charlotte Observer*, had a long perspective on the school. He said in a 2007 interview that the school's mission has been complementary to the university's mission and has had an enormous impact on the state.[10] William Friday has had a perspective on the school as President Gordon Gray's assistant from 1951 to 1956 and as president of the Consolidated University of North Carolina from 1956 to 1986. In 2008, he reflected on what the school has meant to the university and the state with a vivid, personal statement about two problems he faced as president. One was the issue of a speaker-ban law on campus, and the other was the issue of desegregation of the university system.[11] Friday was emphatic in expressing his gratitude for the role of North Carolina newspapers in those struggles: "If it had not been for the editorial support of the newspapers of North Carolina, I would never have survived either one of those fights," he affirmed. He praised Bill Snider of the *Greensboro Daily News*, Pete McKnight of the *Charlotte Observer*, Jonathan Daniels of the Raleigh *News and Observer*, and other editors for their editorial explanations of why those issues were so important to the people of the state. At that time, it was not easy to be an advocate of letting communists speak on campus, Friday said, and the newspapers helped him explain to North Carolina citizens that such a stance guaranteed their right of free speech on other topics. Friday boasted that he attended every meeting of the North Carolina Press Association for 30 years, because he wanted to tell the editors that if it were not for them and the school, the university would not have had a voice:

The press in this state kept the truth in perspective, and I know those journalists got that because of what they experienced in the school. The school saved the university in those two fights. I can't express my gratitude sufficiently. You can tell by the intensity of my feeling even now, 25 years later, that I know where the strength of the university was, and I know it was because of what the professors in the School of Journalism taught those young people about who, what, where, when, how, and why. When they answered those

10. Neill, interview with the author, Oct. 5, 2007.
11. The North Carolina General Assembly enacted a speaker ban law in 1963 to try to prevent communists from speaking on campus. Friday opposed the ban as an infringement on free speech, and the law was declared unconstitutional in 1968. The desegregation controversy began in 1970, when the U.S. Department of Health, Education and Welfare ordered the university to dismantle what HEW called a "racially identifiable" system of higher education in the state. Friday and the Board of Governors submitted various plans while resisting what they felt were overly intrusive remedies proposed by HEW, including the elimination of academic programs at some institutions because duplicate programs existed on other campuses. The matter was finally settled by a consent decree in 1983.

questions authoritatively and translated them editorially, I rested my case. I knew it would be done right. That's how important that school has been to this place. It will always be, and the thing that troubles me now more than anything else is seeing how the sale of newspapers to financially oriented corporations has taken away that personal identity. It has happened to the *News and Observer*, the *Charlotte Observer*, and the *Greensboro Daily News*, and it is not a healthy thing. I wish I could go back to Coffin and say, "Skipper, let's get the *Franklin Times* cranked up again. We need it!"[12]

Throughout its history, the leaders of the School of Journalism and Mass Communication have been visionaries who have marshaled resources and taken advantage of intangible factors to make the school one of the premier programs in the world. That reputation and the resources of the school, backed by the respect and esteem of thousands of alumni and friends, will ensure that current and future leaders can continue the school's tradition of excellence. Regardless of how the media evolve, the school will be a leader in teaching the uses of new technology, conducting research, and serving the media within an ethical framework. The outlook for the next 100 years is bright.

12. Friday, interview with the author, June 16, 2008.

Appendix: Who, What, Where, When, and Why

This is a guide to people, places, and things that have been important in the story of journalism–mass communication education at UNC–Chapel Hill. Although the author has tried to be as accurate and inclusive as possible, some errors of omission or commission may have occurred. An updated version of this appendix will be maintained at the school's Web site: www.jomc.unc.edu/history. Comments, corrections, and additions should be sent to jomchistory@unc.edu.

Abernathy, Penny Muse. Faculty member, 2008–present. Knight Chair of Journalism and Digital Media Economics. Teaching area: digital media economics. B.A. (UNC–Greensboro); M.S., M.B.A. (Columbia).

Accreditation. In 1948, UNC President Frank Porter Graham, who was under pressure from influential newspaper editors in the state to improve the Department of Journalism, invited the American Council on Education for Journalism (ACEJ) to evaluate and accredit the department. ACEJ's denial of accreditation that year led to significant changes, including the creation of the School of Journalism and the School of Journalism Foundation. The school was later accredited by ACEJ in 1958 and reaccredited in 1965, 1971, 1977, 1985, 1991, 1997, and 2003. The 2003 accreditation report said the school was "probably the best in the country."

Adams, Ansel. The famous photographer visited with students in the school's news photography course on April 18, 1969.

Adams, John B. Faculty member, 1958–85; dean, 1969–79. Teaching areas: media law, international communication. B.A. (California); M.S., Ph.D. (Wisconsin).

Aikat, Debashis "Deb." Faculty member, 1995–present. Teaching areas: media futures, new technologies. B.A., M.A. (Calcutta); Ph.D. (Ohio).

Aikat, Jay. Staff member, 1996–99. Computer systems administrator.

Alexander, David. Staff member, 2006–present. Computer support. B.S. (Virginia Tech).

Allred, Michael. Staff member, 2004–05. Computing consultant.

Almers, Jay. Staff member, 2008–present. Education content and Web site developer.

Alumni Building. The Department of Journalism occupied two rooms on the south side of the main floor in 1924–35. Former students recalled how "Skipper" Coffin cursed pigeons that roosted outside the windows of Alumni Building.

Amana, Harry. Faculty member, 1979–2006. First African-American faculty member. Teaching areas: reporting, minorities and the media. B.A., M.A. (Temple).

Anderson, Cindy. Staff member, 1998–present. Graduate program manager.

Anthony, Jesse O. "Jay." Faculty member, 1988–2004. Teaching area: graphic design. B.A. (UNC–Chapel Hill); M.A. (Missouri).

Arledge, Mary. Staff member, ca. 1983. Undergraduate secretary.

Association for Education in Journalism and Mass Communication (AEJMC). Faculty members in the school have been active in this national organization of journalism educators for many years. Three faculty members have been AEJMC presidents: Neil Luxon in 1957, Richard Cole in 1983, and Tom Bowers in 1989. On Aug. 26–30, 1962, when it was known as the Association for Education in Journalism, it held its 50th annual convention on the UNC campus, with 216 members from 86 schools, 80 wives, 66 children, and 67 guests. Despite the oppressive heat, they were reported to be impressed by Howell Hall, the Carolina Inn, Parker and Teague dormitories, and Lenoir Dining Hall.

Barnes, Marla. Staff member, 2007–present. Student records assistant. B.A. (UNC–Chapel Hill).

Bass, Jo. Staff member, 1991–present. Secretary to the dean, administrative assistant to the dean. A.A. (Alamance Community College).

Bechtel, Andy. Faculty member, 2005–present. Teaching area: news editing. B.A. (South Carolina); M.A. (UNC–Chapel Hill).

Beckman, Richard J. Faculty member, 1978–2008. James L. Knight Professor. Teaching areas: photojournalism, multimedia. B.J.A. (Ohio State); M.A. (Minnesota).

Belk, Mark. Staff member, ca. 1997–98. Assistant student records manager.

Bigelow, Patricia. Staff member, 1991–98. Undergraduate secretary, assistant student records manager, financial secretary.

Biocca, Frank. Faculty member, 1987–96. Teaching areas: advertising, new media technologies. B.A. (McGill); M.S. (San Jose State); Ph.D. (Wisconsin).

Bishop, Michael. Faculty member, 1969–75. Teaching area: international communication. B.A. (Baylor); M.S. (Columbia); Ph.D. (Wisconsin).

Bittner, John R. Faculty member, 1991–2002. Faculty member in the Department of Radio, Television and Motion Pictures, 1980–91. Teaching area: electronic communication. B.A. (Dakota Wesleyan); M.A., Ph.D. (Purdue).

Blake, Terry. Staff member, 1986–93. Financial secretary, accounting manager.

Blanchard, Margaret. Faculty member, 1974–2004. William Rand Kenan Jr. Professor. Teaching areas: media law, First Amendment freedoms. B.S.J., M.A. (Florida); Ph.D. (UNC–Chapel Hill).

Board of Visitors. Created to strengthen the school's ties with media executives, utilize members' expertise, and assist with fundraising. Gene Roberts, executive editor and president of the *Philadelphia Inquirer*, was the first chairman. The first meeting was held Sept. 8, 1989, at the Siena Hotel in Chapel Hill. The name was changed to Board of Advisers in 2008.

Bogas, Nicole. Staff member, 2005. Student records assistant.

Boone, Katherine. Staff member, ca. 1948. Secretary.

Bowers, Thomas A. Faculty member, 1971–2006; associate dean and senior associate dean, 1979–2005; interim dean, 2005–06. James L. Knight Professor. Teaching areas: advertising, pedagogy. B.A., M.A., Ph.D. (Indiana).

Boynton, Lois. Faculty member, 2001–present. Teaching areas: public relations, ethics. B.A. (Lenoir-Rhyne); M.A., Ph.D. (UNC–Chapel Hill).

Braxton, Beth Gardner. Staff member, 2002–03. Assistant dean for development and alumni affairs. B.A. (UNC–Chapel Hill).

Brown, Jane D. Faculty member, 1977–present. James L. Knight Professor. Teaching areas: research methods, media and society, honors. B.A. (Kentucky); M.A., Ph.D. (Wisconsin).

Brown, Levi Ames. He received his B.A. in English from the university in 1910 and wrote an undergraduate thesis about the history of journalism at UNC prior to that time. He was a Washington correspondent for the Raleigh *News and Observer*, White House correspondent for the *Philadelphia Record*, and director of publicity for the U.S. Committee on Public Information, 1917–18. When the university raised money in 1931 to honor Graham with the Graham Memorial Building, Brown donated $80,000.

Buhrman, Cassandra. Staff member, 1976–83. Graduate secretary, student records assistant.

Bunn, Terry. Staff member, ca. 1975. Secretary.

Burton, Flynt. Staff member, 2003–04. Assistant to the development director.

Byars, Napoleon. Faculty member, 2005–present. Teaching areas: news writing, public relations. B.A. (UNC–Chapel Hill); M.A. (Northern Colorado, Greeley); Air War College; Air Command and Staff College.

Byars, Queenie. Faculty member, 2008–present. Teaching areas: news writing, public relations. B.A. (UNC–Chapel Hill); M.A. (Northern Colorado, Greeley); Air War College; Air Command and Staff College.

Byerly, Kenneth Rhodes. Faculty member, 1957–71. Teaching area: newspapers. B.B.A. (Minnesota); M.A. (UNC–Chapel Hill).

Bynum Hall. The Department of Journalism moved from Alumni Building to larger quarters on the east side of the top floor of Bynum Hall in 1935. The university used Works Progress Administration funding to renovate the building, which had been the university's gymnasium. See note about Henry S. Snow.

Cairo, Alberto. Faculty member, 2005–present. Teaching area: multimedia. B.A. (Universidad de Santiago de Compostela); M.A. (Instituto de Artes Visuales).

Caldwell, William "Willie" Stuart. Faculty member, 1955–58. B.A., M.A. (Minnesota).

Carolina Business News Initiative. Program created by Professor Chris Roush that trains business journalists through workshops, other special programs, and a blog.

Carolina Communicator. A school publication created in October 2000 to combine the *UNC Journalist* and *JAFA News*.

Carolina Community Media Project. Program created by Lecturer Jock Lauterer to strengthen community media in North Carolina.

Carolina Poll. Survey of North Carolina residents that was first conducted by journalism students in 1975.

Carpentier, Francesca Dillman. Faculty member, 2005–present. Teaching area: electronic communication. B.A. (Northern Arizona); M.A., Ph.D. (Alabama).

Carr Building. Because of the lack of space in Howell Hall, offices for professors Bob Stevenson and Frank Biocca and Ph.D. students were moved to Carr Building in 1991.

Carr, Shanea. Staff member, 2006–07. Student records assistant.

Carroll, Craig. Faculty member, 2007–present. Teaching area: public relations. B.S. (Freed-Hardeman University); M.A. (Abilene Christian University); Ph.D. (Texas).

Carroll Hall. Home of the School of Journalism and Mass Communication, July 1999 to the present. The older (front) part of the building was completed in 1953 and named after Dudley Dewitt Carroll, founder of the School of Commerce. The addition to the building was completed in 1972. In the summer of 1998, while the actor Robin Williams was filming the movie "Patch Adams" on campus, Carroll Hall was being renovated. The front of the building served as the background for the commencement scene in the movie, and set designers covered the name on the front of the building and replaced it with "Virginia Medical University" for the movie.

Carson, Lester. First African-American student to graduate from the School of Journalism in 1963, after transferring from North Carolina College, which was later called North Carolina Central University.

Carter, Roy Ernest Jr. Faculty member, 1954–58. Teaching area: research methods. B.A. (Fort Hays Kansas State College); M.A. (Minnesota); Ph.D. (Stanford). He received one of the first doctoral degrees in mass communication research from an American university.

Cauthren, Benji. Staff member, 2004–present. Assistant director of development and alumni affairs. B.A. (UNC–Chapel Hill).

Cavin, Winston. Visiting lecturer, 1999–present. Teaching area: news writing. B.A. (UNC–Chapel Hill).

Chamberlin, William. Faculty member, 1976–87. Teaching area: media law. B.A. (Washington); M.A. (Wisconsin); Ph.D. (Washington).

Chambers, Lenoir. Director of the University News Bureau, 1919–21. Editor of the *Tar Heel*, 1913–14. He received a master's degree from the Columbia University School of Journalism in 1917 and was listed as an assistant professor of journalism at UNC in 1919 but did not teach. As editor of the *Virginian-Pilot* in Norfolk, Va., he was considered one of the leading progressive Southern editors who championed civil rights and integration. B.A. (UNC–Chapel Hill).

Chapel Hill Newspaper. Successor to the *Chapel Hill Weekly* newspaper that was founded by Louis Graves. Publisher Orville Campbell renamed the paper when he changed to daily publication in the early 1970s. In an editorial marking the school's 50th anniversary in 1974, Campbell wrote that nearly 100 graduates or students from the school had worked at the newspaper. Jim Shumaker had an especially strong influence over those journalists while he was editor, before he joined the school's faculty.

Chapel Hill Weekly. Newspaper founded by Louis Graves, professor of journalism in the Department of English, in 1924.

Choate, Dorothy. Staff member, 1970–90. Librarian.

Chuck Stone Program for Diversity in Education and Media. Diversity workshop for high school media students, 2007–present. Funded by Ethics and Excellence in Journalism Foundation and Gannett Foundation.

Cloud, George William "Bill." Faculty member, 1982–present. Teaching area: news-editorial. B.A., B.J., M.A. (Missouri).

Cobb, Collier. As chairman of the UNC Department of Geology and a founder of the University Press in 1893, he supported student journalists and the University Press Association.

Coffin, Oscar Jackson. Also known as "O. J.," "Skipper," or "Ock." Faculty member, 1926–56; chairman of the Department of Journalism, 1926–50; first dean of the School of Journalism, 1950–53. After serving as editor-in-chief of the *Tar Heel* and graduating from UNC in 1909, he taught school for one year in Asheboro, N.C., before becoming a reporter for the *Winston-Salem Journal* in 1911. He was news editor of the *Charlotte Observer* in 1912–16 before going to the *Raleigh Times* as city editor in 1916–18 and editor in 1918–26.

Cole, Richard R. Faculty member, 1971–present; dean, 1979–2005. John Thomas Kerr Jr. Distinguished Professor. Teaching areas: feature writing, international communication. B.A., M.A. (Texas); Ph.D. (Minnesota).

Commencement exercises. The school began holding a separate May commencement ceremony for graduates in Howell Hall in the late 1960s. As the number of graduates grew, it became increasingly difficult to accommodate them and their families in Howell. In some years, family members sat in the auditorium, and the graduates marched in from outside the building. When that became impractical, the school moved the ceremony to Hill Hall. That venue also became too small, and for a few years the ceremony had to be divided by sequence into two sessions. In 1982, the ceremony was held in the Morehead Banquet Hall. After being held in Memorial Hall for a few years, the ceremony was moved to Carmichael Auditorium. Heat and acoustics were a problem there, and the school held its first ceremony in the Dean E. Smith Center in 2006. The first December commencement ceremony for the school was held for approximately 40 graduates in Carroll Hall on Dec. 18, 1999.

Conway, John. Staff member. Director of career services and special programs, 1994–95; assistant dean for distance education and executive education, 2002–2004. B.A. (UNC–Chapel Hill).

Cook, Sandra. Director of the Newspapers in Education program based in the school, 2001–present.

Cotton, Kendra. Staff member, 2006–07. Assistant director for programs.

Cuadros, Paul. Faculty member, 2007–present. Teaching area: news-editorial. B.A. (Michigan); M.A. (Northwestern).

Cupp, David. Faculty member, 2005–present. Teaching area: electronic communication. B.A. (Central Oklahoma); M.A. (Virginia).

Curtin, Patricia. Faculty member, 1996–2006. Teaching area: public relations. B.A. (Earlham); M.A., Ph.D. (Georgia).

Danielson, Wayne. Faculty member, 1958–69; dean, 1964–69. He became dean at age 34, the youngest dean in the history of the university, and was one of the first scholars to predict that computers would change newspapers. Teaching areas: research methods, computers. B.A. (Iowa); M.A., Ph.D. (Stanford).

Davis, Sabrina. Staff member, 1999–2001. Assistant to the dean for executive education. B.A. (UNC–Chapel Hill).

Davison, Pat. Faculty member, 2001–present. Teaching area: photojournalism. B.A. (Missouri); M.A. (Ohio University).

Diagnostic Writing Exam (DWE). Instituted in 1982 as part of an entrance requirement to the school. Students had to complete English 30, "Advanced Expository Writing," or pass the DWE before they could enroll in "News Writing." The requirement was eventually eliminated.

Dixon, Judy. Staff member, ca. 1973. Secretary.

Dougall, Elizabeth. Faculty member, 2003–present. Teaching area: public relations. B.Bus. (Queensland University of Technology); M.A. (Charles Sturt University); Ph.D. (Queensland University of Technology).

Dougall, Malcolm. Staff member, 2008–present. Equipment room manager. B.E. (University of South Queensland).

Elam, A. Richard Jr. Faculty member, 1993–99. Faculty member in the Department of Radio, Television and Motion Pictures, 1977–93. Teaching area: electronic communication. B.A., M.A. (Texas); Ph.D. (UNC–Chapel Hill).

Ellis, Morgan. Staff member, 2007–present. Special projects editor. B.A. (UNC–Chapel Hill).

Ethridge, Mark Foster. Faculty member, 1964–68.

Eubank, Jay. Staff member, 1996–present. Director of career services. B.A. (Baylor).

Evarts, Audrey. Staff member, ca. 1964. Dean's secretary.

Faculty Council. The school was allotted its own seat on the university's Faculty Council in 1992, and Richard Beckman was elected as its first representative, followed by John Sweeney. Jane Brown was chair of the UNC Faculty Council in 1994–97.

Fee, Frank. Faculty member, 2000–present. Teaching areas: news editing, history. B.S. (Cornell); M.A. (SUNY–Brockport); Ph.D. (UNC–Chapel Hill).

Field, Dylan R. Staff member, 2005–present. TV producer and director. B.A. (UNC–Chapel Hill).

Fiftieth Anniversary. In 1974, the school marked the 50th anniversary of the creation of the Department of Journalism with programs about "Journalism and the Real World" and reminiscences of former students. More than 300 former students and other guests attended the festivities at Howell Hall and the Carolina Inn. The featured speaker was Tom Wicker, a 1948 graduate and associate editor of the *New York Times*, who predicted a new age of journalism because it was assuming a new relevance in American life, beginning with reporting of the Vietnam War. At the banquet, Dean Jack Adams recognized the presence of four men who had played important roles in the department and school: Phillips Russell, Neil Luxon, Holt McPherson, and Walter Spearman.

Folkerts, Jean. Faculty member, Alumni Distinguished Professor and dean, 2006–present. B.A., M.S. (Kansas State); Ph.D. (Kansas).

Foundation. See School of Journalism Foundation of North Carolina.

Foust, Robbie. Staff member, 2000–2003. Computing assistant.

Freedom Forum Ph.D. Program. Established in 1995 with funding from the Freedom Forum foundation. Generous stipends supported 19 former media professionals who wanted to teach at the college level and enabled them to complete the school's regular Ph.D. in 24–27 months instead of 36 months or more. The program ended in 2002 when the Freedom Forum cancelled funding so it could build its $450 million Newseum in Washington, D.C.

Friedman, Barbara. Faculty member, 2004–present. Teaching areas: history, news editorial. B.A. (Webster); M.A., Ph.D. (Missouri).

Gaines, Lisa. Staff member, ca. 1998. Assistant student records manager.

Gallina, Jennifer K. Staff member, 2007–present. Director of research administration. B.A. (Gonzaga); M.A. (Maryland).

Gardner, Paul. Staff member, 1989–98. Director of development, assistant to the dean for development and alumni affairs. B.A. (UNC–Chapel Hill).

Gaulden, Elaine. Staff member, ca. 1974. Receptionist.

Gibson, Rhonda. Faculty member, 2001–present. Teaching areas: news-editorial, media and society. B.S. (Tennessee); Ph.D. (Alabama).

Gifford Courtyard. In 1967, Mr. and Mrs. L.C. Gifford, publishers of the *Hickory* (N.C.) *Daily Record*, donated $25,000 to create an azalea garden in memory of their daughter, Sara Lee Gifford, who had studied journalism in the school and was working in the advertising department of the *Daily Record* when she was killed in an automobile accident. The garden and courtyard were dedicated on Jan. 18, 1969, on the south side of Howell Hall. A new azalea garden, given by Gifford's sister, Suzanne Millholland, was created on the west side of Carroll Hall after the school moved.

Glaxo Wellcome Program in Medical Journalism. Created in 1997 with a $333,000 contribution from Glaxo Wellcome. Professor Tom Linden, M.D., was the first Glaxo Wellcome Distinguished Professor of Medical Journalism and created the medical journalism program.

Gorsuch, Elizabeth. Staff member, 2007–08. Assistant director for programs.

Graduate program. The M.A. program was launched in 1955, and the Ph.D. program followed in 1964. The first master's degree was awarded to Robert Pittman in 1957, and the first Ph.D. was awarded to Grover Cleveland Wilhoit in 1967.

Graham, Edward Kidder. He taught the first journalism course—in the Department of English—in 1909–10 and perhaps again in 1912–13. He received his bachelor's degree from UNC in 1898. As a student, he was an associate editor of the *Tar Heel* in 1896 and editor-in-chief in November and December of 1897. He was also president of the University Athletic Association, which published the *Tar Heel*. He was named dean of the College of Liberal Arts in 1909 and president of the university in 1913 at age 37. He died at age 42 in the Spanish influenza epidemic of 1918. According to the 1900 U.S. Census, he was a boarder in the household of Julia Graves, Louis Graves' mother. Louis Graves was 16 at the time and living in the same house. Graham married Susan Williams Moses on June 25, 1908, and their son, Edward Kidder Graham Jr., was born on Jan. 31, 1911. Susan Moses died in 1916, and the younger Graham was raised by his uncle, Louis Graves.

Grammar Slammer. See Spelling and Grammar Exam.

Graves, Louis (pronounced "loo-ee"). Faculty member, 1921–24. First and only person with the title of Professor of Journalism in the Department of English. After graduating from UNC in 1902, he worked at the *New York Times* in 1903–1906, was manager of Parker and Bridge publicity company in New York City, and worked for the New York City government. In 1921–23, he also served as director of the University News Bureau while teaching journalism. He left the university when he started the *Chapel Hill Weekly* in 1923.

Graves, Ralph. Older brother of Louis Graves. Editor-in-chief of the *Tar Heel* and on the staff at the same time as Edward Kidder Graham. He was later the Sunday editor of the *New York Times*. B.A. (UNC–Chapel Hill).

Grist, Lucy. Staff member, ca. 1990. Secretary.

Guillory, Ferrel. Faculty member, 1997–present. Teaching area: media and politics. Director of the Program on Public Life. B.A. (Loyola University, New Orleans); M.A. (Columbia).

Gunter, Stephanie. Staff member, 2005–06. Assistant director of development and alumni affairs. B.A. (UNC–Chapel Hill).

Habel, Barbara. Staff member, 1987–89. Director of development (part time).

Hales, Ken. Staff member, 1998–present. Accounting manager. B.A. (UNC–Wilmington; M.A. (UNC–Chapel Hill).

Hallman, Speed. Staff member, 2004–present. Associate dean for development and alumni affairs. B.A. (UNC–Chapel Hill); M.A. (Appalachian State).

Halls of Fame. The first members of the North Carolina Journalism Hall of Fame were inducted on April 12, 1981. The Halls of Fame for Advertising and Public Relations were added in 1988. They recognize individuals who are natives of North Carolina or who are distinctively identified with the state and have made exceptionally distinguished and career-long contributions to journalism and mass communication.

Hamann, Susan. Staff member, ca. 1990. Assistant to the financial secretary.

Harden, Glenn. Graduate of the school who was the first woman editor of the *Daily Tar Heel,* in 1950.

Hargraves, Lewis. Janitor in Howell Hall, 1967–77.

Hearst Visiting Professionals Program. Created in 1990 with a $200,000 endowment from the William Randolph Hearst Foundation to bring visiting professionals to the school.

Hefner, Jim. Faculty member, 2008–present. Professor of the practice. Teaching area: electronic communication. B.A. (UNC–Chapel Hill), M.A. (Duquesne).

"Hell No, I Won't Go!" Video produced by Professor Richard Simpson to mark the school's departure from Howell Hall in 1999.

Hennink-Kaminski, Heidi. Faculty member, 2006–present. Teaching area: advertising. B.A. (Michigan); M.A. (Western Michigan); Ph.D. (Georgia).

Hester, Joe Bob. Faculty member, 2001–present; associate dean for undergraduate studies, 2008–present. Teaching area: advertising. B.A., M.A. (Texas Tech); Ph.D. (Alabama).

Hibbard, Clarence A. Taught journalism courses as a faculty member in the Department of English, 1919–21, and later became dean of the College of Liberal Arts. B.A., M.A. (Wisconsin).

Hill, Monica. Staff member, 2002–present. Director of high school media programs. B.A. (Auburn); M.A. (Alabama); M.Ed. (Montevallo).

Hill, Terry. Staff member, 1996–present. Television engineer.

Hirth, Andrea Lee. Staff member, ca. 2001. Assistant to the development director.

Hoefges, Michael. Faculty member, 2003–present. Teaching areas: media law, advertising. B.S., J.D., M.A., Ph.D. (Florida).

Holley, Lester. Staff member, 2000–present. Assistant to the accounting manager. B.A. (Campbell).

Honors program. Program for outstanding undergraduates that was started by Neil Luxon in 1964.

Hoskins, Zachary. Staff member, 2000–2004. Assistant to the dean for communications. M.A. (UNC–Chapel Hill).

Howell, Dottie. Staff member, 2004–present. Administrative manager, assistant dean for business and finance.

Howell Hall. Home of the School of Journalism, 1960–99. It cost $45,000 when it was built in 1905, and it was described as being "architecturally inharmonious with other buildings." The Chemistry Department moved from Person Hall to Howell in 1906 but outgrew the building and moved to Venable Hall in 1926. The School of Pharmacy moved from Person Hall to Howell in 1926, and in 1931 the name was changed from Chemistry Building to Howell Hall to honor Edward Vernon Howell, first dean of the School of Pharmacy, who died that year. In 1959, the School of Pharmacy moved to Beard Hall near the UNC Hospitals, and Howell Hall was renovated for the School of Journalism, resulting in 27,000 square feet of usable space. The school moved to Howell at the start of the fall 1960 semester, and formal dedication ceremonies were held on Oct. 21, 1960. For a time, starting in 1962, the auditorium and three classrooms were used by the Church of Jesus Christ of Latter-Day Saints for Sunday School. When the university assigned building numbers to campus mailing addresses, Howell was 021A.

"Howelling Times." Newsletter produced in the school in the 1970s.

Jackson, Walter. Third African-American student to graduate from the School of Journalism, 1967.

Johnson, Gerald W. First faculty member (and chairman) of the Department of Journalism, 1924–26, and the only faculty member at the time. He later worked with H. L. Mencken at the Baltimore *Sun* and became known as the "Sage of Baltimore." B.A. (Wake Forest).

Johnson, Jayson. Staff member, ca. 1998. Computer systems administrator.

Johnston, Anne. Faculty member, 1993–present. Associate dean for graduate studies, 2007–present. Faculty member in the Department of Radio, Television, and Motion Pictures, 1986–93. Teaching areas: media and society, political communication, women and media. B.A. (Central Florida); M.A., Ph.D. (Oklahoma).

Jones, Paul. Faculty member, 1995–present. Director of ibilio.org. Teaching areas: Internet and new media technologies. B.S. (N.C. State University); M.F.A. (Warren Wilson College).

Jones, Sharon Horton. Staff member, 1985–present. Graduate secretary, undergraduate secretary, student records manager, director of student services and assessment.

Jones, Weimar. Faculty member, 1953–54, while editor of the *Franklin Press and the Highlands Maconian* in Franklin, N.C.

Journalism Alumni and Friends Association (JAFA). Founded at a meeting of 30 people at the Carolina Inn on Jan. 30, 1980, with Reed Sarratt as its first president. Chapters have been in Washington, D.C., Atlanta, Charlotte, Chicago, and New York City. The first issue of *JAFA News* appeared in August 1980.

Journalism Days. An annual program that was first held April 12–14, 1981, and featured special programs and activities. It ended in the mid-1990s. (See Journalism Week.)

Journalism Newsletter. A school publication that first appeared Dec. 1, 1954, and was distributed to alumni and friends of the school. A mimeographed publication called the *Journalism Newsletter* was for faculty and students and was started on Dec. 15, 1969. A weekly newsletter called the *Howelling Times* appeared during the 1970s. The *J-School Newsletter* first appeared on Sept. 4, 1979, and carried announcements of interest to students. On Nov. 7, 1983, the title was changed to *J-School News*, and the issues of April 1 and 15, 1991, were titled *JMC School News*. From Sept. 4, 1991, to April 20, 1992, it was called *JoMC School News*, and the title changed to *JOMC News* on Sept. 8, 1992. It continues to the present and is available via e-mail.

Journalism Organization for Black Students. An organization created in 1978 to address concerns of black students in the school. A later organization with similar aims was called Carolina Association of Black Journalists.

Journalism Week. March 13–20, 1965. The school consolidated several meetings into a week of special activities, including programs for editorial writers, feature writers, nondaily newspaper editors, and the North Carolina Press Women. Journalism Week was held again in March 1966 but not after that.

The Journalist. Also the *UNC Journalist.* Laboratory publication of the school, 1962–2000.

Journalist-in-Space. In 1985, the school was the regional site for the selection of a journalist to participate in a space mission with the National Aeronautics and Space Administration, and preliminary selection interviews were held on campus. The program was cancelled after the explosion of the space shuttle Challenger on Jan. 28, 1986.

Kalyanaraman, Sriram "Sri." Faculty member, 2002–present. Teaching areas: research methods, Internet and new media technologies. B.E. (Mysore University, India); Ph.D. (Pennsylvania State University).

Kappa Tau Alpha. National honorary fraternity for outstanding journalism students established in the school in 1955. It was designated as the "Norval Neil Luxon Chapter" on July 15, 1969.

Kelleher, Thomas. Faculty member, 2004–06. Teaching area: public relations.

Kelly-Scholle, Janet. Staff member, 1998–2000. Assistant to the development director.

Knight Advertising Center. A classroom and research facility created in room 107 of Howell Hall in 1984 with a $900,000 grant from the Knight Foundation. It was sometimes called the "Star Wars room" because of the computers and other technological features of the room.

Knight (James L.) Professorships. Created with an endowment in 1984 from the Knight Foundation and expanded with additional contributions and interest from earnings. James L. Knight Professors have included Robert Lauterborn, Tom Bowers, Jane Brown, and Rich Beckman.

Kokai, Mitch. Staff member, 1998–99. Assistant to the dean for executive education. B.A. (UNC–Chapel Hill).

Kollar, Joe. Staff member, 1996. Assistant student records manager.

Krishna, Samir "Sam." Staff member, 2003–04. Computer systems administrator.

Kuka, John. Staff member, 2004–06. Assistant to the dean for communications. M.A. (UNC–Chapel Hill).

Lamb, Jennifer. Staff member, 2000–2001. Assistant dean for development and alumni affairs.

Lamb, Larry. Faculty member, 2001–08. Teaching area: public relations. B.A., M.B.A. (Pennsylvania State University).

Lane, Walter. University mail service employee who delivered mail to Howell Hall in the 1980s.

Lassiter, Thomas J. Faculty member, 1948–49 and 1951–53. B.A. (Duke).

Last Big Blowout in Howell Hall. Celebration on April 23–24, 1999, that featured an open house, informational presentations about the school, a dinner, and tours.

Lauder, Val. Part-time lecturer, 1980 to present. Teaching area: feature writing. A.A. (Stephens).

Lauterborn, Robert. Faculty member, 1978–2008. James L. Knight Professor. Teaching area: advertising. B.A. (Columbia).

Lauterer, Jock. Faculty member. 2001–present. Teaching areas: community media, news-editorial, photography. B.A. (UNC–Chapel Hill).

Leftwich, Suzette. Staff member, 1998–2004. Student records assistant.

Lewine, Janice. Staff member, ca. 1993–98. Secretary.

Lillis, Rachel. Staff member, 2002–present. Assistant director of distance education and executive education. B.A. (UNC–Chapel Hill).

Linden, Thomas R. Faculty member, 1997–present. Glaxo Wellcome Distinguished Professor of Medical Journalism. Teaching areas: medical journalism, electronic communication. B.A. (Yale); M.D. (University of California, San Francisco).

Lipka, Phyllis. Staff member, ca. 1985. Undergraduate secretary.

Liu, Peizhu. Staff member, ca. 1993–95. Accounting manager.

Lloyd, Rhonda. Staff member, ca. 1990. Receptionist.

Locations of the school. The first journalism courses were probably taught in Smith Hall (later called Playmakers Theater). When the Department of Journalism was created in 1924, it was located on the second floor of New West, above the *Tar Heel* offices and below a room where the UNC wrestling team practiced. The department moved to rooms on the main floor of Alumni Building in 1926 and to a larger space on the east side of the top floor of Bynum Hall in 1935. Howell Hall was the home of the school from 1960 to 1999, when it moved to Carroll Hall. For a few years in the 1990s, the school had additional faculty offices and research facilities in the Carr Building and the Porthole Building near Franklin Street.

Luxon, Norval Neil. Faculty member, 1953–69; dean, 1953–64. Alumni Distinguished Professor, 1966–69. He was chairman of the Accrediting Committee of the American Council on Education in Journalism when the Department of Journalism failed in its bid for accreditation in 1948. B.S., M.A., (Ohio State); Ph.D. (UCLA).

Lyle, Vivian. Staff member, 1961–65. Secretary to the dean.

MacNeill, Eleanor. Staff member, ca. 1948. Secretary.

Madry, Robert Wilson. First director of the University News Bureau, 1918–19. After serving in World War I and working as a journalist in New York City and Paris, he returned as director of the News Bureau in 1923 and served until his death in 1955. He taught two educational publicity courses in the Department of Journalism in 1926–27. B.A. (UNC–Chapel Hill); B.Litt. (Columbia University).

Mai, Richard. Staff member, ca. 2000–2002. Computer systems administrator.

Mann, Raleigh. Faculty member, 1978–2000. Teaching area: news editing. A.A. (Miami-Dade Community College); B.A. (South Florida).

Matrix Society. Founded at UNC in 1957 and intended to be a chapter of Theta Sigma Phi, the national honorary organization for women.

McCloskey, Ann. Staff member, ca. 1990. Administrative secretary.

McCombs, Maxwell. Faculty member, 1967–74. Teaching area: research methods. B.A. (Tulane); M.A., Ph.D. (Stanford).

McDonald, Betsy. Staff member, 2003–05. Assistant director of development and alumni affairs. B.A. (UNC–Chapel Hill).

McMahan, Dana. Faculty member, 2008–present. Teaching area: advertising. B.F.A. (James Madison).

McPherson, Holt. He claimed to be the first student in the Department of Journalism in 1924 and graduated in 1928. In 1946, while he was managing editor of the *Shelby Daily Star*, he was on the Accrediting Council of the American Council on Education for Journalism and led an effort by North Carolina newspapers to pressure UNC to seek accreditation for the Department of Journalism. Later, when he was editor of the *High Point Enterprise*, he was instrumental in the hiring of Norval Neil Luxon as dean and creating the School of Journalism Foundation.

Meade, Judy. Staff member, 1989–99. Business manager.

Medical Journalism Program. See Glaxo Wellcome Program in Medical Journalism.

Meyer, Philip E. Faculty member, 1981–2008. Kenan Professor, Knight Chair in Journalism. Teaching areas: research methods, newspaper management, media economics. B.S. (Kansas State); M.A. (UNC–Chapel Hill).

Mills, Quincy Sharpe. He was editor-in-chief of the *Tar Heel* in 1906–07, graduated in 1907, and worked for New York *Evening Sun*. An infantry officer in World War I, he was killed while attacking German lines at Chateau Thierry, France, on July 26, 1918. A scholarship fund in his name was created by his mother, Nancy Mills, in 1956, and scholarships have been awarded ever since.

Minor in technical writing. The university approved the concept of academic minors in 1991, and the school created a technical writing minor in cooperation with the Department of English. It included three courses from the school ("News Writing," "News Editing," and "The World of Graphic Design"), a technical-writing course in the English department, and an elective in biology, chemistry, or physics. The minor did not attract many students and was discontinued in 1998.

"Miss Spell." See Spelling and Grammar Exam.

Morgan, Andi. Staff member, 2004–07. Assistant student records manager. B.A. (UNC–Chapel Hill).

Morrison, Joseph Lederman. Faculty member, 1940–70. Teaching areas: history, business journalism. B.A. (UNC–Chapel Hill), M.A. (Columbia), Ph.D. (Duke). He was born Joseph Lederman and later changed his name because of a concern about anti-Semitism.

Mortensen, Jennifer. Staff member, ca. 1981. Clerk-typist.

Mullen, James J. Faculty member, 1959–86. Teaching area: advertising. B.B.A., M.A., Ph.D. (Minnesota).

Mullins, L. Edward. Faculty member, 1974–77. Teaching area: news writing. He taught courses as a Ph.D. student beginning in 1969. B.A. (Alabama); M.A. (Ohio State); Ph.D. (UNC–Chapel Hill).

Mustard, Lola Lee. First female faculty member, 1948–53. Teaching area: advertising. B.A. (UNC–Chapel Hill).

Nagelschmidt, Billie. Staff member, 1979–93. Business (administrative) manager, placement director.

News Bureau. The University News Bureau was established in 1918 to gather and disseminate news about the university. Prior to that time, publicity work was done by students in journalism classes or on their own. Robert Madry was director in 1918–19 and 1923–55. Lenoir Chambers was director in 1919–21, and Louis Graves in 1921–23 while he was teaching journalism courses in the Department of English. A. G. "Pete" Ivey was director in 1955–75. At one time, Jake Wade, director of sports information for the university, was part of the News Bureau.

New West. The Department of Journalism occupied space on the second floor in

1924–26, above the *Tar Heel* offices and below a room where the UNC wrestling team practiced.

Nipper, Wendy. Staff member, ca. 1990. Assistant to the accounting manager.

North Carolina Press Association (NCPA). Organization of North Carolina newspapers. In 1916, the Department of Journalism held a newspaper institute in Chapel Hill, the first of what became the annual NCPA Winter Newspaper Institute. NCPA held the institute on campus until 1989, when parking problems on campus prompted NCPA's officers to move it to another location. In 1946, NCPA pressured the UNC president to seek accreditation for the Department of Journalism.

North Carolina Scholastic Media Advisers Association (NCSMA). A group of high school press advisers met at the School of Journalism in Chapel Hill on Nov. 20, 1976, and organized the North Carolina Scholastic Press Advisers Association to help improve the quality of high school journalism. The name was changed to North Carolina Scholastic Media Advisers Association in 1995 to reflect the variety of student media. Part-time directors of NCSMA were Walter Spearman, 1941–72; Richard Cole, 1973–76; Jan Elliott, 1979–82; Bill Cloud, 1982–88; and Rich Beckman, 1988–93. After the North Carolina Department of Public Instruction and the school established a three-year liaison to promote high school journalism, Kay Phillips became the first full-time director on Jan. 18, 1994, and she was succeeded by Monica Hill in 2002. The first North Carolina Scholastic Press Institute in 1936 was sponsored by the *Daily Tar Heel* and was intended to promote closer coordination among high school newspaper editors. The first institute was directed by UNC student Stuart Rabb, and the second by David Stick.

O'Connor, Paul. Part-time lecturer, 1986–present. Teaching area: reporting, opinion writing. B.A. (Notre Dame); M.A. (Minnesota).

Packer, Cathy L. Faculty member 1988–present. Teaching area: media law. B.A. (UNC–Chapel Hill); M.A., Ph.D. (Minnesota).

Pardun, Carol. Faculty member, 1997–2005. Teaching area: advertising. B.A., M.A. (Wheaton College); Ph.D. (Georgia).

Parker, J. Roy. Faculty member, 1941–46. Teaching area: advertising and newspaper management. One of his frequent class assignments was to develop an advertising campaign for the "lowly peanut." B.A. (Wake Forest).

Parker, Karen. First African-American female undergraduate student at UNC–Chapel Hill and in the School of Journalism. 1963–65.

Park Foundation. Located in Ithaca, N.Y., it was divided by family members in 2003, and the Triad Foundation assumed support for the Roy H. Park Fellows Program and other programs in the school. As of 2008, it had supported the school with gifts totaling more than $20 million.

Park (Roy H.) Fellows Program. The Park Foundation of Ithaca, N.Y., gave $5.5 million in 1995 to create a program of financial support for graduate students, the largest of its kind in the country. The first group of Park Fellows entered the school in 1997. The Triad Foundation has continued to fund the program.

Park, Roy Jr. Graduate of the school and president of the Triad Foundation, 2003–present. B.A. (UNC–Chapel Hill); M.B.A. (Cornell).

Park, Roy Hampton. A North Carolina native who built Park Communications Inc., a media empire that included newspapers, radio and television stations, and outdoor billboards in 23 states. Through the Park Foundation created at his death in 1993 and the subsequent Triad Foundation, the Park family became a major benefactor of the School of Journalism and Mass Communication. B.S. (N.C. State University).

Park, Roy III. Graduate of the school and an officer of the Triad Foundation. B.A. (UNC–Chapel Hill).

Pawlow, Nancy. Staff member, 1992–present. Secretary, office assistant. B.A. (SUNY–Albany).

Peterson, Linda. Staff member, 2005–present. School receptionist.

Peterson, Meg. Staff member, 2008. Assistant director for development. B.A. (UNC–Chapel Hill).

Phillips, Cathy. Staff member, ca. 1968. Secretary.

Phillips, Kay. Staff member, 1994–2001. Director of the North Carolina Scholastic Media program.

Pittman, Susan Andes. Staff member, 1958–ca. 1960. Secretary. B.A. (UNC–Chapel Hill).

Placement service. From the beginning of journalism instruction at UNC, faculty members have helped students find internships and employment. The service was formalized by the appointment of part-time directors (Billie Nagelschmidt and Jim Shumaker) and full-time directors (John Conway and Jay Eubank).

Pollander, Leon M. Faculty member, 1946–58. He taught advertising and was sometimes listed in the catalog as "director of advertising." Pollander had 25 years' experience in retail advertising, including daily newspapers and department stores. He was also a part owner of the *Chapel Hill News-Leader*.

Poole, Lucinda. Helped to coordinate the school's move from Howell Hall to Carroll Hall, 1998–99, and was the "finisher" for completion of interior design work after that.

Porthole Building. This university building on Porthole Alley between the campus and Franklin Street was once the home of a restaurant called "The Porthole," which was famous for its bread rolls. In the early 1990s, the school had outgrown Howell Hall, so four faculty members moved to the Porthole Building and remained there until the school moved to Carroll Hall in 1999: Robert Stevenson, Donald Shaw, Frank Biocca, and Xinshu Zhao.

Press Club. An organization in the school from 1953 to 1971. Dean Neil Luxon hosted meetings at his home from 1955 to 1960. It had a record-high membership (up to that time) in 1963 of 40 students and faculty members. For several years, the club and the school held a banquet to distribute awards, but declining student interest in 1971 prompted the faculty to substitute an awards ceremony in the student lounge instead.

Preston Cup. A list of medals and prizes on page 113 of the 1909–10 UNC catalog included this entry: "The Preston Cup, given by the Hon. Edmond Randolph Preston in memory of his brother, Ben Smith Preston, will be awarded annually to the undergraduate student who during the months of September to April has done the best work of a journalistic nature." The prize was announced in the *Tar Heel* on April 1, 1909. According to Levi Brown's history of journalism at UNC, Ben Smith Preston was a former UNC student who died several years before 1910 while working as a reporter on the *Atlanta Georgian*. Records of the General Alumni Association show that he attended one summer session in 1905. The award was given until 1931. E. R. Preston was a graduate of the university and an attorney in Charlotte.

Public Pulse. The school first conducted this public opinion survey of residents in the towns of Chapel Hill and Carrboro in 1992, but the poll lasted only a few years.

Pulitzer Prizes. School alumni winners have included Horace Carter, 1953 prize for meritorious public service by the *Tabor City Tribune* (the first nondaily to win the public service award); David Zucchino, 1989 prize for features for the *Philadelphia Inquirer*; Joel Brinkley, 1990 prize for international reporting for the *New York Times*; and Eugene Roberts, 2007 prize for history. Carter donated his gold medal to the school, and it was put on display in Howell Hall on Feb. 4, 1991, and later moved to Carroll Hall.

Purdy, Carol. Staff member, ca. 1949. Secretary.

Radio, Television, and Motion Pictures (RTVMP). This academic department was in the College of Arts and Sciences and not part of the school. In 1993 the university "disestablished" the department, and many of its faculty members were assigned to the newly created Department of Communication Studies. Four RTVMP faculty members transferred to the School of Journalism and Mass Communication: John Bittner, Richard Elam, Anne Johnston, and Richard Simpson.

Rainbow Institute. Program for minority high school students in the school, 1992–96. It ended when The Freedom Forum terminated its funding, but a similar program was initiated in 2007 as the Chuck Stone Program for Diversity in Education and Media.

Reuss, Carol. Faculty member, 1976–96. Teaching areas: public relations, magazine writing. B.A. (Saint Mary-of-the-Woods); M.A., Ph.D. (Iowa).

Reynolds Center. The Reynolds Industries, Inc., Center for Editing and Graphics was created in Howell Hall in 1981 with a $150,000 gift and was updated in 1988 with a gift of $100,000 from the R. J. Reynolds Tobacco Co.

Rhyne, Mary Ann. Staff member, 1998–2000. Assistant dean for alumni affairs and development. B.A. (UNC–Chapel Hill).

Riffe, Daniel. Faculty member, 2008–present. Richard Cole Eminent Professor. Teaching area: research methods. B.A. (Dayton); M.S. (Ohio University); Ph.D. (Tennessee).

Rigsbee, Betsy. Staff member, ca. 1971. Secretary.

Rollinson, Joan. Staff member, ca. 1992. Secretary to the dean.

Roukema, Ashley. Staff member, 2006–07. Assistant to the graduate program manager.

Roush, Chris. Faculty member, 2002–present. Walter E. Hussman Sr. Distinguished Scholar. Teaching areas: business journalism, news-editorial. B.A. (Auburn); M.A. (Florida).

Royster, James F. Second member of the Department of English faculty to teach a journalism course: English 16 in 1910–12 and 1913–14. He joined the faculty of the Department of English in 1907 and later became dean of the College of Liberal Arts and then dean of the Graduate School. He was a relative of Vermont Connecticut Royster. B.A. (Wake Forest); Ph.D. (University of Chicago).

Royster, Vermont Connecticut. Faculty member, 1971–86. William Rand Kenan Jr. Professor of Journalism and Public Affairs. Teaching area: politics and journalism. He was editor of the *Wall Street Journal* before he joined the faculty. B.A. (UNC–Chapel Hill).

Rubinstein, Eli A. Adjunct faculty member, ca. 1990. He endowed the Minnie S. and Eli A. Rubinstein Research Awards for graduate students in the school.

Ruel, Laura. Faculty member, 2004–present. Teaching areas: graphic design, multimedia. B.A. (Colgate); M.A. (Missouri).

Russell, Brian. Staff member, ca. 2006–07. Computer support analyst.

Russell, Charles Phillips. Faculty member, 1931–56. In 1931–37, he was also on the faculty of the Department of English. As a student, he was editor of the *Tar Heel*. After graduation, he worked at the *Charlotte Observer*, *New York Times*, New York *Herald Tribune*, and *Philadelphia Record*. When he worked in London, he was a publicist for the boxer Jack Dempsey. He had published five books by 1931, and he came to UNC to teach creative writing in the English department. Former students who took the course said it dealt more with clear writing than with fiction. He was a part owner of the *Chapel Hill News-Leader*. B.A. (UNC–Chapel Hill).

Sarratt, Reed. UNC alumnus and first president of the Journalism Alumni and Friends Association in 1980. The school created the Reed Sarratt Distinguished Lecture Series in 1987 to honor him. B.A. (UNC–Chapel Hill).

Schanno, VeAnn. Staff member, ca. 1966. Typist.

School of Journalism Foundation, Inc. Founded in 1949 by North Carolina newspaper executives with an initial gift of $1,000 as a tribute to Beatrice Cobb, NCPA's secretary. The foundation first awarded scholarships in 1956—four scholarships worth $300 each. It later became the School of Journalism and Mass Communication Foundation of North Carolina.

Scroggs, Janice. Staff member, 1974–ca. 1980. Student records clerk.

Scroggs, Mary A. Staff member, 1953–58. Secretary.

Sechriest, Stuart W. Faculty member, 1946–78. Teaching areas: newspaper photography, news editing. B.A. (UNC–Chapel Hill).

Secrest, Andrew McDowd "Mac." Faculty member, 1971–76. Teaching areas: newspaper management, news writing, media and society. B.A., M.A., Ph.D. (Duke).

Semonche, Barbara. Staff member, 1990–2009. Librarian, director of the Park Library. She also taught courses in online reporting. M.A., M.L.S. (UNC–Chapel Hill).

Sequences. Undergraduate specialty areas in the school's curriculum. The news-editorial sequence grew out of the school's original mission of preparing students for careers on North Carolina newspapers, and it was first identified as a sequence when the advertising sequence was started in 1971. The broadcast journalism sequence began in 1975 and included courses taught in the Department of Radio, Television, and Motion Pictures. It was later changed to an option in the news-editorial sequence and then a sequence called electronic communication. The public relations sequence was created as an option in the news-editorial sequence in 1982 before becoming a separate sequence in 1991. The photojournalism sequence began as an option in the news-editorial sequence in 1988 and became known as the visual communication sequence in 1991, encompassing photojournalism, graphic design, and multimedia. Under a curriculum revision approved by the faculty in 2008, the five sequences were merged into two: journalism and advertising/public relations.

Sevick, Chris. Staff member, 1999–2000. Computer systems administrator.

Shaver, Mary Alice Sentman. Faculty member, 1983–2000. Teaching area: advertising. B.A. (Saint Mary-of-the-Woods); M.S., Ph.D. (Indiana).

Shaw, Donald Lewis. Faculty member, 1966–present. Kenan Professor. Teaching areas: history, news writing. A.A. (Mars Hill); B.A., M.A. (UNC–Chapel Hill); Ph.D. (Wisconsin).

Shaw, Eugene F. Faculty member, 1970–74. Teaching areas: research methods, news writing.

Shepherd, Flora. Staff member, 1979–86. Financial secretary.

Sherard, Regina. Faculty member, 1983–89. First African-American female faculty member. Teaching area: advertising. B.A. (Fisk University); M.A. (Michigan State); Ph.D. (Missouri).

Shorthand course. Mildred Stout, the school's secretary, taught a noncredit shorthand course for 14 journalism students in the spring 1967 semester.

Shumaker, James Hampton. Faculty member, 1973–2000. Teaching areas: news writing, editorial writing. Before he joined the faculty, he was editor of the *Chapel Hill Weekly*. In the late 1960s and early 1970s, Jeff MacNelly was the editorial cartoonist for the newspaper. When MacNelly later created his nationally syndicated comic strip, "Shoe," the main character, P. Martin Shoemaker, was editor of the *Treetop Tattler-Tribune* in the strip and was modeled after Shumaker. B.A. (UNC–Chapel Hill).

Sigma Delta Chi. A chapter of this national professional journalism fraternity was established at UNC on March 14, 1959. It later became known as the Society of Professional Journalists.

Sijthoff, Carolyn. Staff member, 2007. Assistant director of development and alumni affairs. B.A. (UNC–Chapel Hill).

Siler, Dan. Staff member, 2008–present. Television producer and director. B.A. (UNC–Chapel Hill).

Simons, Jason. Staff member, 2003–06. Computing consultant.

Simpson, Richard. Faculty member, 1994–present. Faculty member in the Department of Radio, Television, and Motion Pictures, 1981–94. Teaching area: electronic communication. B.A. (Southern Methodist); M.S. (Wisconsin); PGD (London International Film School).

Sinclair, Janis. Faculty member, 2004–present. Teaching area: advertising. B.A., M.A., Ph.D. (Florida).

Singh, Ranjeev. Staff member, 1992–96. Computer systems administrator.

Sluder, Miriam. Staff member, 1999–2003. Administrative manager.

Smith Hall. Also known as Playmakers Theater. Probable location of journalism classes in the Department of English. It was completed in 1853 and known as Library and Alumni Building because it housed the university's library and was the site of commencement ceremonies and alumni meetings. In April 1865 at the end of the Civil War, Union cavalrymen stabled their horses in the basement of Smith Hall while occupying Chapel Hill. That led Union General William T. Sherman to claim that his horses were smarter than those of the Confederacy.

Smoke-free policy. To comply with university policy, the school's faculty voted on Sept. 4, 1990, to ban smoking inside Howell Hall. Prior to that, students and faculty members regularly smoked throughout the building, including classrooms. Joyce Fitzpatrick, who graduated in 1976, recalled a 1974 attempt to ban smoking in all university classrooms. She was a student in Richard Cole's "News Writing" course, and when students walked into Cole's classroom the day after the ban was announced, Cole was sitting there, puffing on a cigarette as usual. He explained his behavior to the class: "If I am to prepare you to work in a newsroom, I can promise you that you will not find a single smoke-free one in this country. Therefore, the smoking ban will not be observed in this class. End of discussion."

Snow, Henry "Hank." Fictitious journalism student known as the "ghost of Bynum Hall" in the 1940s. He was blamed for posting fake notes on bulletin boards and rearranging the letters on a faculty directory so that one faculty member's office appeared to be in the men's room.

Spearman, Walter. Faculty member, 1935–80. Teaching areas: reporting, book reviewing and dramatic criticism. One of the most popular teachers in the school's history, he was also called the "Mr. Chips of Chapel Hill." B.A., M.A. (UNC–Chapel Hill).

Spelling and Grammar Exam. The need for such an exam was first discussed at a faculty meeting in 1973. Initially, the test was the New Purdue Placement Test in English, but Richard Cole and Tom Bowers developed their own test, based on common student mistakes they collected from faculty members. Vermont Royster mentioned the exam in his *Wall Street Journal* column on Dec. 4, 1974, which led to a note about it in James J. Kilpatrick's nationally syndicated newspaper column. NBC News sent a reporter and crew to the school on Jan. 28, 1975, to film a story about the exam that appeared on NBC's national news telecast on Feb. 1, 1975. Starting in the fall semester of 1974, students had to pass the exam to receive credit for the "News Writing" course, and scores on the test become part of students' placement records, available to potential employers. A minimum score of 70 percent was made a graduation requirement in 1975. In 1981, the faculty instituted a series of remedial review sessions that came to be known as "Grammar Slammer." Professor Bill Cloud and Kathy McAdams, a Ph.D. student, also created a computer program called "Miss Spell" to help students study spelling rules. In the early 1990s, students had to attain a score of 60 percent before they could take "News Writing" or "Advertising Copywriting." That requirement was rescinded when enforcing it became too cumbersome.

Spieler, Louise. Staff member, 2004–present. Assistant dean for distance education and executive education. B.A. (UNC–Chapel Hill); M.A. (Maryland).

Sports Communication Program. Created by John Professor Sweeney in 2002 with a $1 million gift from an anonymous donor. It includes courses about sports and the media, offers internships and scholarships, and brings visiting lecturers to the school.

Stablein, Billie. Staff member, ca. 1969. Typist.

Stevenson, Robert Louis. Faculty member, 1975–2006. Teaching areas: international communication, research methods. He was a consummate host to scores of international students and scholars. Kenan Professor. B.A., M.A. (Wisconsin); Ph.D. (Washington).

Stone, C. Sumner "Chuck." Faculty member, 1991–2005. Walter Spearman Professor. Teaching areas: censorship, magazine writing. B.A. (Wesleyan University); M.A. (Chicago).

Stout, Mildred. Staff member, 1966–79. Executive assistant to the dean, administrative manager. She also administered the school's placement service.

Straughan, Dulcie. Faculty member, 1987–present. Associate dean for undergraduate studies, 2005–07; senior associate dean, 2008–present. Teaching area: public relations. B.S., M.S. (Virginia Commonwealth); Ph.D. (UNC–Chapel Hill).

Student organizations. Over the years, these have included Society of Professional Journalists, Women in Communication, Advertising Club, Association of Minorities in Media, Journalism Organization for Black Students, International Association of Business Communicators, National Press Photographers Association, Public Relations Student Society of America, Society of Newspaper Design, Carolina Association of Black Journalists, Radio-Television News Directors Association, Radio-Television News Directors Association of the Carolinas, and Electronic News Association of the Carolinas.

Studies in Journalism and Communications. A series of research studies published by the school and mailed to North Carolina newspapers and other schools and departments of journalism in the United States. No. 1 (November 1962) was "Readership of the *Hickory Daily Record*, Issue of Friday, May 18, 1962"; No. 2 (April 1963) was "Correspondents: How Editors Can Ease Their Problems, Improve Their Product"; and No. 3 (January 1964) was "News Sources: Three Points of View."

Sweeney, John. Faculty member, 1981–present. Distinguished Professor in Sports Communication. Teaching areas: advertising, sports communication. B.S. (Northwestern); M.Ed. (UNC–Chapel Hill).

Taylor, Michelle. Staff member, 1995–present. Accounting manager, accountant.

Theta Sigma Phi. National honorary society for women students in journalism. A UNC chapter was organized as the Matrix Society in 1957.

Thomas, Susan. Staff member, 1970–79. Financial secretary.

Thomsen, Fred. Staff member, 1999–present. Director of information technology and services. B.A. (Swarthmore); Ph.D. (Pennsylvania).

Thornburg, Ryan. Faculty member, 2007–present. Teaching areas: news-editorial, new media. B.A. (UNC–Chapel Hill).

Thornton, Richard H. Faculty member in the English department who taught journalism courses in 1916–18, guided by the journalism program at the University of Wisconsin. B.A. (Virginia Christian College); M.A. (Columbia); Ph.D. (Chicago).

Towns, D. Leroy. Professor of the practice, 2006–present. Teaching area: media and politics. B.A. (Kansas State); M.A. (George Washington).

Triad Foundation. See Park Foundation.

Tuggle, C. A. Faculty member, 1999–present. Teaching area: electronic communication. B.S.J., M.A., Ph.D. (Florida).

Twenty-Something Program. Program that brought young professionals to the school in the early 1990s to talk to classes and meet with students.

University Athletic Association. Student organization that controlled intercollegiate athletic teams on campus by the late 1890s and into the 1900s. It was responsible for creating the *Tar Heel* in 1893.

University Press. In February 1893, the same month as the founding of the *Tar Heel*, five faculty members (John Manning, F. P. Venable, J. W. Gore, Collier Cobb, and R. H. Whitehead) incorporated a private print shop in New West building. It printed the *Tar Heel*, produced official university publications, and engaged in commercial printing. It also provided employment opportunities for students, including Oscar Coffin, who were interested in learning the practical aspects of journalism. The University Press was later moved to a separate building near the Phillips Annex building north of the current site of Carroll Hall.

University Press Association. Organization of students that was founded sometime before 1893, because it was listed as a student organization in the first issue of the *Tar Heel* in 1893. Members were students who were correspondents for newspapers in their North Carolina hometowns, and its object was to disseminate university news. Students may have acted as correspondents for their hometown newspapers as early as 1875; Judge Francis D. Winston told the North Carolina Press Association in 1926 that he had been a correspondent for the *Raleigh News* while a student in 1875.

Vargas, Lucila. Faculty member, 1994–present. First Latina faculty member. Teaching areas: media and society, international communication. B.A. (Universidad Autonoma); M.A., Ph.D. (Texas).

Walden, Ruth C. Faculty member, 1985–present. Associate dean for graduate studies, 2000–2007. James Howard and Hallie McLean Parker Distinguished Professor. Teaching area: media law. B.A., M.A., Ph.D. (Wisconsin).

Walsh, Linda. Faculty member, 2000–2005. Teaching areas: graphic design, advertising design.

Walters, Sally. Faculty member, 1991–97. Teaching area: news-editorial.

Whitehead, David. Staff member, 2007–present. Technical support analyst. B.S. (Swarthmore).

Williams, Anita. Staff member, ca. 1992. Assistant student records manager.

Williams, Jackie. Staff member, 1979–2005. Assistant to the dean, receptionist, secretary.

Williams, Michael. Faculty member, 1994–2000. Teaching area: photojournalism. B.S., M.S. (Kansas).

Windsor, Cheryl. Staff member, 1971–ca. 1973. Secretary.

Wittekind, Don. Faculty member, 2006–present. Teaching area: graphic design. B.A. (Central Florida).

Worksheet. Form used to record undergraduate students' progress toward meeting degree requirements. It was kept in the student's folder in the student records office, updated every semester, and photocopied for the student's adviser. Worksheets were color-coded by sequence: blue for news-editorial, yellow for advertising, pink for public relations, green for visual communication, and white for broadcast journalism (later called electronic communication). When the school's undergraduate enrollment neared 800 in 2004, the worksheets were abandoned in favor of electronic records maintained by the Office of the University Registrar.

Yopp, Jan Johnson Elliott. Faculty member, 1977–81 and 1987–present. Assistant to the dean, associate dean for undergraduate studies, senior associate dean, 2005–2007; dean of the UNC summer school, 2008–present. Walter Spearman Professor. Teaching areas: news writing, reporting. B.A. (UNC–Chapel Hill); M.A. (Florida).

York, Kyle. Staff member, 2007–present. Assistant to the dean for communications. B.A. (UNC–Chapel Hill).

Zhao, Xinshu. Faculty member, 1990–present. First Asian faculty member. Teaching areas: advertising, international communication. B.A. (Fudan University); M.A. (Stanford); Ph.D. (Wisconsin).

Zimmerman, Babs. Staff member, ca. 1968. Secretary.

Zoom-Zoom. Restaurant in Chapel Hill that was the location of Press Club awards banquets.

Index